PREGNANT BODIES, FERTILE MINDS

PREGNANT BODIES, FERTILE MINDS

Gender, Race, and the Schooling of Pregnant Teens

WENDY LUTTRELL

Routledge
New York   London

Published in 2003 by
Routledge
29 West 35th Street
New York, NY 10001
www.routledge-ny.com

Published in Great Britain by
Routledge
11 New Fetter Lane
London EC4P 4EE
www.routledge-co.uk

Routledge is an imprint of the Taylor & Francis Group.
Printed in the United States of America on acid-free paper.

10 9 8 7 6 5 4 3 2 1

Library of Congress Cataloging-in-Publication Data

Luttrell, Wendy.
    Pregnant bodies, fertile minds : gender, race, and the
        schooling of pregnant teens / by Wendy Luttrell.
        p.   cm.
Includes bibliographical references and index.
ISBN 0-415-93188-6 (hardback)—ISBN 0-415-93189-4(pbk.)
    1. Pregnant schoolgirls—Education—Social aspects—United
        States. 2.
Feminism and education—United States. 3. Ethnicity—United
        States. I.
Title.
    LC4091 .L88 2002
    371.93'086'5—dc21
                                        2002014788

This book is dedicated to the lives and memories of

Joan Marie Luttrell
(1928–1997)
and
Edith Shreefter
(1911–1997)

Contents

List of Illustrations

Preface

It is March 5, 1992, my first day at the Piedmont Program for Pregnant Teens, known as the PPPT.[1] I have arrived to conduct an ethnographic study of the program's history, mission, meanings, and everyday life as a way to understand the relationship between sexuality and schooling. It has taken me eighteen months to gain access and secure permission. These negotiations tell a story of their own about enduring racial conflicts and distrust that divides white and black, city and county school officials, teachers, parents, and students in this southeastern industrial town. I feel the weight of these negotiations as I slowly climb two flights of steps.

The stairwell is cold and dark; out of breath at the top, I wonder how the pregnant teens enrolled in this program manage the stairs. The building feels eerily empty as I walk down the long hallway to find room 310 where I am to meet Ms. Nelson and her students who have generously agreed to participate in the project. I pass by a classroom where the door is propped open, and I notice a banner draped across the blackboard with the slogan, "Education Holds the Key to Combat Teen Pregnancy."

Ms. Nelson's classroom door is closed. It is a few minutes past noon, making me think everyone is at lunch. Being alone here makes me realize just how out of sight the program is, tucked away from the rest of the high school world. Nothing announces the program, nor is there the usual sign instructing visitors to please report to the office. It is as if the program does not exist.

I decide to take a closer look at the bulletin board in the hallway next to Ms. Nelson's classroom. "Safe Sex or No Sex Is the Only Key to Combat Teen Pregnancy" is the "official" message made out of black cutout letters on top of multicolored construction paper. Underneath there are six graffiti messages that appear to be written in response: *"It's a choice of one's own mind." "It's a choice of a gift, a life, Another You." "The only education is the mind! (an educated mother)"* Then in small, but bold letters is the statement,

"PPPT only hides you. Be proud, stay with the regular team." To the left of these messages is a big, scrawled *X* underscored by the even more rebellious message, *"This is a bunch of crap."* And below this in eloquent cursive handwriting, *"Don't be ashamed of your kids cause you weren't ashamed of having sex!"*

I stand there scribbling down these compelling messages. The official version of the meaning of the program doesn't surprise me—*education* holds the key to "combat" teen pregnancy (I notice the warlike language). The other key is presented quite simply ("safe sex" or "no sex"), which takes for granted a host of assumptions about choice, agency, empowerment, and alternatives. The graffiti, on the other hand, suggests that the links between education, sexuality, and teen pregnancy are much more complicated—bound up in cultural constructions about proper and improper sex and personal feelings like pride, shame, and guilt. These are the cultural and personal meanings about pregnancy that I, as an ethnographer, want to understand.

I am lost in these thoughts when playful voices filter up the stairwell. The stairwell door swings open and I recognize Ms. Nelson, who ushers me into room 310, saying, "Girls, ladies, quiet down, I want to introduce you to Dr. Luttrell. She's going to tell you about herself and her project; I have to speak with Ms. Washington and will be back in ten minutes."

There are six girls, all speaking at once.

"Yeah, you better go talk to Ms. Washington."

"If she spoke to me like how she spoke to Shanille, my mother would be up here cussing her out."

"She has a real attitude."

One girl stands up—she places one hand on her hip, and with the other she shakes her finger in another girl's face. "You don't bring the form, you don't come back," she says in a squeaky, high-pitched voice. I assume she is mimicking Ms. Washington (who, I later learn, is the program's counselor). I glance at Ms. Nelson, who seems to be fighting back a smile.

"Ms. Washington is a teacher; you better show respect," Ms. Nelson says sternly. Again six responses call out at once; I can only clearly hear two.

"She's no teacher."

"You are just taking up for Ms. Washington, but we don't have the same trouble with you. She's all about rules."

Ms. Nelson turns as she leaves the room, saying even more forcefully, "Dr. Luttrell is in charge here; you better listen to what she has to say."

I shrink at the thought of being "in charge"—this is not how I want to be viewed in my role as ethnographer. But there are six young faces looking at me in anticipation, expecting me to take charge, so I proceed. I walk toward the group and rearrange the wooden desks—the kind that are all one piece and you have to twist your body in to. I put them in a circle and invite the girls to sit down for introductions.

The girl closest to me, the most visibly pregnant of the group asks, "Is this how you have the desks in your college class?"

"Yes, especially when the class is a seminar," I reply.

"What's a seminar?"

"Don't be stupid, Shanille," interjects the girl who just mimicked Ms. Washington. Her tone is light and teasing. [It has been sixteen years since I've spent time in a high school classroom.] "A seminar is a small class with lots of discussion—the teacher doesn't stand up and lecture to the students, but joins the students in conversation about what they understand from the book they have just read," I explained.

"So are we having a seminar?" This question comes from the girl who imagined her mother cussing out Ms. Washington.

"Well, yes, I guess it will be like having a seminar, but I am here doing a research project." The girls speak again in unison.

"Ms. Hayes teaches us about research—science experiments."

"I did a research report last year, it was a lot of work reading and then putting the ideas in my own words."

"What are we going to talk about? Ms. Nelson said you are going to ask us about things that matter to us, like being pregnant in school and what we think about the PPPT."

"How often will you come?"

"Will you be here tomorrow?"

"I hope this isn't going to be like that time the white lady counselor came and said we couldn't tell anybody else what anybody said in the group—is it that kind of group conversation?" I take notice of this racial identification because I am the only white person in the room.

"Yeah, and then everybody knew my business. I'm not doing that."

"Everybody already knew your business, girl."

The girls' energy and enthusiasm are overwhelming and I am eager to correct any misconceptions about my project, especially that it will be like group therapy. "Let's slow down. I'll explain everything—but first, I don't even know your names!" I am relieved when the girls take their seats and, one by one, introduce themselves.

For five years (1992–1997) I did some "deep hanging out"[2] at the PPPT. I spent time in classrooms, ate lunch with the girls, sat in on parent-teacher conferences, and drove the girls on field trips and sometimes to their homes or clinic appointments when their transportation fell through. I also conducted one-on-one interviews with students, teachers, and school officials, and collected and analyzed school documents. But the unique dimension of my fieldwork focused on eliciting the girls' self-representations. I designed a series of activities (three class periods a week throughout the academic year) in which the girls were invited, through multiple modes of expression, to describe themselves to themselves and to each other. These activities included weekly journal writing; "Who Am I?" media collages; improvisational role plays of their "pregnancy stories"; and a collaborative book of self-portraits accompanied by texts. I was particularly interested in the questions the girls asked one another, the free associations they made about others' self-representations, and the concerns they expressed about how others would view these materials. I asked each girl to formally present her piece to the group to explain the choices she had made and the meanings she intended to convey. Her classmates were then encouraged to ask questions about the self-representation. Then I asked my own series of questions to elicit further individual and group observation and reflection (Appendix 1). All these sessions were tape-recorded and transcribed.

Over the five-year period, I met with fifty girls enrolled at the PPPT. They were at different stages of their pregnancies and over the course of each academic year, a few girls would give birth and return to the program as young mothers. Of the fifty girls, forty-five are black; three are Mexican American, and two are white. All grew up in poor and working-class families, and most of the girls were between fourteen and fifteen when we met. I have wrestled with how best to describe the girls. Whereas I might have referred to them as "young women," they called themselves girls. Whereas I would have referred to the majority of the girls as, "African American," they call themselves black. Whereas I might have referred to three of the girls as recent Mexican immigrants, the daughters of migrant workers who have settled in this Piedmont region, they called themselves "Mexican and American." And whereas I have chosen to refer to two of the girls as white, this was not a label I heard them use to describe themselves. Their black classmates referred to each as "the white girl," but not in her presence. I have also wrestled with how best to describe myself in relation to the girls: as a mother; as a middle-class, middle-aged university professor; as a self-consciously white woman in an educational setting with predominantly black students, teachers, and administrators. All these labels are problematic and incomplete. Moreover, as the girls would attest, these categories of fitting in and belonging are elusive and fluid; in fact, they can be bones of

contention among people. Arguments between the girls about racial identification occurred frequently—"If she says she is black then that's what she
is, I don't care if she looks white." Nonetheless, these same labels have un-
deniable force in our lives.[3] And one goal of this book is to take readers
inside one such label—pregnant teenagers—to get up close and examine
what it is like to live inside it so that the dynamic inter-relationships of inequality, social distinction, and personal meanings can be made more clear.

Shanille arrives late to class. She appears upset; she keeps twisting in her
seat. And I notice again how she can't fit her swelling body into the one-
piece wooden school desk. Ms. Nelson asks how her meeting with Ms.
Washington went, and Shanille shakes her head no, crossing her arms over
her chest.

The other girls in class start offering their views. Keisha says, "Ms.
Washington gives us all a look, she has an attitude. I know three girls who
left PPPT 'cause of trouble with Ms. Washington."

Everyone is talking at once about their troubles with Ms. Washington.
"What happened?" I asked.

Shondra jumps up out of her chair, "I'll tell it 'cause I saw it." Ms. Nelson takes a seat, looks toward Shanille who nods approvingly.

Shondra stuffs her backpack under her shirt and swings her newly extended belly from side to side, which makes the girls laugh before beginning her narration.

"She's walking down the hallway, minding her own business and
scratching her belly. [Shondra enacts these motions, then, turns and throws
the backpack on the desk, taking up Ms. Washington's part, speaking in a
high shrill voice and waving her finger.] "What are you doing scratching
your belly like that in school? You wouldn't carry yourself like that at
church or on the street." [Shondra turns and puts the backpack under her
shirt again taking up Shanille's role.] "You never seen me at church or on
the street."

The back and forth switching of characters continues. Ms. Washington
says, "Don't talk to me like that." Shanille says, "I wouldn't have to if you
didn't talk to me like a dog in a pound." Ms. Washington says, "Well, that's
where you belong."

Now several other girls join in the storytelling, explaining that after the
hallway exchange, Ms. Washington stormed into class, telling Ms. Nelson,
"I don't know what is wrong with that girl." She turns to Shanille and says,
"I don't know what is wrong with you, girl." Then Shanille starts fussin' Ms.
Washington out. "There was a lot of language and confusion."

"I just stay away from Ms. Washington; that's the only thing you can do," Keisha says. Keisha pretends to hit Shanille's shoulder and repeats her advice, "Stay away from her, that's the only thing you can do."

Later, out of the girls' earshot, Ms. Nelson puts this unfortunate incident into a larger context—what she calls "politics in the black community." She says, "There is a lot that goes on here. I am glad you are here to see some of it. It is not easy being a teacher in this system; it has really tired me out."

One week at the PPPT and already the ground is shifting under my researcher feet. I am struck by the adversarial "official" messages of the PPPT and the not-so-subtle everydayness of regulation. Something as simple as the too-small wooden desks remind the PPPT girls that they have not only done something wrong by being pregnant, but that they themselves are wrong; "misfits" who don't belong in school. I am also taken with the "Ms. Washington incident" and the way the girls talked about her "attitude" and regulatory ways, both of which brought to mind the subtle force of institutional discipline and punishment. And while this analysis makes sense, there was so much more going on here. There is the girls' exuberance; their unbounded energy. There is the force of emotion that was evoked by the incident and then again by Shondra's performance that quickly drew me in. The girls had made distinctive personal associations to the event, ranging from commentary about authority, rules, and what makes a "teacher," to feelings about powerlessness and vulnerability, to wishes for maternal protection ("My mother would come up here and cuss Ms. Washington out"). Shondra's retelling of the incident through performance also made the pregnant body come alive for her audience, and the girls had responded appreciatively with laughter, clapping, and gestures, including patting one's stomach. What also seemed to incite the girls about the incident were the negative judgments being directed toward them and the limited options they had available for answering back ("Just stay away, that's all you can do"). I was struck by the parallels made between how one might carry oneself "in church" or "on the street" compared to in school, and the attention paid to "respectable" manners of deportment. What did this have to do with being pregnant, being a black girl in a racially segregated town, or being of a certain class? I had admired Shanille's reported ability to defend herself, her sparring with Ms. Washington and the girls' seeming support of this. But I was unsettled by Shanille's reference to feeling treated like a "dog in a pound" and deeply troubled by Ms. Washington's reported collusion in sustaining such a disparaging image. Meanwhile, Ms. Nelson remained vague about her allegiances.

This incident and its performance foreshadowed many aspects of what my time at the PPPT would be like, including how I would learn to enter the girls' worlds through narrative, performance, and creative expression. It also pointed up multiple and complicated layers of social forces and personal meanings to which I would need to attend—the institutional force of discipline and punishment; the force of personal conflicts and emotion; and cultural/class-based meanings of self, respect, and respectability—that lie at the heart of the relationship between education, sexuality, and pregnancy.

I have organized this book in three parts after arranging and rearranging it many times. With each draft I tried to weave together the elements of form, content, analysis, and reflexivity; and with each draft I learned something new about the limits of representation. In my elusive search to get it "right," my main aim has been to keep the girls' stories and self-representations at center stage. Toward this end, I have placed an extended discussion of methodology in Part III. I encourage readers to move between each part depending upon their own interests, to consider the visual images through their own interpretive lens, and to mine the material for alternative analyses.

Part I considers the PPPT girls' everyday experience of school in light of competing discourses and stereotypical images about teenage pregnancy. My point is not to provide an account of the politics of teenage pregnancy—other scholars have already done an excellent job of this, most notably Deirdre Kelly (2000), Kristin Luker (1996), Constance Nathanson (1991), Wanda Pillow (1994, 1997), and editors A. Lawson and D. L. Rhode (1993). Rather, my goal is to consider what we can learn from a single school program in a particular time and place, about the layers of social and psychological forces at work in the education and/or miseducation of pregnant teenagers.

Part II examines the girls' self-representations, both in terms of *what* they construct as well as *how*. I have "curated" the girls' art forms, the stories they told, and the conversations we had to speak to dominant themes in their transition from girlhood to motherhood, including the power of their feelings and their sense of agency. My hope is that this section, with its more expansive reach into the girls' thoughts and feelings, will convey something about selfhood, identity, and agency that many other books about poor and working-class pregnant teenagers have not. That being said, in my effort to counter disparaging images of teenage mothers, I do not want to substitute one stereotypic representation with another. The girls and their self-representations are far more complex, and the social relations affecting their lives are too wide-reaching to draw simplistic conclusions.

Part III speaks to a set of theoretical and methodological concerns about the politics of representation—about evolving fieldwork relationships; the fuzzy line between standing apart and becoming part of what is seen; the discomforts and difficulties of writing against dominant representations of pregnant teens; and making one's writing make a difference with audiences whose perspectives and actions you want to change. Both chapters in this section are meditative and reflect upon what I learned about the power of empathy, observation, and tolerating conflict in ethnographic and pedagogic relationships. I do not provide a neat, handy tool kit for improved ethnographic or educational practice, but I do offer some concrete examples—a "this is how it happened, this is what she said, what I said, and what we came to understand together" set of discoveries that I hope will be useful to others. Most important, I make a case for providing young people more opportunities for "play"—a protected space of moral and creative reflection that is increasingly at risk of disappearing in our contemporary culture and education.

PART I

SEXUALITY, PREGNANCY, AND SCHOOLING

CHAPTER 1

Separate and Unequal

To the real question, "How does it feel to be a problem?" I answer seldom a word. And yet, being a problem is a strange experience.—W. E. B. Du Bois, The Souls of Black Folk

Everyone has an opinion about teenage pregnancy and why it is a problem. It is straightforward, said former president Bill Clinton: "Teenage pregnancy is just plain wrong." But personal opinions, cultural prescriptions, and political rhetoric are not enough, especially for educators whose business it is to understand the "strange experience" of being a "problem."

Teenage mothers' motivations have already been scrutinized in ways that are racialized, class-blind, and, in far too many cases, stigmatizing.[1] But how do pregnant girls themselves experience disparaging public attributions and directives that they are "babies having babies" or are "looking for love" in ways other than so-called normal mothers? This book examines the experience of being a pregnant teenager as a struggle *between* a girl and her world, not simply *within* an individual girl. This distinction is ever so important if we are to avoid pathologizing and stigmatizing the life choices and trajectories of poor and working-class girls. Rather than focusing on individual girls and their "problem," my aim is to consider the cultural and psychological mine fields through which they must walk, particularly within school settings.

Rerepresenting the Pregnant Teenager

This identified problem group—pregnant teenagers—is highly visible in the public imaginary and in political rhetoric about what is wrong with

3

America. In terms of the dominant image that gets evoked, the "pregnant teenager" is seen as a black, urban, poor female who is more than likely herself the daughter of a teenage mother. She is probably failing in school, has low self-esteem, sees no future for herself, and now must deal with the untimely end of her youth and face the harsh realities and responsibilities of adulthood. Research about this group, whether the researcher acknowledges it or not, must engage in, and respond to, these dominant discourses and representations of the "pregnant teenager."[2] It is not as if one can present a distinct "narrative" or set of alternative images about teenage pregnancy without engaging the dominant discourse. Moreover, there is a class- and race-based history of teenage pregnancy that shapes how these representations are understood by different groups of Americans. Kristin Luker (1996) examines this politically charged history in her book, *Dubious Conceptions*, and explodes many myths. She shows that "teenage mothers" are no more common today than in 1900; that despite the dominant image, pregnant teenagers in America today are more likely to be white than African American; and that the greatest increase in "unwed mothers" is not among teenagers, but among women in their mid-thirties. Most important, what most characterizes American culture since colonial times, according to Luker, is the tenacious hold of racial stereotypes and the scapegoating of pregnant teenagers for social ills.

These politics of representation are further complicated by the force of personal feelings. In addition to conflicting messages, images, and expectations about becoming young mothers, there are psychologically particular ways in which girls make meaning.[3] Pregnancy presents a girl or woman with the unique challenge of becoming conscious of two people living under one skin. I like the way Joan Raphel-Leff, in her book *Pregnancy: The Inside Story* puts it:

> In pregnancy, there are two bodies, one inside the other—a strange union that recalls gestation of the pregnant woman herself in the uterus of her own mother many years earlier. When so much of life is dedicated to maintaining our integrity as distinct beings, this bodily tandem is an uncanny fact. Two-in-one body also constitutes a biological enigma, as for reasons we do not quite understand, the mother-to-be's body suppresses her immunological defenses to allow the partly foreign body to reside within her. I suggest that psychologically too, in order for a woman to make the pregnancy her own, she has to overcome threats posed by conception. (1995: 8)

Raphel-Leff calls this the inside story of pregnancy and argues that it differs for each pregnancy; every mother (no matter what her age) infuses the experiences of pregnancy with her personal feelings, hopes, memories, and powerful unconscious mythologies.

Meanwhile, there are external, "public" interests that also infuse the meanings an individual woman attaches to this two-in-one relationship between herself (woman) and inside other (fetus). Indeed, competing meanings of pregnancy continue to be debated within the law, especially regarding women's reproductive rights. Regardless of one's position on these issues, the point is that there are interests beyond the individual pregnant woman that mediate how she makes sense of her pregnancy. And whether she is consciously aware of it or not, these "outsider" interests affect her "insider" experiences. Is the pregnancy legitimate or illegitimate, planned or unplanned, wanted or unwanted, natural or inseminated, in or out of wedlock? In short, individual girls or women are not "free" to forge their own distinct relationships with the other they carry.

All of this is to say that this duality—the inside and outside story of pregnancy and the blurred boundaries between self and inside other— complicates the already politically charged problem of how to represent pregnant teenagers. Each girl holds personal images, ideals, associations, and feelings that are unique to her alone *and* that are part of a system of regulation and social control. This is where we must start when we consider how the PPPT girls live the personal and cultural phenomenon and social "problem" called teenage pregnancy.

"Use Theory, Don't Let It Use You"[4]

The "teenage pregnancy is just plain wrong" perspective is, sociologically speaking, a deviance theory. And, to paraphrase sociologist Howard Becker (1986), for deviance theorists, the important question, the question most worth asking, is, "Why would girls do a wrong thing like that?" The favored way of answering this question is to find a psychological trait (i.e., girls who get pregnant are "looking for love" or have low self-esteem) or a social attribute (i.e., urban poor and working-class girls who have low aspirations for the future) that differentiates girls who do get pregnant from girls who don't. The underlying premise is that "normal" girls wait until they are older, financially secure, and, preferably, married to have babies. And, those girls who do get pregnant as teenagers are not just "different" but "wrong" in one way or another. Meanwhile, boys, and their part in this phenomenon of deviance, drop out of the picture.

All this being said, I didn't realize the extent of and tenacious hold of deviance theory until I began to explain my project and present conference papers on my preliminary findings. It seemed next to impossible to move beyond the scripts and stereotypes of my audiences: Were these pregnancies planned? Were the girls knowledgeable about or practicing safe sex? Did these girls ever think about having abortions or about giving their babies up for adoption? Were these girls having trouble in school? Had their mothers been teenage mothers? What about the boys? Do any of the girls plan to marry their babies' fathers? It seems like having a baby for some of these girls was like having a toy, and that their motivations were somewhat selfish. It was next to impossible to move away from public discussions scrutinizing the girls' motivations, in ways that sometimes felt like a modern-day version of the Puritan's public stockades. I still remember my moment of frustration when responding to an audience member's question, "So, what do you think is the underlying reason these girls have babies?" I replied, "I've worked with fifty girls and there are at least fifty reasons."

Thinking about my own distinctive motivations and feelings about each of my three pregnancies, I wondered aloud, "Do you think there is one underlying reason that an adult, married woman has a baby?" And then it dawned on me that I was missing an opportunity to reframe the terms of debate. What if I could find a way to turn these audience questions of "judgment" into questions of *interest* about the girls' self and identity-making? This is, after all, the art of ethnography—taking something that is perceived as "strange" and making it "familiar" to audiences who might otherwise cast aspersions on groups unlike themselves.

It is in this spirit that I have taken a person-centered approach to ethnography, attempting to develop an experience-near way of describing and understanding the PPPT girls' personal and cultural meanings of pregnancy. Rather than providing an aerial (or *experience-distant*) view of a community or culture, person-centered ethnographies attempt to "tell us what it is like to live there" (*experience-near*) (LeVine 1982: 293). Person-centered ethnography has important parallels with psychoanalysis. Indeed, "experience-near" and "experience-distant" are borrowed from psychoanalyst and theorist of selfhood Kohut (1971, 1977), as noted by cultural anthropologist Doug Hollan (2001) in his review of recent trends within person-centered ethnography. Kohut (1971, 1977) used the distinction to describe "his own (experience-near) efforts to ground psychoanalytic theory in the language and subjective experience of the analysand from the more abstract (experience-distant) metapsychological theorizing of Freud" (Hollan 2001: 49). Person-centered ethnographers and psychoanalysts share a similar goal. Both wish to engage people to talk about and reflect upon their subjective experiences.[5]

Cultural anthropologist Robert LeVine, who first coined the term person-centered ethnography, offers a way to learn about subjective experiences and distinct social worlds through what he calls "canonical narratives (cultural dramas)" (1999: 23). Analysis of cultural dramas and people's forms of self-presentation focuses on three things. The first is to identify and compare the constellation of emotions—including those emotions that can be expressed and those that must be suppressed; second, is to identify cultural patterns and continuities of meaning that occur within and across the narratives; and finally, to uncover social divisions or cultural conflicts and corresponding inner personal conflicts that individuals seek to manage or resolve through these narratives and forms of self-presentation.

I adapted LeVine's method for my purposes. I was interested in what I could learn about the PPPT girls' social worlds and subjective experience of being a "problem" through the "cultural dramas" they told. I searched for different ways that the girls could narrate their experiences—through informal classroom conversations, through the self-representation activities, journal writing, and formal interviews. I sought to identify and compare the constellation of emotions, continuities of meaning, and recurring conflicts and responses that were expressed within and across the girls' varied forms of self-representation.

Person-centered ethnography also requires an experience-near relationship between the researcher and researched, including an awareness on the part of the ethnographer that his or her own subjectivity (emotions, presumptions, and preoccupations) shapes what she or he hears, sees, and understands about the other.[6] I have written elsewhere about how my own biography, identities, social position, and experiences in the field shaped what I have been able to know about the subjects of my research (Luttrell 1997, 2001). But my work with the PPPT girls posed new dilemmas, which I discuss in Part III.

Centerville and the Piedmont Region

The aerial view of Centerville, a mid-size industrial city in the Piedmont region of North Carolina, shows two things in common with other towns in the region: both a railroad and a highway cut through it. But, what it is like to live there is distinctive and depends upon whether one is white or black, Christian (or not), and how long one's family has resided there. Centerville has close to 200,000 residents, most of whom are employed in either manufacturing or service jobs. Over the past twenty years Centerville's population has almost doubled; today, it boasts of being large enough to provide the cultural diversity of an urban center, yet small enough to offer a hometown atmosphere.

Black and white communities, dependent in different ways on the textile mills and the tobacco factories until the 1980s, have given way to a somewhat more diverse set of communities tied to the booming computer, medical, and pharmaceutical industries. Hispanics and Asians now make up close to 10 percent of the population, with the rest being divided evenly between whites and African Americans. Centerville's historically thriving middle-class African American community sits alongside a working-class community of African American service workers, who are gradually losing their long-held jobs to contract service workers. These contract workers are, increasingly, migrants from Mexico who have decided to settle in the area after having begun their sojourn to the United States as farm laborers in the neighboring agricultural counties. Meanwhile, drug traffic and trade, made more possible by a nearby interstate highway, have created havoc within a once stable and more prosperous African American working-class community. Old and middle-age African American residents remember a thriving downtown neighborhood bustling with black-owned businesses that represented hope for its industrial workforce, especially those whose families had escaped the harsh life of tenant farming. Centerville residents, black and white alike, worry about violence and crime on city streets, warning newcomers away from certain downtown neighborhoods. Several of the PPPT girls had lost family members in drive-by shootings that occurred in low-income housing units in which the victims were either living or visiting friends. The homicide rate is staggering for a town this size. At the same time, Centerville has numerous lively and engaged citizen groups and active religious communities, including a Catholic parish, two Jewish congregations, a mosque and Muslim school, numerous Protestant mainstream churches, and a strong evangelical movement.

The housing pattern in Centerville is segregated, largely according to both race and class. Most white, middle-class professionals and middle-class African Americans live in the areas surrounding the largely abandoned downtown district. White, working-class people who used to work in textile or tobacco are being pushed out of their mill homes as middle-class professional newcomers (from other parts of the United States and world) move into city and county neighborhoods. Giant shopping malls now line what was once a two-lane highway between Centerville and the nearby town, causing residents to complain about traffic once unheard of for these parts of the Piedmont region. Whereas it used to take twenty minutes, at most, to travel from one end of town to another, now it can take forty minutes, and it is best to get on the highway.

Over the past twenty years, the look and pace of life in Centerville has changed. For some, these changes have brought prosperity, for others poverty, and for everyone, more diversity. But, there are stark vestiges of racial segregation, especially in the city schools and when one uses the sorely inadequate bus system, which is the PPPT girls' main mode of transportation.

The Piedmont Program for Pregnant Teens

Today I joined the PPPT girls for lunch in the cafeteria at a table that is the farthest from the cafeteria line. The table sits close to the door leading out to the annex building, which houses the PPPT program.

"This is the table we always sit at," explains Cheri.

With the exception of one boy who waves to Shanille, there is no interaction between the PPPT girls and the other students.

Shanille doesn't wave back to the boy and Cheri asks, "Why? He's cute."

"I don't pay attention to that nappy-headed boy. The other day he said he wanted to feel my stomach. I told him he wouldn't be feelin' nothin' when I was finished with him," replies Shanille.

Ms. Nelson had told me that the girls would have much to say about getting hassled by their peers. One particular example she gave occurred yearly on school picture day. Students enrolled at the high school are called into the auditorium and sit in rows according to their home rooms. Each home-room class is called onto the stage where the photographer, who is set up with lights and backdrop, takes individual portraits. The PPPT girls are assigned the back row of the auditorium. When they are called to the stage, numerous "students, I should say boys," according to Ms. Nelson, start hooting and hollering insults as each PPPT girl walks across the stage. Despite teachers' admonitions, this shaming practice continues year after year. I ask why the photographer can't set up the equipment in some less public space and Ms. Nelson replies, "tradition, that's always how it's been done. It breaks my heart to watch it. I don't think it is worth putting the girls through it just to have their school photo; but they insist. You can't blame them for wanting to have a school photo like everyone else."

The girls' cafeteria seating arrangement parallels their auditorium seating on school picture day. I ask how they came to sit at this particular table. The girls look at me as if this were an odd question. "I don't know, nobody else sits at this table," replies Shanille. "Next question?" (said in what I heard as a flippant tone of voice).

"Don't mind her, what do you want to ask us about?" Keisha says with a smile.

"I was wondering what you all think about the graffiti on the bulletin board—'PPPT only hides you. Be proud, Stay with the regular team,'" I ask.

Despite Shanille's previous curtness, she is the first to answer. "It is sort of true, the PPPT does make us different. And you can see no one eats lunch with us. We're the same as the other girls, but. . . ."

Cheri interrupts. "My mother enrolled me, her sister was in the program when she got pregnant [the program was founded in 1979]. She said it was good for her sister and it would be good for me. But I think they want to keep us from setting bad examples to the other students."

I am about to ask Cheri if she feels like she is a "bad example," when Keisha interjects, "They want to keep pregnant teenagers from dropping out of school, and they help us do that."

Cheri agrees and explains, "Yeah, we don't have to take gym. And we get excused for more things than other students, like going to the clinic and if we need to be on bed rest."

Melissa adds, "Sometimes Ms. Nelson lets us eat if we are hungry during class—and she sends our homework to us if we miss class."

Yvonne adds, "Yeah, I appreciate the PPPT because school rules can't always be followed and PPPT is flexible. Anyway, I'm not ashamed of being pregnant. I feel bad, but I'm not ashamed. Everyone is entitled to one mistake."

The bell rings, and a loud, crackling voice booms over the intercom announcing bus delays.

The PPPT program exemplifies typical post–Title IX educational responses to teenage pregnancy and motherhood. (Title IX refers to legislation that mandated equal educational opportunity for all female students, including school-aged mothers). During the course of its eighteen-year history (the PPPT was dissolved in the summer of 1997), it has seen many changes. The program was established through federal grants that provided comprehensive services such as prenatal health care, mental health services, counseling, and on-site childcare for high-school-age pregnant teens and mothers. One of the founders of the program whom I interviewed referred to these as the "golden years" because the program had more autonomy from the school district, could hire its own staff (including a full-time counselor, an outreach worker, and several classroom teachers), could develop its own curriculum, and had comfortable surroundings, including sofas for quiet reading and a kitchen where a nutritionist held classes. The program served high school students—grades nine through twelve—and as many as fifty students were enrolled during an academic year. As federal funding evaporated and the school district took up the cost of running the program, the PPPT program suffered. Teachers who did not necessarily want to be teaching at the PPPT were assigned there and important staff positions were eliminated (for example, the outreach worker, herself an alumnus of the PPPT, and the full-time counselor). The program moved from its original location to the annex building of the city's most troubled high school. This facility was wholly inadequate; while spacious, it lacked sufficient heat, had no carpeted or comfortable spaces, was furnished with the oldest and most traditional desks (the wooden ones, too small for the most pregnant girls, that I described in the preface), and was isolated from important resources (i.e., the library, computers, and science labs) of the "regular" school upon which the girls depended. The textbooks were outdated. Ms. Nelson described these textbooks as being like the students who had been "dumped at the PPPT because there was no better place for them." When I arrived in 1992, the program's funds had been even more drastically cut so that only ninth-grade girls were being served, although in some cases, girls from the county school system's middle schools (sixth through eighth grades) could also enroll.

As a voluntary program, PPPT students could enroll as soon as they became aware they were pregnant. Students were encouraged to return to their "regular" school within three months of giving birth, although girls could elect to stay throughout the school year. This meant that at any one time in the program there were girls at different stages of pregnancy and motherhood. The enrollment at any point in the academic year could be as high as twenty students, with six to twelve girls attending class on any one day. The program offered a small set of "regular" school course offerings—offerings that met basic graduation requirements but limited the girls' future curricular choices. For example, more advanced math courses were not offered and, thus, students wishing to take college preparatory math classes would not have the prerequisites. The same was true for science. In addition to the academic course offerings, there was a course on prenatal and infant care (taught by a school nurse who visited twice a week); a sharing group run by a volunteer public heath educator; and for the first two years of my study, a writing project staffed by area university students in which the PPPT girls produced a literary journal. The PPPT also coordinated with various after-school social service programs and parenting classes, and secured transportation for those PPPT girls who wanted to attend.

The PPPT's deterioration did not go unnoticed by school officials. The program, along with several others, had come under review and a report had been released a month or so before I started the study. Ms. Nelson was distressed by the report—most especially, its characterization of the girls as "depressed." There was no discussion of the social conditions that might give rise to the girls' lost interest in school (such as poverty at home, sorely lacking school resources); there was no consideration given to the physical demands of pregnancy on the girls (for example, there was no mention of the lack of any elevator, making it necessary for the girls to climb two steep flights of stairs to get to their classes). There was no evidence (other than observations, made on a single day, of one student sleeping in class and others looking "bored") provided to support the conclusion that the girls were depressed. Like Ms. Nelson, I found this way of pathologizing the PPPT girls' circumstances troubling, but all-too-familiar in light of the literature and public attitudes toward teenage pregnancy. Moreover, given the schooling hardships the girls faced, it struck me that being depressed might be an appropriate response.[7] The challenge, as I saw it, was to tap into the girls' feelings and conflicts, and present these without feeding into stereotypes, as the report had.

The release of the report was timely because there were finally plans in the works for a newly configured, unified city and county school district. The town had been debating the merger of its segregated system since 1924! There was a "county" system, populated largely by white, middle-class students and some middle-class African American students and a "city," system, populated predominantly by African American, low-income students. The potential for change was in the air, as the merger had been formalized (forced by court order to be more precise), but not yet implemented. Ms. Nelson was cautious about the possibilities, given the racially divided interim school board. The board, predominantly white save for a single member, was split along racial lines regarding various strategies for implementing the merger.[8] Whereas the school board embraced two goals—improving academic achievement of all students and achieving racial balance across the whole system—these would not be easy to attain. There was the continued declining enrollment of white students and a perceived lack of confidence among white parents in former city schools, a perception that many black residents resented. Despite the system's growth by almost 10 percent, the percentage of white students was dropping, and in 1992 had fallen below 50 percent. Strategies for enticing white families to send their children to former city schools and to attract middle-class black students (e.g., magnet programs) were especially controversial. Debates would continue until 1995, when a final settlement, that included student redistricting, teacher reassignment, and the creation of magnet programs, was reached.

The PPPT teachers met several times to discuss the recommendations they wanted to present to the new school board. These included reinstating important elements of the program that had been eroded—most important, serving all high school students. The teachers also recommended instituting an on-site childcare program for participants that would also serve as a learning lab; providing parenting classes to teen fathers, and support groups for the parents/guardians of teen mothers and fathers; offering *all* required courses and *some* electives (emphasis included in the document) for PPPT students; providing transportation for teen mothers and their babies—in the words of the document, "this transportation should be separate from that of the 'regular day student';" and finally, updating the facility, including installation of an elevator. Ms. Nelson, a key architect of this proposal, was not hopeful. She proved to be right. Members of the unified district school board and its new superintendent rejected the proposal. The PPPT program hobbled along for several years. It was moved from the annex building to an even more remote site at the other end of town. This facility, an old, small white wooden house that sat at the edges of an abandoned elementary school building, had "bad lighting, but better heating," in the words of one PPPT teacher. Access to resources was even more limited (the girls could not walk to a school library for example). In this setting there was a kitchen where the girls could store favorite food items in the refrigerator and where they ate hot lunches delivered to the site. As PPPT student Shani put it, "At least we don't get hassled here." In the summer of 1997, the program was closed. The PPPT teachers were not informed about this decision until two weeks before school was to start. As one teacher put it, "The superintendent decided the program was inadequate, and he's right about that. There's a committee to study the situation and come up with a proposal, but none of us are on it. You know how those things work."

Over five years, I worked with six groups of PPPT students. (See Table 1.1 of the girls and their ages in each group.) Most of the girls had been born and raised in Centerville or in the surrounding Piedmont region. The majority lived in families headed either by a single, working mother, or by a grandmother, or aunt. Less than a fourth of the girls lived in two-parent households, including all three Mexican American girls and both of the two white girls. A few of the girls currently lived in foster care or had in the past. Besides the most basic demographic information provided in school records, much of what I learned about the girls' households and family life came from the girls themselves. The family members I met were those who

Table 1.1   PPPT Girls in the Study*

Spring 1992		1992–93		1993–94		1994–95		1995–96		1996–97	
Name	Age	Name	Age	Name	Age	Name	Age	Name	Age	Name	Age
Shanille	15	Brandi	14	Grace	15	**Eliza**	15	**Teresa**	15	Kaela	14
Keisha	15	Tskaie	14	Shantae	16	Vaquan	14	Charmine	15	Sonya	15
Shondra	16	Malika	15	Stella	14	Tarisha	15	*Celia*	14	Tara	16
Cheri	15	Alisa	14	Monica	14	Louise	13	Charlene	15	Ebony	14
Melissa	14	Shanika	14	Aysha	14	Rhonda	14	Alisha	16	Shannon	15
Yvonne	16	Nicole	16	Patrice	15	Crystal	14	Sara	15	Kendra	14
Angelica	16	Tanna	14	Donna	14	Shani	15	Tanya	16	Clarise	15
						Carlotta	14	Violet	14	Shadra	14
								Tracey	15	**Marisa**	15
										Michelle	17
										Twana	15
										Alice	14

Key for Ethnicity/Race:

Regular print: African American—these girls called themselves Black.

Bold Regular Print: Recent immigrants from Mexico—these girls called themselves Mexican and American.

Bold Italicized Print: White—these girls did not refer to themselves in racial or ethnic categories.

Not all girls enrolled in the program participated in the study. All names are pseudonyms.

attended school celebrations and events and the end-of-the-year art shows and book exhibits held to honor the girls' art work.

The Changing School Context for Pregnant Teens

The evolution of the PPPT program reflects national trends regarding the education of pregnant girls. For decades the prevailing policy in public school systems required that pregnant students be expelled as soon as the pregnancy was known. In my previous research with older, white, and black working-class women seeking their high school diplomas, I had heard personal stories from those who had been forced to leave school when they had become pregnant (Luttrell 1997). These women were clear that, for them, the problem was not being pregnant but the school's response. I was interested in learning what might have changed. I expected to learn that Title IX, which legitimated the educational rights of pregnant students, had changed things for the better. Instead, I found the end of de jure but not de facto discrimination against pregnant students—discrimination by way of subtle forms of discipline, punishment, and racial segregation.

It is important to realize that negative responses to pregnancy have not been confined to students. As late as the 1920s it was common practice to dismiss or not hire a woman to teach if she was *married,* and only recently have pregnant teachers been welcomed in the classroom.[9] Kristin Luker writes:

> Until the mid-1970s visibly pregnant *married* women, whether students or teachers, were formally banned from school grounds, lest their swelling bellies cross that invisible boundary separating the real world (where sex and pregnancy existed) from the schools (where they did not). The idea that a pregnant *unmarried* woman would show herself not only in public but in schools, where the minds of innocent children could be corrupted, was more unthinkable still. (1996: 2)

Prior to the passage of Title IX, school districts cited various reasons for expelling pregnant students from school. These included the impact of pregnancy upon the girl and her ability to function in a school situation, and the detrimental effects of an obvious pregnancy on the sexual morals and activities of other students (Osofsky 1968). School personnel also argued that allowing pregnant students to remain in the classroom could be viewed by other students as a sanction for premarital sexual activity. (These sentiments are reflected not only in official PPPT documents describing the program and its mission but also in the PPPT students' self-perceptions that they are setting "bad examples.")

Meanwhile, local and national controversies about sex education in schools led many school districts to be wary of promoting any policy or practice that might call attention to teenage sexual activity (Tebbel 1976). Caught between the demands of constituents on both sides of the debate, and expectations to respond each time a new demand is made (or contested) about how to best serve the health and sexual needs of adolescents, schools have perhaps intentionally avoided developing clear policies and practices for teenage pregnancy and parenthood. Indeed, as Burdell (1998) points out, educators have not been at the center of research and policy construction regarding the school-age parent, relying instead on "experts" in other fields. Despite their key "frontline" position in matters relating to adolescent sexuality and parenting, educators have been curiously quiet.

Hunter (1982) notes that it wasn't until the federal government got involved in funding programs for pregnant teenagers in 1963, that school policies really began to change. This decade of social and racial unrest made it very difficult for school officials to continue to ignore the rising dropout rates among pregnant teens and the disparity of services to school-age pregnant students, particularly black students. As a result, some school districts initiated special programs, some of which stressed comprehensive services, including medical, education, and mental health services for unwed school-age mothers (Visotsky 1966; Goodman 1968).

The program most frequently cited as the prototype for comprehensive services for pregnant school-age students was the Webster School in Washington D.C., which was the first full-time, full-curriculum public school for pregnant teenagers in the United States. Operating as a demonstration research project and funded by the Children's Bureau, the program's primary goal was to meet the educational, medical, and social needs of predominantly black, low-income, pregnant teenagers who had either dropped out of school voluntarily or were forced out. School administrators, worried that pregnant teens might corrupt the morals of other students, but also committed to the importance of schooling for pregnant teens, stressed that these students should be educated in separate facilities. As a result, the Webster program was established in a building that had not been used as a school for thirty years (Howard 1968). Subsequent programs were developed in many other cities, increasing in number from thirty-five in 1967 to close to three hundred in 1972 (M. Howard 1972).

These special programs could not keep pace with the numbers of teenagers needing services. Howard (1968) estimated that only 40,000 of those teenagers who had become mothers each year were being served through these programs. At the same time, legislative efforts to secure the rights of pregnant teenagers were succeeding; Florida became the first state to relax its policies governing pregnant students. Meanwhile, controversies were erupting over the value and effects of special programs for pregnant students. Most notable, according to Holmes et al. (1970), was the racial imbalance found in these programs, in most of which non-white students constituted the majority. Segregation and discrimination were also cited as problems of special programs for pregnant teenagers.

The racial imbalance of the PPPT was strikingly evident, and when I asked about it, there were interesting and distinct explanations, according to who was providing the reason. Teachers responded with either hesitation or suspicion to my question about why there were so few white girls enrolled in the program. Ms. Nelson, on first reflection, said she thought it had to do with the fact that the program was part of the city system, which was populated by black students and controlled by middle-class black educators. Thus, the program was no different from any other city school in its identification as a "black" school. Later, however, she added that she thought "white people think about teenage pregnancy differently," because there was no similar program available for white students in the county system. Meanwhile, another teacher at the PPPT, Ms. Peterson, responded to my question by asking why I wanted to know: "Why would that be an issue? Black people have run schools for black students for a long time, it is part of a tradition of education." Different PPPT girls had their own explanations, including one girl's observation that "white girls who get pregnant don't want to be associated with us," and another girl's observation that all the white girls she knew who got pregnant dropped out of school.

Ricki Solinger (1992) puts this racial segregation into a larger context. In *Wake Up Little Susie* she describes the differences between the treatment and education of black and white pregnant girls from the 1950s to the 1970s. She points out that white girls during this time were treated as if they had a psyche—their deviance could be cured, and thus they were sent away to "homes for unwed mothers" to be reformed. Black girls, on the other hand, were not treated as if they had psyches or inner lives. Rather, their deviant motherhood was said to stem from their unruly and unredeemable sexual conduct. Twenty years later, in this particular local school context, pregnant, white working-class girls were still being educated separately from working-class girls of color.[10] The two white girls who were initially enrolled in the PPPT during the five years I was there ended up in the "homebound program." This was a program in which girls were assigned a tutor who would bring course work to their home and provide guidance, and the work was graded by the teacher in whose class the girl was enrolled. This option was used by girls enrolled in the PPPT when they were "put on bed rest by their physicians," according to Ms. Nelson. I met two homebound tutors who told me that the majority of the girls with whom they worked were white. The two white girls enrolled at the PPPT switched to the homebound program because they had been put on bed rest; but, in the words of their black classmates, they "went missing."[11]

Part of the Title IX mandate was to protect pregnant students enrolled in separate programs from getting an unequal education. Schools were required to provide separate programs for pregnant students that were "comparable" to those for regular students. The legislation also required that special programs be voluntary. Burdell (1998) reviews various evaluation studies of teenage pregnancy programs, including that of Zellman (1981), who describes three types of school-based programs that evolved in response to Title IX. The most common type, *inclusive* curriculum programs, offers a general education curriculum as well as supplemental courses dealing with parenting and child development. These programs may also include counseling and health care advice and referrals and on-site childcare (Zellman 1981). Students attend these programs in place of regular high school classes. These programs purport to be separate from (but equal to) the regular school program. Zellman argued that inclusive programs, like the PPPT, are most prevalent because they are designed around a medical model, one treating "school-age pregnancy as a trauma" (1981: 17).[12] The other two types of programs provide relevant course work for students who remain in their regular classes. *Supplementary* curriculum programs provide school credit, whereas *noncurricular* programs do not.

Zellman's (1981) assessment of school-based teen pregnancy programs is sobering. She concludes that academic learning is secondary, and that most staff believe that, regardless of a student's capability, her pregnancy and early motherhood forecloses the possibility of educational and career success. "Having wasted her potential, many staff do not want to invest a great deal of effort in her" (Zellman 1981: 95). Ten years later, writing about a teen pregnancy program she studied, McDade heard the same assumption from teachers she interviewed. One teacher explained her reaction in the following way:

> There is no doubt that when Pam began to show I got uncomfortable and even annoyed. How could she? Sure we have a high rate of pregnancy here, but it usually happens in other classes and not in honors. So when she started to show I spoke to her and asked her what she was going to do with the baby and school and what about the father. She got belligerent and told me to mind my own business. Can you believe it? I always thought that she would be one to go on. (1992: 50)

It is worth noting that it was Pam's "showing" that precipitated her teacher's discomfort. In my observations at the PPPT, I also sensed that the "showing," of pregnancy was what was most problematic in the school context.

The politics of "showing"—but especially the regulation of "proper conduct" for "girls in their condition" (and the girls' resistance to this regulation)—was a recurring source of conflict between some PPPT teachers and the girls. The incident between Shanille and Ms. Washington about how Shanille should not draw attention to her stomach, relayed to me on my first day and described in the preface, would not be the last time "showing" and proper ways to "carry oneself" would be issues. On the one hand, "showing" was used by the girls (often enhanced in playful performance) to mock a teacher behind her back or as part of a girl's "show and tell" description of the events of her weekend. The girls seemed to know just how to move their bodies in a way that would provoke a negative reaction. On the other hand, teachers routinely discussed the related issues of "showing," proper attire, and deportment, but especially before field trips where the girls were reminded that they would be seen as public representatives of the program. In one instance, a field trip was canceled because, according to a school official, "we have to be more restrictive with students in that condition." In another case, a girl was suspended who, in the words of one teacher, had a "bad attitude," wore improper outfits to school, and carried herself in a way that was not "respectable."

This incident, along with many classroom discussions about the girls' misconduct (sexual and otherwise) brought to mind Karla Holloway's (1995) analysis of racial codes of conduct, which, she argues, fragments black girls' and women's sexual subjectivities. She writes about her grand-mother's warning that "nice" black girls should not wear red dresses as part of her "ongoing lecture series to me and my sisters on morality, values, and proper conduct for young Negro girls. . . . I am still conflicted about the intersection between public and private, and ever aware of the subtext of my grandmother's intimate awareness about public bodies—dark skinned, daringly colored, and female" (1995: 16–17). I suspect the same subtext was being passed on by the black, PPPT teachers, who sought to protect their charges by insisting they uphold their honor in a racially and sexually divided and dangerous society. But, as Holloway argues, this pro-tection takes its toll on black women's minds, hearts, and bodies. Speaking again of her grandmother's admonition, Holloway observed that "when she warned us away from red, she reinforced the persistent historical reality that black women's bodies are a site of public negotiation and private loss" (1995: 21). I will return to this issue in part II, as part of my discussion of the girls' self-representations.

Whatever can be said about the PPPT teachers' differences of opinion and personal conflicts about, and treatment of, the girls' "showing," it was clear that the teachers were aware that the girls faced problems of stigma and isolation. While not using these terms exactly, Ms. Nelson pointed out the ironies of the program: that at the same time it was designed to protect the girls from undue harassment in the "regular" school, and to provide special encouragement to the girls to continue their education, the pro-gram (especially in its cut-back form) was isolating the girls from needed educational resources and thus stigmatizing them in another way.[13] It is questionable whether this dominant model of "delivery services" to meet the "specific needs" of pregnant teens is possible or desirable. Lesko (1995) takes a distinctly critical view, arguing that school districts define "specific needs" in ways that reflect a conservative discourse (what she calls "New Right" themes of family decay, sexual permissiveness, and dependency).

Lesko argues that the main problem with schoolgirl mothers is that their needs are "leaky"; these needs cannot be construed as either "just economic" issues (making sure the girls are employable) or "just family" issues (making sure the girls are good mothers). Pregnant schoolgirls' "leaky needs" speak to the artificial separation between public and private, and indeed, Lesko argues, provide a perfect example of how these segregated spheres no longer hold, if they ever did.

McDade (1992) raises yet another problem regarding the isolation of special programs, noting that these programs are most often physically and administratively separated from "regular" school and most often administered by special education, handicapped, or homebound staff. Many state educational codes permit schools to classify visibly pregnant students as chronically ill and disabled—classifications that allow schools to receive special education funds. Thus, pregnant students may be placed in special programs, rescheduled for homebound instruction or encouraged to attend an alternative school, or transferred to another school site with proper resources for pregnant teens. Such reclassifications "not only represent a *structural* dislocation of visibly pregnant students in the everyday practice of schooling, but also mirror a *social* dislocation that results from the public knowledge of their sexual and reproductive behaviors" (my emphasis) (McDade 1992: 51). I would argue that this structural and social dislocation is coupled with a psychological dislocation that results from shaming practices and undue hostility in school settings and that require pregnant girls to cope with their tainted identities. All three of these dislocations are represented by the graffiti messages at the PPPT: "PPPT only hides you, be proud, stay with the regular team." "Don't be ashamed of your kids cause you weren't ashamed of having sex!"

Special programs that tend to target one segment of students (often low-income, urban, African American students) can serve to restigmatize those who enroll.[14] This pattern reinforces the public perception that teen pregnancy/teen parenthood is a poor and minority problem and constructs a dynamic of self-selection into and out of the programs (Nathanson 1991). This seemed to be the case at the PPPT, especially in terms of the perception that white girls were opting for the homebound classes so as to disassociate themselves from black girls. Meanwhile, families with resources are likely to seek (and are often encouraged to do so) less stigmatized educational options for their daughters. (Zellman 1981; Weatherly et al. 1985; Nash and Dunkle 1989).

One lesson to be drawn from the evolution of educational responses to pregnant and mothering students is that Title IX may have ended de jure discrimination but it did not end de facto discrimination against pregnant schoolgirls. Programs like the PPPT, organized around the special needs of pregnant girls, while intending to solve one problem (protecting girls from being hassled by their peers, providing homebound tutoring services or creating less stringent attendance requirements) may create other problems at another level. A current Women's Educational Equity Act Grants (WEEA) Equity Resource Center report (2002) gives schools a C+ on the treatment of pregnant and parenting teens, citing examples of continuing discrimination.[15] The three most egregious ongoing discriminatory practices cited are "excluding of pregnant students from school, denying pregnant students the opportunity to make up missed classes, and requiring pregnant students to attend a separate, frequently less rigorous, school or counseling designed to steer pregnant students to such a school." They recommend that the Office for Civil Rights more actively enforce Title IX by focusing on the more subtle forms of discrimination that undermine pregnant girls' education. Meanwhile, despite the fact that the 1996 Personal Responsibility and Work Opportunity Reconciliation Act requires teen mothers who receive welfare to be participating in educational activities that lead to a credential, the actual provision of educational services is uneven, at best (AAUW 1992; Burdell 1998; Lesko 1995; Pillow 1997a and 1997b; Weinstein 1998).

The Curricular Context

Alongside the shaping force of school policies, resources, and practices is the powerful and paradoxical role of curriculum in the education of pregnant girls. Whereas Title IX cast *education as a right* to which pregnant teens and teen mothers are entitled, much of the curriculum designed for this special population focuses on *education as a responsibility of the teens themselves.* At the PPPT, this emphasis took many forms. There was the "do it for your baby" version to which both teachers and girls subscribed. As many PPPT girls told me, "If I hadn't gotten pregnant I wouldn't still be in school; I'm here for my baby." There was the "you got yourself into this mess and now you're going to get yourself out of it by getting an education" version. One teacher, who said she favored a "tough love" approach to the girls, thought providing childcare was a mistake because it made it "too easy"; moreover, she felt that some teachers were "too soft" on the girls— that they needed more, not less discipline, especially if they were to be well prepared for motherhood. Another teacher's favorite remark to establish order with the girls was to say, "Okay, enough fun and games. You are going to have to get serious and work hard now that you are becoming mothers—you are responsible for more than yourself now." There was also the "don't give up on yourself" version of education as responsibility. This message, often presented by a teacher through personal example, was meant to provide inspiration, which it often did, according to the girls. Nonetheless, the "don't give up on yourself" version still emphasizes that the goal of education is to become a good mother and be able to provide for oneself and one's child.[16]

Both Lesko's study of Bright Prospects School (1990) and McDade's ethnography of the "Family Life Center" in "New Town" (1992) provide similar examples of education framed as responsibility rather than a right. Lesko found that despite good intentions, the school curriculum reinforced images of teenage mothers as sexually irresponsible, likely to be bad mothers, and destined to become dependent, nonproductive citizens. She argued that the curriculum helped the girls to "redeem" themselves, providing ways for them to prove that they can deliver themselves from their problematic status as teenage mothers. The curriculum falls short, according to Lesko, because it offers no critique of the way in which teen pregnancy is framed as a problem, no examination of the disparity between women's and men's economic opportunities, and no way for the girls to question sexist stereotypes about women's proper roles.

Laurie McDade tells a rich, complicated story about the closing of a teen pregnancy program, a story that has many parallels to struggles faced by the PPPT. Her analysis of the curriculum, and the teachers' commitment to "educated motherhood," is more optimistic than what Lesko found at Bright Prospects School. Teachers in the Family Life Center (FLC) stressed that education and a high school diploma would benefit a woman and her child. The FLC's curricular philosophy, which did not distinguish between these two identities—being pregnant (and a mother) and being a student—was key to the educational success of FLC students. McDade quotes one veteran FLC teacher, "If you're not gonna' do it for ya'self, then do it for your child, girl. Lord knows, the little one is gonna' need a mother who can think" (1992: 63). McDade says the teacher offered this advice to her students as a way to instill in them a "seriousness" and a desire to work harder at their studies. Meanwhile, those students who believed their babies were "going to be a hopeful promise of better things to come" (64) saw graduating high school as key to their babies' futures. Nonetheless, McDade also is critical of what she calls the maternalism of FLC teachers who sought to protect the FLC girls from knowledge about what was happening politically in the community. Keeping the FLC girls unaware of events leading up to the closing of the school left them unprepared for the outcome, McDade argues. She also points out curricular "absences and silences"—especially about sexuality, bodies, and pleasure—and argues that this curriculum gap disempowered the FLC students. She notes that part of the conflict over the program had to do with "New Town" residents, who believed the most dangerous aspect of the FLC was that it was "teaching teens to say 'yes' to sex and pregnancy" (59). The fact that the FLC program had no curriculum dealing with female sexuality meant there was no effective way to respond to this attack on the program.

All three of these curricular features—the messages of social redemption, and educated motherhood, and silence about female sexual pleasure—found expression at the PPPT. Meanwhile, during the course of my study, North Carolina laws regarding sex education changed from supporting a dialogue about sexual options (learning the consequences of saying yes or no to sex) to "abstinence only" discussions.[17] Michelle Fine (1988) describes the prevalence of this muted and suppressed discourse of female sexual desire throughout public school settings (a discourse that ironically may be even more suppressed in school-based programs for pregnant teens). In part II I will discuss how the girls took up and avoided conversations about female sexual desire; my point here is to emphasize that this was not an official curricular topic at the PPPT. Likewise, informal sex education, if and when they occurred, followed the *education as a responsibility* approach—how as girls, *they* were responsible for practicing "safe sex" or abstaining from it, and not that, as girls, they were entitled to an education that would provide them with a sense of their own sexual desires and their power vis-à-vis boys. (I will return to this topic in part II). My point is that the *education as a responsibility* approach, whether related to pregnancy or motherhood or sexuality, frames educational conflicts and decisions in terms that may limit a girl's sense of self-regard and importance. "If you are not going to do it for yourself, then at least do it for your child."

We are back from lunch, and in Ms. Nelson's classroom there is an assignment written on the board: Write an essay on the most influential person in your life.

"The essay needs to convince the reader why this person is influential—you need to provide examples," explains Ms. Nelson.

Shondra announces, "I am going to write about my mother."

"Good, what are two outstanding things that she has done to influence you?" asks Ms. Nelson.

"Well, she has taught me to read behind the lines. She says that no one can make a fool out of you if you can read behind the lines."

"And what is an example of reading behind the lines?" asks Ms. Nelson.

"Boys, all they want is one thing and that's sex [there are giggles from the girls at this]. So my momma has always said, 'Don't be a fool, you need to read behind the lines.'"

"She's right, your mother is speaking the truth and you should all listen up—being pregnant does not make you a fool, but giving up on yourselves does. Okay, Shondra, do you have another example of how your mother has influenced you?" asks Ms. Nelson.

"Yes, I have learned that you can learn from your mistakes, and go on with your life."

Not being ashamed, being entitled to at least one mistake, not being a fool, not giving up on yourself, learning from mistakes—I am thinking about how these are all linked in the girls' minds, especially in light of dominant discourses of blame, shame, and stigma in the "war against teenage pregnancy" to which I now turn.

CHAPTER 2

Shame, Blame, and the Stigma Wars

I'm not ashamed of being pregnant. I feel bad, but I'm not ashamed.
Everyone is entitled to one mistake.—Yvonne, PPPT student

There are complex social and psychological forces that shape how pregnant girls see themselves—how Yvonne arrives at feeling bad, but not ashamed of being pregnant. This chapter deals with a mine field of competing discourses, stereotypical images, and public representations through which girls must walk as they make decisions and take actions in their lives. These public (mis)representations frame the way we think about teenage pregnancy as a cultural phenomenon and as a social, political, or moral problem. Here I will consider the range of meanings made possible by these representations and discourses; meanings that become part of girls' inner dialogues about who they are, who they are becoming, how they are seen by others, and how they see themselves. Having said this, I want to make clear that my focus on these public images and representations is not meant to trivialize the consequences of teenage pregnancy for those concerned. In the present social and political climate in the United States, especially in the wake of welfare "reform," the conditions under which many young women give birth and raise their children are wholly inadequate.

What do I mean by discourse? Discourses are institutionalized and taken-for-granted ways of understanding relationships, activities, and meanings about the way the world works, in this case sexuality, pregnancy, and motherhood. These understandings emerge through language and symbols (from media images, to laws, to educational curriculum, to medical practices, to folk wisdom, and common sense), and influence what people take to be true, "right," or inevitable. Discourses direct our relationships—both with ourselves and with others. For example, educational discourses direct us to value intellectual development and provide us the means to gauge our "progress" in accordance with grade levels and standardized test scores, thus shaping our self-assessments as learners and our views of others as "slow" or "fast" learners. This is not the only, or even the best, way to think about the acquisition of intellectual skills, but it is the way that coordinates, manages, and regulates children's trajectories through schools (see Anderson-Levitt 1996). There are varied ways to construe any one person's learning curve. But in schools, only certain assessments predominate and those are the ones that correspond with institutional aims.

Discourses are not neutral; they rest on and are responses to power relations. Competing interests shape dominant discourses—medical, religious, legal, governmental, to name a few. For example, in terms of sexuality, there are religious discourses that direct us to put a moral premium on certain sexual behaviors (as either bad or good; sinful or obligatory); whereas medical discourses direct us to view these same sexual behaviors as more or less "risky." Meanwhile, legal discourses sanction sexual behaviors as more or less "criminal," and psychological discourses endorse sexual behaviors as more or less "normal." Together, these discourses work to ensure that people will come to regulate themselves, policing their sexual desires and actions to be in line with proper, heterosexual norms.[1] All of these discourses are part of the same governing force of what has been called "compulsory heterosexuality," which, while appearing to be "natural" or "given," is actively enforced through all of the above (Rich 1981). The point is that the same sexual behavior holds multiple meanings—there is no single, "pure," outside-of-a-discourse-or-power-relationship meaning for a sexual act.

Indeed, neither the PPPT girls nor I can find a voice or fashion a representation that is independent of these discourses. One of the aims of this chapter is to clarify my stance toward a variety of media, political, and social science discourses about the topic of my research—teenage sexuality, pregnancy, and motherhood. The other aim is to consider what identity- and self-making processes are made available to the PPPT girls by these dominant discourses.

The Stigma Wars

Deirdre Kelly (2000) characterizes discourses about teen pregnancy as a "stigma contest"—a contest I saw played out over and over again in the PPPT:

This contest is waged among those who continue to believe that adolescent pregnancy should be stigmatized as a deterrent to early sexual activity and welfare dependence, and those with rival interpretations of the meaning of teen pregnancy and motherhood. (2000: 67)

She describes four contending groups and discursive frameworks: bureaucratic experts and their "wrong-girl frame"; social, religious, and economic conservatives and their "wrong-family frame"; oppositional movements, including feminism and their "wrong-society frame"; and teen mothers' own "stigma-is-wrong" frame. The latter two frames do not command media attention or shape policy.

These four frames co-exist and shape the schooling of pregnant teenagers as well as the experiences of individual girls. But understanding how this works requires a closer examination of each discursive frame in conversation with the others.

The "wrong-girl" discourse, in my view, is the most complicated to unravel because there are several versions of it. According to Kelly, it is also the *dominant* discourse, meaning that it currently holds the most sway in public understandings of the phenomenon of teenage pregnancy.[2] The "wrong girl" discourse scrutinizes pregnant teens' motivations, as distinct from older (and especially married) women's. These "wrong-girl" motivations are understood not so much in terms of being "immoral," but as individual flaws. Examples of psychological flaws include a girl's "wish to receive unconditional love from a dependent object, in this case, the baby" (Gordon 1990: 349 quoted in Kelly 2000: 74) or as a way to find a "love object to ward off a depression or to counteract it" (Landy et al. 1983).[3] I wish to make it clear that I do not mean to suggest that such psychological or relational conflicts are nonexistent for individual pregnant girls or women. Quite the contrary; rather, my point is that the "wrong-girl" discourse directs our understanding of these conflicts, not as part of a complex constellation of emotions experienced by an individual, but as the *source* of a girl's problem.

"Wrong-girl" discourse also distorts our understanding of how social conditions and cultural forces converge to create isolation, troubled relationships, and little support for many teenage girls (but especially girls living in poverty) at a pivotal point in their lives.[4] Thus, the way individual girls navigate these relationships (i.e., making "bad" or "good" choices) becomes the focal point of attention. This is the "choice-making" version of the "wrong-girl" discourse and it points the finger of blame at those girls who make "choices" that do not adhere to a "normative" life trajectory (i.e., finish school, get a job, find a male partner, marry, and have children). Young women who don't follow this trajectory can be viewed as "deviant" or as having made a "mistake" for which they must account. Yvonne's reference to making a mistake, quoted in the epigraph to this chapter, is in dialogue with this version of the "wrong-girl" discourse. She wants to make it clear that her "mistake"—and she is entitled to at least one—does not make her "wrong" (i.e., ashamed or immoral). Kelly (2000) points out that this discourse of wrong "choice-making" attempts to separate out the "practice" from the "person"—which, in the case of teenage pregnancy and motherhood, means rejecting the "lifestyle" rather than the individual teen mother or her child (47).

There is an extensive body of research, dating back to the Alan Guttmacher Institute 1976 report entitled, "11 Million Teenagers: What Can Be Done About the Epidemic of Adolescent Pregnancies in the United States," that casts the phenomenon in "epidemic" terms (Singer et al. 1993; Vinovskis 1988). According to this version of the "wrong-girl" discourse, teenage pregnancy is out of control and requires intervention. Ironically, this epidemic logic occurred during a time when birthrates among young women were actually at their *lowest*. What was different was that the teen population itself (and the number of teenage girls) had grown, so numbers (but not rates) of teenage pregnancy were higher. But the social context had changed (Vinovskis 1988). The most notable of these changes, according to Lawson and Rhode (1993), was that the racial gap was closing between white women and women of color regarding sexuality, unmarried motherhood, and single parenting. In particular, *white* girls were reported to be increasingly sexually active outside of marital relationships. This new social context created a perception that teenage pregnancy was a serious problem.[5]

Research about risk factors associated with teen pregnancy grew in response to the public concern.[6] It tended to support "epidemic logic" even if unwittingly in that it tended to ignore the structural dynamics of racism, poverty, and social and economic injustice and its effects. Identifying girls by their risk factors (or their ability to overcome risks) is yet another version of the "wrong-girl" discourse insofar as it redirects attention from larger forces at play in girls' lives, including the profoundly inequitable distribution of resources. Debold et al. (1999) provide a compelling discussion of the problems created by such research:

> The methodological emphasis on the individual as the unit of analysis in the search for factors that protect children and lead to

resilient outcomes has led a number of researchers to raise serious concerns. . . . The implication and endpoint of such individually based conceptualization and measurement becomes the search for a "cure" to apply to children suffering from the extreme stress generated by a profound lack of resources rather than for ways of addressing those inequities more directly. (185)

Insofar as the resilience framework reflects white, middle-class expectations of achievement and assumptions about what a successful or "normative" life trajectory should be, then those who fall short risk being viewed in pathological terms (Erkut et al. 1995: 55 quoted in Debold et al. 1999).[7]

For example, researchers Arlene Geronimus and Sanders Korenman (1992) argued that for young black girls living in poverty, having children when they are young may be an effective adaptation to economic deprivation. Younger girls who are in better health, with greater access to nutrition and social support, may be better equipped to become mothers than their older counterparts whose health and well-being has been compromised by living more years in poverty.[8] Geronimus' and Korenman's research began to turn the tide in the debate over the causes and costs of teenage pregnancy. J. Dryfoos (1988) put it most boldly: "Teenage parenthood is much more an issue of class than we have been willing to admit: *low socioeconomic status children become parents, high status children do not*" (213, author's emphasis).

Identifying class inequality as the root cause of teenage pregnancy is part of the "wrong-society" frame that was first presented by feminists. Rosalind Petchesky (1984), noted for being one of the first to articulate a feminist position on teenage pregnancy, took issue with the notion of individual "choices," arguing that personal sexual and reproductive choices are highly contingent on a girl's access to material resources, including opportunities for sex, birth control methods and delivery systems, as well as the distinct cultural meanings associated with sexuality and motherhood. Rather than focusing on the "good" or "bad" choices girls make, feminists drew attention to social inequalities that shape the range, quality, meaning of, and conditions under which choices are made, especially unequal relations of power between men and women.

Nonetheless, the language of "choice-making" had the advantage of investing teenage mothers with agency and positioned them as architects of their own lives. Perhaps this is what underscores teen mothers' own "stigma-is-wrong" discourse that Kelly (2000) identifies. She describes teen mothers' self-interpretations as stressing the positive and empowering aspects of their situations. She writes about girls' rejection of stigmas associated with teenage motherhood including, "messages that portray them as victims, childlike, welfare abusers or morally tainted." She found teen mothers stress the following themes:

> [F]irst, the right to choose, including motherhood and adoption, is essential; . . . second, choosing to keep one's baby should not be stigmatized; . . . third, choosing to give one's baby up for adoption should not be stigmatized; . . . fourth, high school programs dealing with sexuality as well as mothering should carry less stigma; . . . fifth, teen mothers are each other's best support system, which schools can encourage; . . . sixth, teen mothers have matured and taken responsibility, they deserve to be treated accordingly; . . . and seventh, teen mothers not only recognize stigmas against them, they fight back. (2000: 81–83)

That teenagers are "bad mothers" is a stigma against which the PPPT girls felt they had to fight. When I asked the girls to complete the following sentences: What others think they know about me is . . . ; and What I know about myself is . . . , the overwhelming response was to fill in the first blank with "that I will be a bad mother" (80 percent of the girls). And somewhat fewer (70 percent) filled in the second blank with some variation on the statement "that having a baby is going to make me a better person."[9]

Oftentimes, noting the demands placed on them to shoulder domestic and childcare responsibilities, the PPPT girls said they were as likely to be prepared for these responsibilities, if not more so, than women who "did not know how to do for themselves." Indeed, this was one of the PPPT girls' biggest complaints about how they were viewed by others: that, given the adult responsibilities they had been forced to assume at young ages, they viewed the "bad mother" stigma and the "babies having babies" rhetoric as out of touch with the realities of their lives, and indeed, the reality of many women's lives.[10] In the words of one PPPT student, "You don't have to be young to be a bad mother—you can be a bad mother at any age, taking drugs, drinking, only thinking of yourself."

The PPPT girls' "stigma-is-wrong" frame focused on their resistance to stereotypes, including being viewed as inadequate mothers. Indeed, many girls emphasized that their pregnancy was in fact, changing them for the better. The same student (Marisa) went on to explain: "I know I can't be thinking only of myself now. The good thing about being pregnant is that it has made me change some bad habits, including eating better and taking vitamins, getting more sleep." Other girls talked about "cleaning up" and how getting pregnant gave them "more reasons to finish school, to work hard and keep on track."

These conversations brought to mind Martha McMahon's (1995) research on differences between white, working- and middle-class motherhood. Despite their obvious differences, the PPPT girls echoed many of the same sentiments about pregnancy and motherhood as did the white, working-class mothers in McMahon's study. Most similar was the notion that motherhood is a pathway to maturity, an opportunity to become a better person by taking on the responsibility of motherhood.[11] According to McMahon: "Whereas middle-class women indicated they felt they had to achieve maturity before having a child, working-class women's accounts suggest that many of them saw themselves as achieving maturity through having a child" (1995: 91). McMahon argues that "moral reform" is a centerpiece of white, working-class motherhood, and that pregnancy can serve as a motive to reform a life; to revise bad habits for the baby's sake, including doing better in school. These were views held in high regard by the PPPT girls that will be examined more closely in chapter 5.

Moreover, I will argue that the language of "choice" was not used by the PPPT girls. Rather than having "choices," they spoke about making "decisions," which I will argue complicates conventional notions of agency.

Historical Antecedents

The "wrong-girl" discourse has its roots in early nineteenth-century American constructions of what Constance Nathanson (1991) terms "sexually unorthodox" women, and institutional methods for social control of them. She links current views about the problem of adolescent pregnancy "to its predecessors under other names—unwed motherhood, white slavery, ruined or delinquent girls." Her book, *Dangerous Passage: The Social Control of Sexuality in Women's Adolescence,* provides the most comprehensive discussion of sexual categories and sexual social movements that shape our understandings of teenage pregnancy as a social problem. Nathanson shows that earlier labels for sexually unorthodox girls as "immoral" have given way to constructions of the "sexually active" high school teen.

She examines three overlapping campaigns in the early twentieth century: (1) raising the "age of consent"; (2) eliminating prostitution and ending "white slavery"; and (3) combating venereal disease. She links these to contemporary debates about and campaigns against teenage pregnancy. What ties them together, according to Nathanson, is the way in which all these campaigns serve to reassert society's moral order against the threat of deviant (wrong-girl) behavior. Her point is that these campaigns represent more than public concern about *individual* transgressions, which could be "quietly consigned to the discreet management of reform schools, maternity homes, and the offices of amendable physicians" (14). Through these campaigns, young women's sexual unorthodoxies were elevated into *cultural symbols* of disorder, moral decay, and social instability. Social changes and conflicts (i.e., changes in the structure of class, race, and gender relationships brought about by industrialization, urbanization, immigration, and so forth) fueled these campaigns. These social conflicts were translated into moral terms, wherein order and stability were represented by the "family" and, more specifically, by the homemaker mother.

Efforts to reestablish a stable, moral order are central to social and economic conservatives associated with the "wrong-family" discursive frame that Kelly describes. For this constituency, teenage pregnancy *should* be stigmatized, and pregnant girls *should* be excluded from public settings to ensure that the moral fabric of adolescents unravels no further than it already has. But Nathanson is careful to distinguish these moral, "wrong-family" discourses from the racialized, "wrong-family" construction, which casts *black teenage women on welfare* (which is a distortion of demographic evidence) as the problem.[12] This racialized construction dates back to the 1960s and the characterization of "the black family" and its matriarchal household structure as the cause of poverty. This controversial hallmark of the Moynihan Report sparked a flurry of scholarship about the strengths and adaptability of African American family life.[13]

More recent constructions of teenage pregnancy have shifted from being a black, "wrong-family" problem to being a welfare problem (which does not mean that racialized images of and stereotypes about pregnant teenagers no longer hold sway). The Personal Responsibility Act and recent welfare reform legislation (e.g., Title I Block Grants for Temporary Assistance for Needy Families Public Law 104-193 [August 22, 1996]) combine the "wrong-girl" and "wrong-family" frames, targeting "young women 17 and under who give birth outside of marriage." The document stresses that these young women are more likely to go on public assistance and to spend more years on welfare once enrolled, and are least likely to finish high school. Their children are said to be at risk of low birth weight, low cognitive attainment, more child abuse and neglect, and reduced chances of growing up to have an intact marriage. But the most negative consequences of raising children in single-parent homes are said to be poverty and welfare dependence.

This legislation identifies individual men (especially older men) as perpetrators of the problem of teenage pregnancy:

An effective strategy to combat teenage pregnancy must address the issue of male responsibilities, including statutory rape culpability and prevention. The increase of teenage pregnancies among the youngest girls is particularly severe and is linked to predatory sexual practices by men who are significantly older. (Public Law 104-193)

Two things are disturbing about this representation. First, blaming the phenomenon of teenage sexuality and pregnancy on predatory, older men, while ignoring the fact that young girls are increasingly eroticized throughout the media seems shortsighted. The eroticization of girls is found not only in child pornography, but "in the most respectable and mundane of locations" (Walkerdine 1997: 170). Valerie Walkerdine warns against such simplistic representations of girls' sexuality, which can be extended to representations of pregnant teenagers:

This is not about a few perverts, but about the complex construction of the highly contradictory gaze at little girls, one which places them as at once threatening and sustaining rationality, little virgins that might be whores, to be protected yet to be constantly alluring. The complexity of this phenomenon, in terms of both the cultural production of little girls as these ambivalent objects and the way in which little girls themselves as well as adults live this complexity, how it produces their subjectivity, has not begun to be explored. (1997: 171)

Second, given the continued racialized images of teenage pregnancy, this reference to men's predatory sexual practices is haunting. As several critics note, "phobic images" of black men's sexuality have served, historically to divert attention from the structural violence of racism. The history of slavery and sexuality provides a good example. Some historians have argued that racist stereotypes about black men's sexuality were grounded in white slave owners' misplaced fears about their own part in the institutionalized rape of black women slaves. But official versions of the history of slavery have not cast white slave owners as sexual predators.[14]

There is no mention of abortion or adoption or of their provision—both highly controversial issues—in this welfare reform legislation, as Kelly (2000) would predict. For at the heart of the "wrong-family" stigma is a political agenda of "reprivatization"—a retreat from the notion of governmental provision for basic needs. To put it somewhat differently, unmarried teenage mothers pose a threat to the traditional relationship between families and the state, a threat because it could, if not checked, lead to demands for all sorts of government provisions. Universal childcare and health insurance, greater access to abortion and birth control, and state-run adoptions are just a few examples of provisions. As Lesko (1995) put it: "The construction of the problem of teenage pregnancy is part of broad social engineering toward reprivatization and dismantlement of the welfare state support of women and children" (147).

It is crucial to recognize that not all men, women, and children are affected by reprivatization in the same way. Unmarried women who have the resources to raise their children on their own (without being dependent on the state) can escape the intense scrutiny of being a "wrong-girl" or part of a "wrong-family" form. Those other, "undeserving" mothers who are dependent on others (which is how pregnant teens are viewed) are those who are currently being scapegoated and stigmatized. Meanwhile, men with resources can escape the scrutiny and "criminalization" of their inadequacies as fathers. One of the most unsettling images of my fieldwork, one that remains alive in my mind, was a trip to family court with one of the PPPT girls who was seeking child support. As we sat in the courtroom, fifteen or so African American men were brought before the judge, all wearing orange jumpsuits and chained at their feet. These were the fathers being sought by the state to make good on their financial responsibilities. I do not mean to suggest that the African American men in the courtroom should not be held responsible for the children they fathered, but that they are being disproportionately held responsible because they are easy to access.

Paralleling the trend toward reprivatization is the contemporary, broad-based, bipartisan marriage movement, supported by both religious and political leaders. Writing about the relationship between faith-based approaches to social reform and the marriage movement, feminist sociologist Judith Stacey puts it this way:

> The marriage movement's biggest prize yet was the 1996 welfare law. As the statement of principles that (*presidential candidates*) Bush and Gore endorsed points out approvingly, "three out of the four legal goals of welfare law are now marriage-related;" promote marriage, encourage two-parent families and reduce ... out-of-wedlock births. (2001: 27)

Current marriage-only programs in sex education are another example of the marriage movement's political success. Interestingly, empirical evidence suggests that marriage does not ensure that individuals, especially children, will escape poverty. "In 1999, 4.3 million of America's 10.9 million poor children lived in married-couple families." But when the official poverty measure is changed to reflect a more realistic "self-sufficiency" income standard (roughly 200 percent of the poverty level), Brown and Beeferman (2001) found that the picture is quite different: 14 million of the 25.3 million children living in poor families, were living in married-couple families (Brown and Beeferman 2001).

In summary, the stigma wars over the meaning of teenage pregnancy reflect a cultural struggle over *proper (hetero)sexuality* (i.e., sex should occur only within marriage); *proper families* (two parents—a male breadwinner and a homemaker mom—and children); and *proper family-government relations* (self-sufficient families who need no government supports or provisions). Less explored are the psychodynamic conflicts that fuel these stigma wars.

Precarious Protection and the Loss of Childhood

An ambiguous image appears on the cover of an important collection of essays called *Small Wars: The Cultural Politics of Childhood,* by Nancy Scheper-Hughes and Carolyn Sargent (1998). The image helps to convey the psychological complexities of the cultural phenomenon of teenage pregnancy. First, in keeping with a "wrong-girl" discursive frame, the image features what appears to be an impoverished girl of color. She looks to be sleeping outside, inviting viewers to ask, Does she have a home? Second, there is no male present, suggesting an incomplete, "wrong-family" frame. But perhaps most unsettling is seeing the thumb-sucking "child"-mother asleep nursing her baby. This "baby-having-a-baby" image disturbs our notion of the "right" sort of mother-child bond and taps into primal feelings of both the terrors of dependency and the comforts of being merged in a dreamlike state where mother and child are one. Indeed, the alarming absence in this image is the *mother*, not the father. The pull of this absent-mother image is that it taps into deep-seated feelings, unconscious identifications, and anxieties about being part of, yet separate from, our mothers. From a psychoanalytic perspective, feelings of vulnerability and powerlessness that are part of this early relational pattern are feelings we deny or suppress, but seek alternative expression. One alternative way of expressing them is to project them onto others.

What I am suggesting is that one of the reasons people might be drawn to the "babies having babies" rhetoric to define the social problem of teenage pregnancy, and why people might be compelled by the "looking for love" explanation for why girls would get pregnant, is because these images and stereotypes serve to allay or contain our own deep-seated fears. What seems to be at stake in the current framing of the problem of teenage pregnancy (babies having babies) is the loss of maternal protection—a fear that grabs at individual hearts and that organizes modern notions of childhood. In the context of the current political crisis over *social reproduction*— struggles over who is to provide for children's well-being and needs, and who is to be responsible for children's socialization (the state, families, individual women?)—the campaign against teenage pregnancy serves to translate what is a political problem into a problem of individual dependency. Put slightly differently, social instabilities brought about by globalization, economic restructuring, and diminished forms of social welfare are transposed into cultural symbols of vulnerability and dependency— the sleeping, thumb-sucking, nursing girl-mother—who must be made innocent (i.e., child-like) in order to be seen as deserving of protection.

For Scheper-Hughes and Sargent, the cover image of the young mother is meant to speak to the disappearance of childhood: "[T]he modern conception of the child as vulnerable and needing protection is giving way to that of the child as miniature adult, a full-circle return to Philippe Aries's notion of pre-modern childhood."[15] And this *is* one side of a very important crisis in childhood—the need to shield children from the horrors of war and violence and the harsh demands of the global economy. There are multiple, if not competing political views of the crisis. While one side focuses on improper sexual activity and forms of popular culture that sully the innocence of children, others are focusing on the effects of poverty, political violence and war, and changing global economies that are forcing children into child labor, street violence, and child prostitution. In both cases, children are viewed as losing their protected status. This is an important moment in the evolution of cultural meanings of childhood, and it seems to revolve around the question of whether or not an image of childhood in which innocence, vulnerability and a need for protection can co-exist with a recognition of young people's sexual subjectivities and agency.

Changing views about children's rights, especially the increasing awareness that children can and do have agency of their own, independent of adults (as reflected in the United Nations Convention on the Rights of the Child) present new contradictions and ironies.[16] These changing children's rights discourses make different sorts of self- and identity-making processes available. Ironically, just as children are increasingly viewed as having rights, they are also increasingly being divided into two ideal types: those who are at risk (i.e., those who are still considered "good" and in need of protection) and those who are themselves a risk to the social order (i.e., those who are "bad" and must be punished).[17] These are the divided ideal sexual types from which the PPPT girls can fashion an image of themselves as they strive to grow up in a society that does not offer much room to grow, especially as young black women living in poverty.

I would argue that in addition to the other things I've mentioned, the PPPT girls' "stigma-is-wrong" frame reflects their anxieties about losing their "protected" status (such that it is).[18] And that the identity- and self-making processes made available to the girls through these opposing ideal types inhibits their growth and development. This will become clearer in part II.

Summary

At the heart of America's anxious "war" against teenage pregnancy lie conflicts about changing social conditions—efforts toward reprivatization, changing forms of social welfare, and profound changes in the structure of race, class, and gender relationships brought about by globalization—that resonate with and evoke individual feelings and conflicts about dependency, nurturance, and protection. My concern is that this war (including the stigma contest) deflects attention from economic, political, and social injustices. Perhaps dominant discourses about and representations of teenage pregnancy serve the public imaginary like the love objects that pregnant teens are accused of seeking, images that ward off or contradict depression or anxiety about the future. I would suggest that this is an example of what Homi Bhabha means when he says that stereotypical discourses are "as anxious as they are assertive" (1983: 22).

My other concern, as I have said, is that girls, as individuals and as members of marginalized and stigmatized groups, sift through these representations and come to view themselves as "good" or "bad," powerful or powerless, vulnerable or not. Elements of these processes of self-making and *being made* are what I extract from the PPPT girls' self-representations, to which I now turn.

PART II

PREGNANT
WITH MEANING

Introduction

Part II takes the reader into a rich and complicated archive of images and self-representations[1] that the PPPT girls created in response to my invitation to do three things: first, to "perform" their pregnancy stories; second, to make a "Who am I?" collage using images and words from their favorite teen magazines; and third, to make a collaborative book of self-portraits with written self-descriptions. I discuss these three activities as research methods in part III (chapter 6), which some people may wish to read first. My focus here is on what insights about the girls' sense of self, identities, and agency can be drawn from these creative materials.

These three distinct forms of self-representation are by no means transparent. My aim is to explore and sustain a range of meanings, associations, and understandings that these various art forms may hold without "collapsing their energies into a closed system by consolidating them within any single language, style or theory" (Paley 1995: 6).

My approach to analyzing each form of self-representation is more *listening*-centered than visual-centered. In other words, I have focused my presentation and discussion of the girls' art forms (improvisations, collages, self-portraits) in terms of what they had to say about what they were making.[2] My interest is in the girls' self- and identity-making process—how they saw themselves being "addressed by" and "answering to" others[3] and how they wished to be seen.

I tape recorded all the activity sessions. I hoped that the audio tapes and transcriptions would capture the qualities of the girls' performative style—the rhythms of their conversations and the dramatic pitch of their improvisations. I also took detailed fieldnotes everyday as a backup, which was crucial because oftentimes the girls would speak over each other, which made the transcription process difficult. I did not expect that just because I would work from recorded speech—some directed at me, some spoken as if I were not present—that I would be able to truthfully or fully represent the girls' worlds, identities, and relationships. But I did believe that the re-corded conversations would make me more aware of the complexities and nuance, and therefore, enable me to write a more faithful account. Field-workers have learned to be cautious not to overstate the claims made based on transcribed conversations or interview texts, our "holy transcripts" (Riessman 2002a: 9). These texts, like any other, are embedded in a particu-lar context, at a particular moment of time, between particular people who are in varied relationships of power.

Meanwhile, the tape recorder held different meanings for different girls. There were times when a girl would start to speak about her life and ask, "Are you going to be the only person listening to these tapes?" I would reassure her that only I would have access to the tapes, but that we could turn the tape recorder off any time she wanted. There were a few times when a girl requested that I turn off the tape recorder. Then there were times when a girl would speak directly into the tape recorder. Shaniqua was one of many girls who turned to the tape recorder saying, "I am speaking to the truth here," and then proceed to report on a life event. There were girls who took control of the tape recorder, using it to "interview" each other and sometimes me (e.g., "Long back then when you were coming up, what did you think about black girls?" "Tell us what it is like to live with an artist").

In writing about the girls' conversations, stories, and art forms I have struggled not to set up a hierarchy between the girls' words and my inter-pretations. While I believe the girls' forms of self-representation stand on their own, I don't believe they speak completely for themselves. There is a great deal of interpretive work—the girls and my own—that I have tried to make explicit so that readers can entertain their own interpretations as well.

I have taken certain liberties and made editorial decisions in reporting on classroom conversations and the girls' stories. On occasion I cut repeti-tive, complicating, or exposing details from the conversations and stories in order to make the material readable (and in some cases to protect anonymity). I also was selective in using the girls' dialect; I deleted certain speech utterances (such as um or ah) and I also (reluctantly) deleted some repetition of words and phrases that were a feature of their performative style of speech because I worried about giving the wrong impression of the girls. As other ethnographers have noted, when translating conversational speech or oral storytelling into a written text, the person speaking can be misinterpreted as sounding less articulate, or less educated, than they are.[4]

These decisions notwithstanding, I have stayed as close as possible to a "rendering of the actual, a vitality phrased" (Geertz 1988: 143). I have provided dialogue and built a narrative that is based on the tape recorded and transcribed sessions, one that is both empirically grounded and evocative.

Perhaps the best way to describe what I have done is to say that I have written these three chapters hoping to bring readers into the girls' personal and social worlds. I have selected from and edited the girls' improvisational performances, the characters they created and played, and plots they devised to tell about themselves, their pregnancies, and their transitions into motherhood. And I have "curated" the girls' art forms to speak to dominant themes about how they experience the cultural phenomenon and social problem of "teenage pregnancy." The benefits and limitations of this approach to representing the girls are discussed at more length in part III.

I am not aware of any other ethnographic texts of this sort. Sherry Ortner (1993) identifies two "novel forms" of ethnography, and my approach seems to fit somewhere in between. The first is what she calls "an ethnography of issues" in which the ethnographer focuses on a contemporary conflict (for example, the abortion controversy as in Faye Ginsburg's, *Contested Lives* and urban racial conflict as in Jonathan Rieder's, *Canarsie*). The other form she calls "documentary ethnography" in which the ethnographer strives to "enter relatively small life-worlds and examine how large-scale forces work themselves out in everyday life" (412–413). She cites Judith Stacey's *Brave New Families,* which traces the impact of 1980s Reaganomics and ideological shifts in family norms within the lives of her California subjects, all of whom are part of two kin networks living in Silicon Valley. For lack of a better phrase, I call my project an *ethnography of representation and self-representation.* Like an ethnography of issues, I am focusing on a contemporary conflict from the perspective of those who have been defined as "the problem." Like a documentary ethnography, I have used the self-representation activities as a way to enter the girls' life worlds and to examine how particular psychological and social processes work themselves out in these self-representations.

Each activity offered the girls a different means through which to represent herself to herself and to others and for me to learn different things about the girls. The role-playing skits opened up opportunities for improvisation—for the girls to reenact a drama of firsthand experience and/or to re-play a cultural script by experimenting with new ways of interacting. Moreover, these role plays allowed for audience participation, which I describe in chapter 5, and sparked debate among the girls about inadvertent stereotypes that were being presented by these dramas.[5] The collage-making activity used images or text from teen magazines, and thus allowed for a different sort of cultural appropriation and personal meaning-making. By clipping fragments from a whole, selecting unrelated media images, and re-arranging them on the page in a way that spoke to the question, "Who am I?", the girls could invest these images with their own meanings. Put slightly different, the girls could select dominant images, which were then trans-formed through their personal use.[6] Listening to the girls explain the meaning of their collages and their reasons for selecting each image or text provided insight into their self-which-I-might-be as I discuss in chapter 4. Finally, the self-portrait activity (using collage rather than drawing) al-lowed for yet another type of expression and means to examine psycholog-ical processes. Being asked to fill a blank sheet of paper from assembled bits of hand-painted papers[7] and to produce a sense of one's self-image, offers a view of a girl's relational world—how she placed herself in time, place, and in relationship to parts of herself or to others.[8] Psychologically speaking, we could speculate that the blank piece of paper symbolized a girl's "area of integration and differentiation, giving us her own picture of her inner world with its drama of subtle change and growth" (Naevestad 1979: 18). Reading the girls' texts that accompanied their self-portraits; listening to them elaborate on the particulars of their picture; and hearing their con-cerns about what others might think provided invaluable insight into their way of bridging between external forces and inner realities. All three forms of self-representations proved to be an ideal means to explore the interplay between that which the girls created and that which they "found" already in the culture as part of their self-making process.

Part II begins with the girls' self-portraits to give the reader a sense of them as distinctive individuals who, while sharing many social characteris-tics and common concerns, see themselves in unique and idiosyncratic ways. In the next chapter on the girls' media collages, I describe how they take up and use cultural symbols and images as resources to define them-selves within different social worlds during this time of transition. In chap-ter 5 on telling pregnancy stories, the girls speak to and (re)enact existential moments regarding their pregnancies, accounting for their actions and de-cisions as sexual beings, as daughters, and as future mothers. In each chap-ter I try to put forth what seemed most significant to the girls as they made these self-representations and engaged each other in conversation. At the same time, each chapter is framed by my own interpretations. These inter-pretations are offered in a spirit once defined by anthropologist Clifford

Geertz, who said that ethnographic interpretation is "more like grasping a proverb, catching an allusion, seeing a joke, or reading a poem than it is like achieving communion" (1997: 241).

If there is a punch line for part II it is that when asked to represent themselves through these three forms, the girls crafted responses that shed light on their multiple worlds—worlds of childhood, womanhood, motherhood, heterosexual romance, and consumerism—and that highlight their growing awareness of how race, class, and gender inequities shape their participation in and aspirations about these worlds. The girls' self-representations also illustrate their efforts to manage feelings associated with life events and hardships. I argue that the girls' attempts to "answer" to their worlds, and to portray the complexities of their wants, wishes, and wills, surpass standard notions of agency. This is a piece of the self- and identity-making process that is not well-enough understood, especially regarding girls' sexuality, pregnancy, and motherhood.

Figure 1

This picture is me when I was 4 years old. One day I was standing outside and it was dark and the stars were out. My mom told me to stand still and pose, and so I did it. It was a summer night in 1985. I'm glad that she took that picture of me that young because it lets me know how I look back then. When I look and see that old picture I laugh and say in my mind that I look so cute and small. I remember how crazy the clothes were and how things change over time.

Figure 2
My picture is of me in a thought. A thought of a colorful, magic, genie-like person, me. I'm in my own little world. Life is unreal, crimeless, and bright in this dream world. I'm alone but not lonely. Peaceful. Happy as a child on her birthday. If somebody touched me and made me come alive, I would probably be a cartoon figure dancing the robot.

Figure 3

This picture represents the way I feel. I feel like a big, heavy ball that can't move. I can't pick up things—I can't do what I usually would do, like go out. People look at me as if they've never been feeling like this before. I have nothing to say to them as long as they say nothing to me. The reason for my purple color is because I feel independent. I'm going to have to be independent because nobody is going to do anything for me.

Figure 4

This picture is about me and my baby. I am imagining how I just came home from work and she wants to go out for a walk. I'm thinking how I am going to treat my daughter when she gets a little older. She is one-year-old and I am sixteen. My baby looks happy so I am happy.

I dream of my baby finishing her schooling and being what she wants to be when she grows up. I love my baby a lot. When she is sad or sick I feel the same way.

For myself I dream of being a professional, like a doctor. I would like to help ladies deliver their babies.

Before my baby I didn't have anything to keep me going. But now I have someone who keeps me hoping for a future—liking finishing school and having a career. I am going to do it for my baby and for me. I hope my baby does not go through the same things I am going through because it is really hard.

Figure 5

This picture is about me in the future relaxing in the Jamaican islands. I am around twenty years of age. I am happy that I finally made it to the islands. I have a young boy, Malcolm, as a son. His loving father is my husband. They are both a joy to have in my life. During the time that I was pregnant with Malcolm I felt all types of emotions: happy, sad, funny, glad, angry and mad. But most of all I felt a whole lot of love for my baby.

Figure 6

My name is Alice. I am fourteen years old. I have blonde hair and blue eyes and I have braces. I stand about 5'3" and weigh about 142 pounds. I am going to have a baby in August. I don't like going to school. I don't like to be mean to other people. I have a great personality when I am around my friends and family. Now you know about the unknown girl.

Figure 7
This is a picture of me. I'm
17 years old and so miserable.
All I can do is think of the
things I used to do and will
do after I have my lovely baby.
I only smile when I want to or
if somebody makes me laugh.
The funny feeling about being
pregnant is feeling something
move inside you. I'll never
hold hatred toward my baby
because I know it's my fault
and not my baby's. I have
more problems on me than
usual. But now I have somebody to really love and care
for—somebody who's a piece
of my heart.

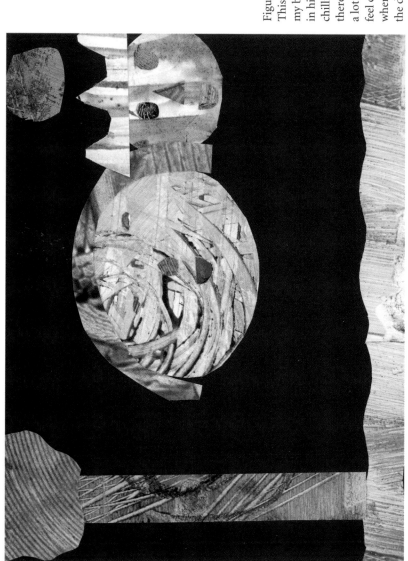

Figure 8

This is a picture of me and my boyfriend at his house in his yard. I'm in his yard chilling. I like being over there with him because it's a lot of fun. He makes me feel comfortable. The tree is where we like to be during the day.

CHAPTER 3

Self-Portraits: From Girlhood to Motherhood

Introduction

"Hello Ms. Wendy, what fun are we having today?" Kaela's unbounded energy fills the room.

"You artists are going to make self-portraits," I pause for the laughter this evokes. "You are going to illustrate and write a book about yourselves—it will include everyone's self-portrait and written description. You can draw yourselves or make pictures from the paste paper.[1] We'll make color Xerox copies of everyone's portrait and bind them altogether. Robert will come in and show you how to do the bookbinding and make the covers. You'll each get your own copy of the book," I explained.

"How many pieces of paper do we get?"

"Can I take some home?"

"I want that purple one," Sonya reaches over Tara to grab the paste paper; she runs her fingers over the paper as if it were silk.

"I'm going to make a picture of me in the future, when I'm eighteen. I'll be married, a singer maybe," says Sonya.

"I'm not getting married until I finish school," announces Tara.

"I'll have my high school diploma when I'm eighteen," says Sonya sounding exasperated.

"I'm talking about finishing *college* [emphasizing this word] before I get married," Tara retorts.

"And how you goin' to do that?" Ebony asks while laughing and poking Tara in the ribs. Tara doesn't reply.

Silence hangs in the room.[2]

"Can we turn on the radio?" asks Kaela. She knows playing music is against school rules.

"Okay, but keep it low," I reluctantly agree.

"This is going to be some book once *we* get through with it" [her emphasis]. Kaela laughs as she starts to sing along with the music.

This chapter is about what we can learn about the girls' self- and identity-making from their self-portraits and texts made into collaborative books, and from the lively, and at times intense, conversations that were sparked by a girl's self-representation. It is difficult to collapse the vitality of these self-portraits into an analytic framework. Because for each self-portrait there is a story. Fifty self-portraits and fifty stories, each one distinct in its making and meaning. A girl might go through several iterations before she discovered what—or settled on how—she wanted to represent herself. These self-portraits also evoked a range of viewer responses from schoolmates, boyfriends, teachers, and family members, some of whom attended the "book signing" parties held at the end of each school year.

The group conversation that surrounded the making of the self-portraits, including my questions, often spurred a girl to see what she had made in a different light. After each girl finished her portrait we would talk about it and I would ask both the "artist" and her "viewers" what they saw (see Appendix 1). Then I would ask a series of questions specifically related to the image; some were "aesthetic" questions about color choices, features of design, and perspective; others were anatomical questions about missing body parts or the varying size of body parts; and others were "autobiographical" questions about the people or places depicted in a picture.[3] I always made a point to ask at least one question about a unique detail provided in a portrait. It wasn't long before the girls would anticipate and imitate my questioning style with light-hearted laughter: "You know, Ms. Wendy is about to ask you about your picture, you better be ready."

Knowing that they were producing a collaborative book in which everyone's work would be included meant that the girls often took on the role of "critic" of each other's illustrations or texts. On a few occasions classmates suggested that a girl needed to "work" more on her art form if she wanted it included in the book. But most often the girls asked for help from their classmates: "Who can make me shoes that will look right?" I actively encouraged and listened carefully to this group "critique" process and the debates it generated as a means to understand the girls' struggles over self-representation.

Throughout this chapter I try to feature both the idiosyncratic and the culturally patterned nature of these self-portraits. Several themes related to the self- and identity-making process can be traced throughout the girls' self-portraits and in their conversations: (1) changing *self- and body images* (about which there is very scant research [Stenberg and Blinn 1993]);[4] (2) reflecting on their *self-worth and value* (i.e., what they have or don't have in life and what they are looking forward to); (3) managing *conflicting emotions* (in relation to their mothers, their soon-to-be-born babies, and themselves); and (4) expressing a desire to control their surroundings, which for now I will call *agency.*

I have organized my presentation of these self-portraits according to how the girls placed themselves in time and place, and through which we gain insight into their social worlds and their class, race, and gendered meanings of selfhood. At the end of the chapter, I consider how the self-portraits also provide a glimpse of a girl's coming into new awareness about herself and her soon-to-be-born baby, what Joan Raphael-Leff (1995) would call the "inside story" of pregnancy.

Time, Place, and Personhood

Most girls portrayed themselves in the present. Twelve of the fifty PPPT girls portrayed themselves as children, ages four to eight (before the onset of puberty). I was struck by the fact that twice as many girls chose to portray themselves in the past, reflecting on their childhoods, compared to those who projected themselves into the future. Only five of the fifty PPPT girls made themselves "grown women" (in Ebony's words); and three of those girls were Mexican American, which I discuss later in the chapter. In light of public discourses that cast pregnant teenagers as those who lack aspirations or a vision of their future or as "babies having babies," I was curious to probe more deeply the meaning of the girls' depictions of themselves in a past time.

In their re-creations of childhood, each girl described herself in the language of ideal girlhood as "innocent," "cute," and "small." Their reflections were nostalgic and evoked a sense of loss about the past.[5] Their portraits of girlhood also sparked discussion among the black girls about beauty, fashion, femininity (what it means to be a girl), racial identity, and culture within African American communities.

Shannon's picture of herself as a child is a good illustration. (See Figure 1) When I met Shannon she was fourteen, a "bright student," who, according to Ms. Washington, was "going places before she became pregnant." Shannon attended the PPPT program for a brief time—only the last three months of her pregnancy—after which she returned to her "regular" high school. Shannon's self-portrait was unusual in that her paste paper, cutout figure took up the entire page. Her picture featured an exaggerated head, with bright *blue* eyes (noticed by her classmates), and a hairstyle (with ribbons) that many of the girls recognized as one they had once worn.[6] The clothes Shannon made for her figure were reminiscent of a midriff fashion many girls remembered wearing when they were "small" or "skinny." Behind the figure Shannon pasted bright, multicolored stars. She described her picture in this way:

> This picture is me when I was four years old. One day I was standing outside and it was dark and the stars were out. My mom told me to stand still and pose, and so I did it. It was a summer night in 1985. I'm glad that she took that picture of me that young because it lets me know how I look back then. When I look and see that old picture I laugh and say in my mind that I look so cute and small. I remember how crazy the clothes were and how things change over time.

The girls were quick to respond to Shannon's portrait and eager to share their own recollections of being cute and small; to express delight in the hairstyles they used to wear, sometimes lamenting the loss of this girlhood ritual. I was especially struck by Kendra's description:

> I remember how my momma would set me on the porch every morning before school combing and braiding my hair, for hours it seemed. I'd say, "Let me go, I'm going to be late for school." But she would be running her fingers through my head saying how tight and curly and BEAUTIFUL my hair was. She'd put ribbons, bows, beads, barrettes, pulling and yanking at my head and when she got finished I looked so cute—"cuter than those white girls," she'd tell me.

Turning toward me Kendra said, "No offense, Ms. Wendy, but that's what my momma would say."[7]

The lesson Kendra learned on her mother's porch is part of a long tradition of racial socialization within the African American community where children "learn more than how to listen and speak. They also learn a way of looking at the world—a way of positioning their experiences in opposition or relation to those of the 'dominant culture'" (Rooks 1996: 286). Indeed, Kendra (and many other PPPT girls) spoke reverently about the practice of braiding hair, as if she were paying homage to a time when she felt cared for, valued, and made mindful of her beauty in relation to white girls.

The girls' portraits of childhood sparked many conversations about gender and racial socialization within their families and community.

Childhood experiences of hairstyling were associated with feelings of "closeness, comfort and community," racial pride, and maternal care.[8] Perhaps in this way, the girls' portraits of childhood are not only about the past, but also about the anticipation of the future world of motherhood, including its rituals of caretaking and racial socialization.

There was a liveliness and immediacy about the PPPT girls' attention to hairstyling—both in everyday life and in their self-portraits. Without a doubt, the most consistent and recurring topic of conversation among the black PPPT girls was about hair. And inasmuch as there was joyfulness, there was also angst associated with having or not having "good" hair.

Triumphant tales of "fixing" their own or another's hair—getting the right texture, curl, or color—were told as often and with as much detail and delight as were the failed efforts. These conversations, whether critical or congratulatory, seemed to serve as a means of girlhood bonding where both creativity and conformity was endorsed.

The girls' focus on hair would not have surprised black feminist author Lisa Jones (1994) who writes about hair and hairstyling in African American communities as an emotional and political battleground. She opens her book with a glimpse into the emotional meaning of hair for one of her interviewees:

> When I was a little girl, about thirteen or so, they told me a woman's pride and glory was her hair. Then they told me mine wasn't any good. I guess I went to war to absolve myself of this grief. (11)

To understand current trends in hair fashion and politics, Jones draws links between African American diaspora hairstyling practices and traditional African cultures, arguing that it is "not the naturalness of the braids, it's the idea of construction. Hair in both traditions suggests spectacle and pageantry. It's always handled and adorned; hair is never left 'as is.' Hair exists to be *worked*" (297). The PPPT girls' art forms and conversations about hair resonate with both this idea of "construction" and establishing a sense of one's own "style" and "attitude."

Creating one's own, distinctive style was not always easy. Stories of being teased or teasing another about hairstyle decisions peppered informal conversations. In one case a girl told about an experience where she had been called into the (black) principal's office at her "regular" school for wearing a hairstyle he described as "a distraction to students who are here to learn not to make fashion statements."[9]

The girls' conversations about hairstyling intermingled several sides of the social world of African American womanhood and motherhood. One is the side of being valued, cared for, and held within the comfort of community (and perhaps being worried about whether they will be able to do the same for their babies). Another is the side of resentment about being scrutinized, including by members of their own community for "looking too black or not black enough" (a statement attributed to their peers) or for looking in a way that is "unbecoming" (a statement attributed to their elders).

Still another side is the girls' struggle to create their "own look" amid multiple and competing tastes and expectations, sometimes expressed as resistance to dominant white standards of beauty and sometimes as assent. This was a salient theme in the girls' self-portraits as well as their media collages (see chapter 4).

The Hardness of Life

The girls' portraits of childhood also speak to a sense of disillusionment about their impending womanhood. Clarise's self-portrait is a case in point (see Figure 2). Clarise was fifteen when I met her. She was admired by her classmates for her quick wit and honesty. She had the best "fashion sense" according to Star, her friend in the PPPT Program. Clarise often spoke about arguments she and her mother were having, and how she regretted not having "listened better to her warnings about boys and how they only want one thing." Clarise described herself as "independent" and "a good friend to have" but "not a good student" because she hates following rules.

Clarise first assembled a frame of colorful (reds, purples, blues) and textured pieces of paste paper around the edge of her paper. In the center she pasted a black piece of construction paper onto which she pasted pieces of a torso—a blue neck, green shirt, brown arms and hands, purple pants, and green shoes "to match the shirt," she explained. Above the neck floated bright red lips, a blue nose, and green eyes; the traditional border outlining a face was missing (an example of disconnected body parts that was found in many of the portraits). Instead, what bordered the facial features was an elaborate hairstyle. Clarise took days to carefully cut, place, paste, and bend layers of colorful strips of paste paper, which she braided, into place. When she was finished and I held it up for the class to observe, the girls exploded with applause and shouts of joy—"I love those lips, I want those big lips." "That hairstyle is CRAZY!" Clarise seemed to appreciate the attention her picture was drawing, as she broke into a smile and threw back her head with laughter. To the next session Clarise brought two pieces of writing to share with the class. The first was about her portrait:

My picture is of me in a thought. A thought of a colorful, magic, genie-like person, me. I'm in my own little world. Life is unreal, crimeless, and bright in this dream world. I'm alone but not lonely. Peaceful. Happy as a child on her birthday. If somebody touched me and made me come alive, I would probably be a cartoon figure dancing the robot.

The second is a poem she had written and wanted to read aloud:

Life

My life is moving so fast
when I get older I doubt if I have much to tell
bout the past.
First it was pubic hairs
then it was breasts
then it was a period
and then it was sex.
Now it's pregnancy
Motherhood will be here soon.
I wonder what's next
Growing up is hard
especially when you're a girl.
Life is so misunderstood
it's just one big swirl.

Clarise's picture and writings hold multiple truths and express mixed feelings about growing up hard and fast.[10] Her picture is colorful and imaginative; she made it with great ease and zest. Her two writings were read soberly and expressed divided emotions about the costs of growing up as a girl. One text speaks in terms of magic, wishes, and a crimeless, dream world (in which somebody touches her and makes her come alive). Her other text speaks directly about her changing body and life world, things are happening to her and her body—pubic hair, breasts, a period, sex, pregnancy, motherhood—and "life is hard, especially when you are a girl." She expresses different responses to these changes, from escapism —"I'm in my own little world"; to solitude—"I'm alone but not lonely"; to fantasy—"I would probably be a cartoon figure dancing the robot"; to reflection, "[*when*] I get older I doubt if I have much to tell about the past."

Clarise's writings express a sense of loss of power that is made explicit by many female characters in coming-of-age stories.[11] As so many feminist literary critics have noted, initiation into the sexual and political realities of womanhood comes in many forms depending on one's class, racial, religious, and regional background. Clarise's stark presentation of the realities of womanhood that she has come to understand, remind me of Paulette Childress White's (1984) autobiographical coming-of-age story, "Getting the Facts of Life." The main character, Minerva, describes her initiation into black womanhood in a similar tone. "And the facts of life, fixed in our minds like the sun in the sky were no burning mysteries" (140).

Some of the research literature on girls' development characterizes adolescence as a time of inner restlessness, anxious concern, and sense of imminent danger associated with changing bodies and blossoming female sexuality.[12] Girls' "voices" and sense of value are said to be driven underground or at least weakened in the face of social pressures and demands. Meanwhile, there are psychodynamic conflicts associated with adolescence. According to psychoanalyst Louise Kaplan:

> This period of life is concerned with the profiling of gender identity, because both inner sexual tensions and outer social demands pressure the young person in the direction of gendered growing up. What does it mean to be a grown woman or man? What desires are there room for—and at what costs? (cited in Nielsen and Rudberg 1994: 93)

It would seem that Clarise is considering the costs of becoming a grown woman and what desires there are room for, costs that are both social and personal.

Particularly striking is Clarise's reference to a world that is "hard," a view of the world shared by the PPPT girls. To survive in a hard world requires a string of qualities that the PPPT girls referenced throughout their conversations. "Standing alone"; "making it on my own"; "facing the world by myself"; being "tough and independent"; "not taking shit"; "depending only on myself"; "not letting anyone walk over me"; "not letting anyone get into my business"—these were all qualities admired by the PPPT girls and were often traits they used to describe themselves.

Cultural anthropologist Adrie Kusserow's work on class-based notions of "hard" and "soft" individualism within American culture is useful in thinking about the meanings of selfhood upon which so many of the PPPT girls seem to draw.[13] Kusserow observed and interviewed parents and teachers in two working-class communities (one more prosperous than the other) and in one professional, upper-middle-class community in New York (1996, 1999) about their views and practices regarding selfhood, childrearing, and concepts of individualism.[14] The working-class parents and teachers she interviewed held Clarise's version of the world as a difficult place, full of hardships. Being able to survive against great odds (financial instability, gang violence, drugs, dangerous life on the street) is a necessary trait among working-class children who are raised to have "tough" and "thickened" boundaries of the self (1999: 229). Kusserow observed that the working-class parents in her study used childrearing strategies that encouraged developing a thick skin and independence. Unlike the upper-middle-class parents in her study, the working-class parents felt there "should be limits on praise so that the child doesn't become too dependent on it or become too 'full or himself' or 'puffed up'" (1999: 218). Being tough, not crying over spilt milk, getting on with one's life regardless of loss and disappointment are important traits that the working-class parents whom Kusserow interviewed wanted to pass on to their children. "The word tough was often part of a constellation of other words and phrases such as 'isn't a pushover,' 'speaks her own mind,' 'is her own person' which portrayed a solidity to the self of which the parent was quite proud" (1999: 218). Meanwhile, tough expressions of discipline and harsh phrases said in the presence of the child were used without worrying that these would hurt the child's feelings or damage his or her esteem. These parents wanted their children to be tough enough to take whatever hardships might lie ahead. Kusserow contrasts this model of the self as a "barricade" against the world, to the middle-class model of the self as a "flower" opening up to the world and a sense of "soft" individualism born of a life of comfort and greater opportunities for self-expression.

People can hold and use two, even contradictory orientations toward the self at once, for example, in the ways in which ethnicity is used by Americans to fulfill a need to feel unique, as well as a need to belong to something larger than themselves, a community (Waters 1990). The girls' self-portraits speak to both modes of individualism; their claims to uniqueness and creativity as well as their attachment to community. But it was the hardness of life as a girl—the coping with life's gendered hardships—that begs for more attention.

British feminist historian Carolyn Steedman, in her autobiographical account of working-class childhood, argues that the effects of life's hardness—a sense of exclusion, envy, and longing for "the good life"—are unexplored in terms of the psychological development of working-class youth.[15] She writes:

Working-class autobiography and people's history have been developed as forms that allow the individual and collective expression of thoughts, feelings and desires about class societies and the effect of class structures on individuals and communities. But as forms of analysis and writing, people's history and working-class autobiography are relatively innocent of psychological theory, and there has been little space within them to discuss the development of class consciousness (as opposed to its expression), nor for understanding of it as a *learned* position, learned in childhood, and often through the exigencies of difficult and lonely lives. (1986: 13)

The black (working-class and poor) PPPT girls' self-portraits spoke to a sorrow associated with growing up "hard." And there are hints about the psychological effects of social injuries, for example, difficulties managing grief or being unable to acknowledge loss and disappointment, what Morgan (1999) refers to as the "strong black woman" syndrome. Anne Cheng (2002) notes that a psychological effect of racism is losing one's capacity for "affective discrimination"—the ability to recognize and distinguish one's feelings, such as envy or longing. Another way of putting this is that the PPPT girls' self-portraits suggest that at the heart of personal conflicts are social divisions—gendered, racial, and class-based divisions through which girls filter their wide range of feelings about the hardships of life, from exclusion, to envy, to defensiveness.

Tara's self-portrait highlights a constellation of feelings that was common among the PPPT girls. Tara was the tallest and most full-bodied girl among her classmates. Her presence was at times regal; "the queen," one classmate referred to her. Tara spoke with a deep, scratchy voice and had earned the respect of her classmates for her poetry writing, which she often shared in class sessions. When I met Tara she was living with her maternal aunt because she had recently lost her mother. Her father had died in a car accident when she was a child, and her mother had died of cancer. She spoke openly about her grief during class sessions, including how she was seeing a counselor whom her aunt had arranged. Tara described what had happened when her aunt had learned of her pregnancy as she made her self-portrait:

My aunt cried and cried when she found out I was pregnant. She just couldn't stop crying. My aunt is overly sensitive and emotional; my mother used to say that about her, that she was too soft for the world. Anyway, if my mother was alive I wouldn't be having the baby. You know, how when a family member dies and you get pregnant as a way to deal with it? My mother died in November and I got pregnant in November so I needed to keep the baby [it is April].

I always wanted to have a baby, but not so soon, and since my mother isn't alive I went ahead and decided to have it. You know she [her mother] told me not to cry at her funeral, so I didn't cry. I didn't cry except on my birthday. I can't cry.

"Why can't you cry?" demanded Shadra. Tara avoided answering and said, "My half sister cries all the time and my half-brother, well he's crazy."

"But you might feel better if you could cry," offered Kaela.

"Yeah, that's what my counselor says. But I need to get on with my life. I can't be crying all the time, and besides, there's always somebody worse off than you, you can't spend your life feeling sorry for yourself."

Tara selected a dark blue sheet of construction paper for her background, saying, "This won't take long. I know just what to make to show how I feel." From a piece of bright purplish red paste paper, Tara cut a large round ball, which she pasted in the center of the page. (See Figure 3)

"Finished," she announced. "I'll do the writing now and maybe a poem later." Here is what she wrote:

This picture represents the way I feel. I feel like a big, heavy ball that can't move. I can't pick up things—I can't do what I usually would do, like go out. People look at me as if they've never been feeling like this before. I have nothing to say to them as long as they say nothing to me. The reason for my purple color is because I feel independent. I'm going to have to be independent because nobody is going to do anything for me.

Tara's image embodies, among many things, her feelings about her changing body, that it is big, heavy, motionless, unable to do what she is used to doing (like pick up things or go out). Speaking as if her body is betraying her or is at least a separate entity from her self reflects a kind of division that was common among the PPPT girls. The girls talked about being eager to "get my body back" and being able to fit into clothes they wore before pregnancy and they spoke of their bodies sending them "signals" or "messages" about what "it" needed. In chapter 5, I discuss this disconnection between self and body, especially as it relates to the medicalization of pregnancy.

In light of the conversation that surrounded the making of her portrait, I see Tara's purple ball as also reflecting a bound-up, toughened sense of self that she has had to develop to cope with unspeakable grief and hardship— her "you can't be crying all the time" stance toward the world. As Tara read her piece outloud she spoke with great force about being the object of others' gaze. She raised her voice as she said, "People look at me as if they've never been feeling like this before." Tara's them-me formulation, her defensive stance ("I have nothing to say to them as long as they say nothing to me") suggests pain or at least concern about what others see, think, or have to say to her. These views of what "others/they" have to say might also reflect her own negative feelings about herself and her body, which she attributes to others, feelings that are hard for her to recognize as her own.

The girls' reaction to Tara's picture drew my attention to how much the girls wrestled with the force of social divisions in making their self-representations. Shadra complimented Tara on her text, "It sounds just like you." Nonetheless, Shadra thought the picture needed some work. "We aren't going to have a big purple circle sitting on a page in the middle of the book. It doesn't look finished," Shadra stated firmly.

Ebony disagreed, "Well, if that is how Tara feels, we can't expect her to change it. Besides, she's talking about feeling like everyone's looking at her, just like in the picture where we're just looking at the ball."

"That's my picture—if you don't like it, you can change it yourself," Tara said defiantly, shaking her head and shrugging her shoulders.

A heated debate followed and the PPPT girls were split over the decision. The debate was in part about the perils of representation. Given the disparaging image of pregnant teenagers, what would viewers think about Tara from her picture? How might they judge her? Those who argued that viewers "might make some wrong assumptions about Tara, like that she is lazy or doesn't care" finally convinced the others. Tara reluctantly agreed to let Shadra add some "scenery." (As far as Tara was concerned, she was finished with her picture.)

The struggle to find a way to represent themselves and their pregnancies so as to break the gaze[16] of those who would judge or belittle them galvanized the PPPT girls' discussions. This struggle was not limited to Tara's self-portrait; rather, the perils of representation persisted throughout each activity where the PPPT girls were called upon to portray themselves and their lives.

The girls' debates, especially when they engaged and talked back to dominant representations, feature what I have come to call their "body-smarts"—their dual awareness that they and their pregnant bodies are being viewed and scrutinized by others. The term "body-smarts" is meant to convey the grief and the insight the girls express about their difference (Massey 1996).[17] On the one hand, the girls express their growing awareness that others are seeing them as "depressed," as "irresponsible," as "babies having babies," as "lazy." And this hurts or smarts. On the other hand, as the girls become more self-aware and express their mixed feelings and fears—from feeling miserable or immobilized, to being in awe of their changing bodies—they become more aware (they become smart) about their power and possibilities as women.

I also want to suggest that the girls' "body-smarts," expressed by their self-portraits and the group conversations, bespeak a wide range of complicated, conflicting emotions about their bodies. Especially striking to me was how much sadness (Anne Cheng [2002] calls it melancholy) was associated with the making of these self-portraits. (Interestingly, this sadness was less pronounced in the making of the "Who am I?" collages and in the pregnancy performances as I will show in the next chapters.) Tara's self-representation is a case in point. She moves between several emotions, from talking about not being able to cry about her mother's death, to mourning the body she used to have, to resisting the objectified gaze of others, to a somewhat sorrowful self-affirmation ("I'm going to be independent because nobody is going to do anything for me"). Anne Cheng (2002) suggests that we do not know enough about how "racialized people as complex psychical beings deal with the objecthood thrust upon them. . . . Within the reductive notion of 'internalization' lies a world of relations that is as much about surviving grief as embodying it" (20). I suggest that the PPPT girls' self-representations provide a glimpse into this inner world of objecthood, resistance, and grief.

Kaela's self-portrait of childhood is another poignant example. Remember that Kaela is the girl who asked, "What fun are we having today?"—her characteristic stance toward the creative activities. Among her PPPT classmates she tended to be the first to agree to do an activity and was both eager and willing to help with the art supplies and cleanup. Kaela was quick to joke around with others and was admired for her "in your face" attitude. When I met Kaela she was living with her retired paternal grandmother who used to work as a housekeeper at a local college. Kaela is the oldest of four children, but only her brother stays with her and her grandmother. Kaela doesn't talk much about her family life, but from what I could glean (from teachers, school records) she has faced difficulties, including moving between schools and living for a brief time in foster care. In her journal she writes about her dreams of becoming a doctor, what it feels like to be in love, how she wishes for an end to street violence and racial discrimination.

Kaela selected a dark blue piece of construction paper for the background. Unlike the other girls who were preoccupied with finding pieces of paste paper, Kaela took a piece of bright yellow construction paper. "This is for the sun," she remarked. Kaela took her time cutting and pasting strips of this yellow paper to make rays of sunshine. She did this activity quietly, meditatively, almost solemnly, as if she were in some far-off place, a demeanor that was unusual for her. She took her time cutting out a doll-like figure with a blue dress, which she put on the middle of the page, saying she remembered having a dress like the one in the picture.

In the next several sessions, Kaela added very specific details to the face, including cut-out ears and eyes; she used a black marker to draw in a nose, a smiling mouth, fingernails and toenails, and, finally, a distinctive hairstyle. She placed a long strip of green paste paper at the base of the picture (grass), added a tree to the left, a round blue object to the right of the figure and announced she was finished. Kaela handed it to me to hold up "for questioning."

"What do you see?" I asked my standard opening question.

"My legs look skinny and bow-legged—that's what people used to say about me as a child."

The girls start talking about who was and wasn't skinny and bow-legged as a child. There were comments about her "cute" hairstyle.

"What do you notice about the colors?" I asked.

"Everything is blue, except for the yellow sun," Tara remarked.

"Does the color blue have any special meaning to you, Kaela?" I asked.

"No, not especially, except for feeling blue, the blues, yeah, singing the blues," she replied haltingly.

The next day Kaela brought a written text about her portrait to class:

This picture represents me as I was a young child. I was seven years old. I was in MacDonald Terrace [a housing project]. It was 5:30 in the afternoon and it was very hot outside. I was getting ready to go the store for some five cent candy with no shoes on. I've always had a good attitude. I don't pick at people, I speak to everyone who speaks to me. I'm not stuck up on myself, and I speak my mind.

Tara offered her opinion, "What you say is true; you are not stuck up on yourself."

Kaela smiled and said that she would never think she was better than anyone else if she had "nice clothes, jewelry, and stuff. That's the way a lot of people are, but not me."

The girls exchanged names of peers who they believed "looked down" on others, who "bragged" about their possessions. As this conversation died down, I asked Kaela, "Why don't you have shoes on?"

She pondered this question, "Because my shoes didn't fit and they made my feet hot. I kept begging my mother (she lived with us then) for new shoes but she said, 'You're too hard on your shoes, you always need new shoes, now go on and get you some candy.' It was such a hot day—hotter than any day I can remember."

"And what do you have to say when you speak your mind?" I asked.

"I don't let anybody take advantage of me. I stand on my own."

Two girls laughed and said, "Well, it's true that you always speak your mind."

References to her toughness, "hard" individualism, and to her grief (expressed through her association with the blues and a time when she lived with her mother) are woven into Kaela's representation of growing up. And there are references to her efforts to be in control of her surroundings. There is her ability to speak her mind, her unwillingness to let others "take advantage" of her, her "good attitude" and treatment of others, her desire for new shoes, her acknowledgment of envy (and being envied) for having nice clothes, jewelry, and stuff.

Kaela's pensive demeanor while making her self-portrait compared to her usual liveliness lingered in my mind as I went back through her writing and the transcription of the class conversation. I noted a break in the story she had begun to tell about her picture. At our next session, I said to Kaela, "I forgot to ask you something about your story. You said you were on your way to the candy store, but you stopped telling us the story and started telling us about yourself. I was wondering what happened—did you go to the store; are you going to put that part in your piece?"

Kaela looked away, something about her reaction made me think she was upset.

"There's a lot that happened at that candy store but I don't want to say."

Kaela's self-representation of childhood referenced an experience about which she did not want or was not yet ready to tell. One of her reasons is that she needs to "move on" despite her feelings, feelings upon which Kaela doesn't like to dwell. Over the course of the year I would learn more about the candy store and the violence that occurred there. But Kaela wished not to speak about it (or for me to write about it); rather, she prefers to talk about her life now—her positive attitude and her ability to stand up for herself. Kaela is wary of people getting "into her business" and making judgments. Kaela's survival of her "hard" growing up strikes me as a central feature of her agency.

Grief and Longing for a Place

The three Mexican American girls presented themselves in the future, as grown up and in their maternal roles. While on the surface, these self-representations were about the future, they were also about the girls' past lives in Mexico and their efforts to manage strong emotions related to physically, socially, and psychologically adjusting to their relocation.[18] All three girls wrote and spoke about missing Mexico: Eliza reflects, "Today I have been thinking so much. I am sad and feeling lonely wishing I could be in Mexico with my father or my godmother." While making her self-portrait, Teresa spoke about her wish to return to Mexico to have her baby. She reminisced about the beauty of the landscape and her feelings of confinement in the city. Upon completing her self-portrait, her baby in her arms, Teresa remarked, "My baby looks happy so I am happy." "I hope my baby does not go through the same things I went through, feeling lonely and longing to see the countryside" (see Figure 4). These self-portraits, and the self- and identity-making processes they suggest, are best understood within the context of immigration, a sense of a traditional, extended family, and a cultural world of womanhood that idealizes Catholic iconic images of motherhood.[19]

Marisa's self-representation illustrates all of these, coupled with her sense of agency. When I first met Marisa, she was fifteen and living with her boyfriend in her parents' home. Marisa's father had migrated to this country from Mexico five years earlier, with the rest of the family joining him three years later. Her father works on subcontracted construction crews (part of a growing labor practice in this region of the country), and her mother "stays at home—she can't drive." Marisa talked about her experience as she was making her self-portrait:

> I was going out with my boyfriend and we had run away during the summer together, so my mother figured I was having sex and I didn't think she would be so surprised. . . . I told my mom that me and my boyfriend were going to move in together, that we couldn't stay at the house. But my mother said it wasn't safe. Something could happen to me while I was alone and it wasn't good for me or the baby. She said my boyfriend should move in. So at home we have my mom, dad, my brother and his girlfriend who is expecting twins (my mother is very excited about this); my younger sister who is nine. She keeps saying, "What am I going to do with three babies coming?"

Marisa often came to class with stories about her overcrowded but lively household, including the squabbles and feelings of jealousy she had with her brother's girlfriend, who she believed received more of her mother's attention than she did. To make her self-portrait, Marisa chose a burgundy colored sheet of construction paper. First she made a landscape of sun, clouds, rain drops, and a waterfall flowing from the sun to a rock.

Then she began assembling her figures. She cut out a female figure (with dress) and added brown legs, feet/shoes, and hands, which held a small oval shape ("My baby," she said). Immediately to the right she pasted a cutout male figure with pants, brown feet/shoes, and large green hands reaching over toward her and the baby. These figures stand to the left of the waterfall and on top of ground that is cut with points, which she explained, were mountains. Here is what she wrote about her picture:

> This picture is in my mind everyday because I can't wait for my baby to come. I am excited and long to be happy with my boyfriend and my baby like a loving family, joyful and united. I see us in a beautiful place, sunny, raining with a waterfall. My baby, my boyfriend, and I are hoping and waiting, never to be separated.

Marisa's picture and writing speak to the tension between her wishes "to be happy with my boyfriend and my baby like a loving family, joyful and united" and the demands of her immigration experience, which include separation and loss (e.g., "My baby, my boyfriend and I are hoping and waiting, never to be separated"). Indeed, many of Marisa's journal entries focus on how much she misses family members still in Mexico, most especially her maternal grandmother who visits every summer.

Marisa's classmates were interested in her beautiful landscape. "But how can it be sunny and raining at the same time?" asked Charmine. Marisa explained that it was a soft, gentle rain, like the rain that sometimes falls in the mountains where she used to live. I asked if the waterfall was imaginary or an actual place she had been in Mexico. In response, she told the following story:

> A few years ago I went on a camping trip with a bunch of kids, including my boyfriend. The guides asked me if I wanted to hike to the top of the mountain where I would see a waterfall, go swimming, and whatever. It was all there. I told them I don't like to walk (even before getting pregnant I didn't like walking). But I decided to go along. The hike up the mountain was long and tiring, but when I got to the top I could see the waterfall and how very beautiful it all was.

Marisa has this picture (and narrative) "in her mind everyday" as she waits for her baby to come. Her picture and narrative take us inside both her cultural and her inner worlds. Above all, Marisa misses Mexico. Besides her family and her attachment to the land itself (the mountains, light, and waterfalls), Marisa laments her lost freedom of movement. "You can't do much here—you can't walk to do or see things. Here it is only the mall or maybe a lake, but you need transportation to do that." Her story about climbing the mountain strikes me as a particularly telling representation of how she sees and feels about her pregnancy. Marisa's story is about being taken somewhere and asked for her preferences about what she wants to do. She decides to climb the mountain (despite her reservations that she wouldn't have the energy). Her story expresses a sense of accomplishment and has a happy, beautiful ending. The story includes her boyfriend, just as her picture portrays him as part of her future traditional family.

Just as some of the black PPPT girls' self-portraits referenced a world of community and comfort and expressed nostalgia for this time in their lives, the Mexican American girls' self-portraits also referenced a lost world of community and comfort for which they longed. This sense of longing, which is also characteristic of art and artistry, could be felt across the girls' self-representations.

Yearning for the Future

Remember that Sonya was the girl in the opening scene of the chapter who said she was going to make herself in the future, as a singer. When I met Sonya she was living with her mother who worked at a local hospital as a blood technician. Sonya was quiet and studious in her PPPT classes and in our sessions. She was short, had a small frame, and wore stylish clothes that often earned her praise from her classmates. Sonya lived in a part of town that had recently been redistricted, which meant that she would attend the "flagship" high school after delivering her baby. The teachers referred to her as one of the best PPPT students.

Sonya's self-representation speaks not of a hard growing up, but of a yearning for an idealized future:

> This picture is about me in the future relaxing in the Jamaican is-
> lands. I am around twenty years of age. I am happy that I finally
> made it to the islands. I have a young boy, Malcolm, as a son. His
> loving father is my husband. They are both a joy to have in my life.
> During the time that I was pregnant with Malcolm I felt all types of
> emotions: happy, sad, funny, glad, angry, and mad. But most of all I
> felt a whole lot of love for my baby.

This self-portrait sparked a heated debate about racial representation and identification (see Figure 5). Sonya's artfully designed picture, but especially the shapely hourglass, Barbie-doll-like figure earned her praise from classmates. They "ooohed" and "aahhed" at the picture—"that girl has style"—and she quickly became the resident artist from whom other girls sought advice and help. When she added the black wavy hair and black eyes, Ebony said, "That makes you look Chinese." Moreover, Ebony added, the figure didn't look like Sonya who is "dark-skinned." From Ebony's perspective, the figure "looked white or Asian—because of the eyes." Tracey said, "I know black people who look Asian," to which Ebony replied, "we are not talking about whether this could be a black person, we are talking about whether this could be Sonya. There's nothing that looks like Sonya here—not the skin, not the hair, certainly not the eyes." The girls were talking all at once. Once again, the problems of race, representation, and "black looks" preoccupied the girls. Meanwhile, Sonya seemed unfazed by the debate; she offered no response or defense for her picture.

I was interested to know how Sonya, who was born and raised in Centerville, was connected to "the islands." I asked her about Jamaica—had she been there before? What was the special appeal of Jamaica to her? She reminded me of her desire to be a singer—"Reggae music, that's my music; I love to sing and dance to it. I used to sing gospel, I was part of my church choir, but that's not where my heart is." She said she hoped to "travel the world" in her future.

Like the others, Sonya's picture and text defies any simple interpretation regarding her pregnancy, her changing sense of self and body image, her femininity, or her racial identification. She writes about what she hopes to have in life—a son, a loving husband, relaxation in an ideal environment. She also speaks of managing "all types of" emotions, which for some of the girls were harder to acknowledge.

Gone Missing

Alice was one of the two white girls enrolled at the PPPT during my five years there. She was part of the cohort of girls mentioned in the opening scene of this chapter. As her classmates put it, Alice "went missing" from the program. In her fifth month, she elected to enroll in the "homebound" tutoring program available to pregnant teens.

When I met Alice she was living with her mother, who works as an unskilled manual worker at a dry cleaning store, and her father, who is on disability because of an injury suffered while operating a machine in a textile mill. She is the youngest of three daughters and has "always made my parents proud of me and my good grades." Alice was quiet and often sat by herself doing her homework while her classmates ate lunch in the kitchen.

She said she didn't care for the school lunches and brought dinner leftovers her mother packed for her in plastic containers. One of the first things Alice told me about herself was that getting pregnant was "one of the best things that has ever happened to me."

> A lot of people talk about the problem of babies having babies, but what they don't know is having a baby is one of the best things that could happen to me. I'm already more responsible and realistic since I got pregnant. Having a baby is settling me down.

Alice said she was not "any good at arts and crafts." She took her time selecting a bright yellow piece of construction paper for the background. Then she cut a big round red circle for her face and placed it in the middle of the page. She cut out equally round blue circles for eyes. She gracefully encircled her face with long strands of yellow paste paper hair, for which she received several compliments from classmates.

After penciling in eyebrows and a nose and adding light red lips, Alice said she was finished. (See Figure 6) "That really looks like you, Alice," said Sonya. Others agreed that she had achieved an amazing likeness. Clarise said she liked the bright colors Alice had chosen, including her red face. "All that yellow reminds me of sunshine. It makes me wonder why you aren't smiling in the picture." Alice didn't reply.

Alice missed the next few weeks of school because she was put on bed rest but sent in the following text about her self-portrait so it could be included in the book. This is what she wrote:

> My name is Alice. I am fourteen years old. I have blonde hair and blue eyes and I have braces. I stand about 5'3" and weigh about 142 pounds. I am going to have a baby in August. I don't like going to school. I don't like to be mean to other people. I like to be nice and sweet to other people. I have a great personality when I am around my friends and family. Now you know about the unknown girl.

What questions are being asked and what conversations are taking place between the lines of Alice's text and her picture? And what does her self-representation suggest about her self- and identity-making process?

Alice's text opens with conventional details of her physical self, as if she were filling out a form—name, age, hair and eye (but not skin) color, height, weight, and one distinguishing feature—having braces. She references the world of family and friends, a world in which she feels she has a "great personality." She also references the world of school, which she does not like. Alice's text makes me think she felt misrecognized by her classmates. "I don't like going to school"; "I don't like to be mean to other people." (Does she think she is perceived by her classmates as "mean" or is she perhaps saying, but not saying that others have been mean to her?) "I like to be nice and sweet to other people." (Is this how she wishes to be perceived but feels in some way thwarted?) "I have a great personality when I am around my friends and family." (She seems to be suggesting that she is not "herself" when she is not around friends and family.) Finally, speaking to a generalized "you" (me? the PPPT girls? the public?) she characterizes herself as the "unknown girl." In what ways does she feel unknown, and to whom?

I suspect that the effects of America's racial and class divisions lie at the heart of Alice's self-representation. Of course we cannot know with any certainty, as neither I nor the PPPT girls could ask Alice to elaborate. Alice is like other white working-class girls who have "gone missing" from public representations about the "problem" of teenage pregnancy. To the question of how it feels to be a "problem," Alice has answered with "seldom a word," she is the *unknown girl.*

Individual "Inside Stories" of Pregnancy

You recall that in chapter 1 I referred to what Joan Raphel-Leff calls the profoundly unique and emotionally laden *inside story* of pregnancy. She notes the particularly "strange union" of "two bodies, one inside the other" and suggests that each woman responds to this experience, in part, based on her own relational history and with unique stakes in "making her pregnancy her own" (1995: 8). In this section I consider two girls—Michelle and Twana—and what their self-portraits suggest about their particular *inside stories* of pregnancy.

Michelle was one of the two (out of fifty) PPPT girls who portrayed herself as pregnant in her portrait. (See Figure 7) This simple fact struck me as remarkable; that so few girls represented their bodies in a pregnant state.[20] Before meeting her, I was told Michelle was "difficult"—a "handful"— she was having lots of "personal problems." She might not even want to participate; "So don't take it personally," Ms. Nelson forewarned. In any case, "Don't let her sleep in class because she will put her head down on the desk and not pull it up again," she advised.

When I met Michelle she was living with her mother and younger sister who has epilepsy. Michelle's mother works as a clerk at the townhall and has been raising her girls on her own for as long as Michelle can remember. Michelle was born "up north" but her mother moved back to raise her daughter in the company of family and extended kin. She was usually quiet during class and often didn't participate in the girls' joking banter with one another. Michelle was most engaged in the journal writing activity, reflecting about her emotions and mood swings ("Yesterday I felt as if everyone was on my back and that I couldn't do anything right but today everything is looking up"). She wrote about her goals of getting a job and moving out of her mother's home, as well as worries about who would care for her sister when she left. Her boyfriend said he wanted to stay involved with her and the baby, but Michelle expressed doubt that he "would keep his promise. Besides, I don't want to get overly dependent on him or anybody." Other girls in the PPPT talked behind Michelle's back, saying that she was "spoiled" by her mother, meaning that they thought Michelle was overly sensitive and "whined" too much about her problems. "Michelle thinks she is the only person going through hard times," complained Ebony one day when Michelle was not in class.

Michelle was eight months pregnant, more visibly so than any of the other girls, and attended class less regularly than most. She began by asking for a black piece of paper to use as the background.

"Why don't you pick a nice color for the background?" Kaela asked.

Michelle didn't reply and Kaela said, "She's in a dark mood I guess."

Michelle took several days to make two pregnant figures facing each other—one she called her "happy" and the other, her "angry" side. Once finished, she held it up, frowned, and said, "There's too much emptiness—I need something to fill me, I mean this space up."

I noticed her slip and wondered if she did as well. I considered asking her about it, but decided against it (a good example of a time I held myself back from making interpretations). Instead I asked if I could hold up her portrait for her to view from a bit of a distance.

"What do you see?" I asked.

"It's too dark, too empty, too much space in between the two figures," replied Michelle. "I'll fix it later."

The next day Michelle returned with a written statement to accompany her picture. I had not seen her appear so enthusiastic and energetic. She asked me to read what she had written and "correct" it:[21]

> This is a picture of me. I'm seventeen years old and so miserable. All I can do is think of the things I used to do and will do after I have my lovely baby. I only smile when I want to or if somebody makes me laugh. The funny feeling about being pregnant is feeling something move inside you. I'll never hold hatred toward my baby because I know it's my fault and not my baby's. I have more problems

on me than usual. But now I have somebody to really love and care for—somebody who's a piece of my heart.

As I was reading her statement aloud, Michelle stopped me on the phrase; "I'll never hold hatred toward my baby because I know it's my fault and not my baby's." At this point in hearing me read her statement, Michelle said, "I know what I need to do," and she picked up pieces of paper and started cutting out hearts that she placed in the empty space. Perhaps the hearts—symbols of love—were substitutes for Michelle's feelings of hatred or aggression because these feelings were too painful or difficult to abide.[22] Some viewers will see Michelle's picture and notice the hearts, unaware that at first there was an empty space. Interpreting the symbolic meaning of these hearts is complicated given competing discourses about teenage pregnancy. On the one hand, one could interpret the hearts as illustrating Michelle's "looking for love"—a popular psychological explanation often offered to explain girls' motivations for getting pregnant. On the other hand, one could speculate that the hearts are symbols of acceptable, traditional femininity upon which Michelle might be drawing to defend herself against the "war on teenage pregnancy" and its stigma.

All three of the above interpretations are plausible, but what the art-making process and our conversation suggests is that Michelle was coming into consciousness about her conflicted feelings, that she would "hold hatred toward her baby," and this made her want to change (in her words "fix") how she feels and sees herself. In making her portrait, Michelle notices or becomes more self-aware of several things about herself and her life: her feelings of "emptiness" set next to "feeling something move inside you"; her fears of holding hatred toward her baby held alongside deep feelings of love; and her conflicting sense of her own value as both "miserable" and as worth "having somebody to really love and care for."[23]

Michelle's self-portrait sheds light on her relational inner world, an "empty space" that could be interpreted in several ways. Perhaps the empty space represents the distance she feels between herself and her baby, or between the opposing sides of herself, or a reverberation of a much earlier, primal sense of loss from her own mother. In any case, Michelle's desire to close the gap, to feel connected, to recuperate her losses, reveals her unique drama of change and growth.

There are additional observations that could be made and interpretations that could be offered about Michelle's self- and identity-making process from her self-portrait. First, she is missing hands, something about which I asked her. She replied, "I didn't want to mess up my picture by putting on hands; I just couldn't make hands that looked good." Second, her classmates argued that her "happy side" didn't look especially happy, to which Michelle said, "I tried to make a cut-out smile—you don't think it looks like a smile?" These both signify what I consider "technical" difficulties Michelle claimed to have with her artistic abilities, and thus I downplay their significance to Michelle (a therapist might disagree). Finally, Michelle chose white paper for her body and made herself a "straight" hairstyle (her classmates' words), which could be said to reflect social issues regarding race and representation as well as her own feelings regarding racial identification.

Twana's self-portrait provides another distinctive example of a girl coming into consciousness about her changing body, self, and identity. When I met Twana she was fourteen and living with an aunt who had recently moved back to town after living "up north." Twana took care of her aunt's four young children in exchange for living with her. I gathered from school records that Twana had lived in foster care for most of her life. When she was eight, she had been assigned a guardian ad litem by the court, whom she liked and continued to see regularly. She had attended several schools during the course of childhood and, in her words, had been "held back because it took me so long to read good." Twana was eager to join in her classmates' jokes and playful banter, especially when it came to play-acting events that had occurred over the weekend or at school. She had never mentioned having a boyfriend before making her self-portrait, and thus, it came as a surprise to her classmates, "You never told about a boyfriend—where does he stay at?—how old is he?" The questions came much more quickly than Twana could answer, and in the end, she said, "Shut up, do you think I want you all to know my business?"

Twana cut out and pasted two adjoining circular shapes that she said stood for her and her boyfriend's faces. She added a "straight hairstyle" that her classmates observed was unlike any they had seen her wear. Then she added eyes, nose, and lips to her face and a hat, eyes, nose, and lips to her boyfriend's face. Twana completed her picture by cutting out and pasting a tree to the far left of the page, a sun in the upper lefthand corner, and a border of grass at the bottom. (See Figure 8) She wrote the following, and asked me to read it out loud before I held her picture up for her classmates to view:

This is a picture of me and my boyfriend at his house in his yard. I'm in his yard chilling. I like being over there with him because it's a lot of fun. He makes me feel comfortable. The tree is where we like to be during the day.

In writing about her picture Twana reflects on what she has in life—a boyfriend who makes her "feel comfortable." When I asked how her boyfriend makes her feel comfortable, she replied, "comfortable with myself, you know how I mean." She explained that she doesn't like being around people who make her feel "big" or "ugly" or who give her "looks." All the while Twana does not acknowledge her pregnancy until later when questioned by her classmates who, among other things, asked why she had made her boyfriend's head so much smaller than hers. Looking at her picture again, Twana turned it on its side and reflected anew on what she had made. "Look at this, this is me, pregnant." Moving her finger along the outlines of the merged circles that, from this new angle, looked like a pregnant figure, she said, "This is all one big, round belly." Twana's new perspective on her self-portrait speaks to her growing awareness of the uncanny fact of her "two-in-one" body. What she first envisioned as being two separate parts (in this case two "heads") comes to be viewed as one whole. Twana's self-portrait sheds light on her relational inner world—what for Michelle was construed as an "empty space," for Twana is construed as a merged, undifferentiated space, perhaps evoking feelings about herself in relation to her baby, or feelings about a form of relationship that she has internalized, which like her boyfriend, makes her "feel comfortable with herself." In any case, what I want to stress is Twana's own surprise about what she had made. This coming into a different awareness speaks to the importance of the critique sessions that enabled the girls to reflect anew on their self-image and representations.[24]

Again, there are other observations and interpretations to be made about Twana's picture, including why she made "only heads," an observation made by her classmates that led to the question about the differential size of each head. Twana did not have an answer. Again, it is her new view of herself that I wish to feature, despite whatever other meanings might be being conveyed by her picture.

The girls' self-portraits illustrate their struggles to express multiple feelings and truths about their changing sense of self and identity. The girls speak about these truths in fragmented ways, and at times elusively. But it is their readiness to and the facility with which they represent themselves and their lives to others that I stress. Each of the PPPT girls' self-representation, in one way or another, and with more or less expression of personal conflict, engages a dialogue between the self (*Who am I?*) and society (*Who do others think I am?*). This dialogue also takes place in the girls' media collages, to which I now turn.

CHAPTER 4

Making the "Self-Which-I-Might-Be"

Introduction

"How many of you have ever made a collage out of pictures from magazines?" Everyone raises her hand. I had placed an array of magazines in the middle of the table, and a stack of 8x11 sheets of colored construction paper for each girl to choose from.

"*Ebony, Essence, People, YM, . . .*"—these are good magazines, and they are this month's!" Charlene exclaims gleefully.

The girls start talking all at once.

"Can we take them home?"

"*Teen Voices*, what magazine is that? I've never seen it," says Alisha grabbing it from Sara's hands.[1]

"How much did all these cost, Ms. Wendy? You got all the ones we told you we read."

"There's a box of old magazines in the closet like *Redbook, Glamour, National Geographic*, we can ask Ms. Pepper if we can cut them up too," suggests Sara.

I start passing out scissors, a small tub of glue, and a brush to each girl.

"In this activity I am asking you to consider the question, 'Who am I?' Look through these magazines and pick any pictures, words, sentences that represent who you are. I've also brought alphabet stamp sets and ink pads for you to write your own words or phrases, if you wish, and markers in case you want to draw your own images."

"Can we make more than one collage? I want to make one for my room."[2]

"How much did these stamp sets cost? Can I have one?"

Alisha is the first to take an alphabet stamp set and a red ink pad. She prints across the top of her construction paper the phrase, BLACK, STRONG, WOMAN! "Okay, now I will look for pictures," she says.

Tanya has been leafing quickly through *Ebony* and selects a picture of a woman wearing a light blue blouse, black stretch pants, and sneakers. Her straight black hair is pulled back in a ponytail. She is bending over to pick up a toddler.

Alisha asks, "Is that woman black?"

This question sparks a lively debate among the girls about skin color; about who is light and who is dark; about people they know who look white, but are "black," and vice versa, people who are "black" but "act white." Celia, who is white, and Teresa, who is Mexican American, are quiet during this discussion.

Tanya ends the argument by saying, "If she says she is black then that's what she is." Pasting her picture into the center of the paper Tanya declares, "This is me—an independent mother."

The debate starts all over again. "It can't be you, that woman is light skinned and you're dark," argues Violet.

"That's not the point. She *represents* me and how I carry myself, [her emphasis]" says Tanya raising her voice. "She's making it on her own."

Tracey throws the *Essence* magazine she has been looking through onto the table, saying, "There is nobody who represents me in this magazine." Teresa agrees, saying the same. Sara hands Tracey her copy of the *Ebony* she has been thumbing through and says, "Here, have a look at this one."

Tracey eventually finds a picture she likes—it is another light-skinned, black woman wearing peach silk pajamas reclining in bed, surrounded by a mound of white fluffy pillows. She is holding a baby up in the air. There is a look of joyful recognition between magazine mom and baby as they rub noses together. Tracey holds the picture up in the air just like the magazine mom and says, "That's me. That's my style. But now I need to find me some food—I need some food."

She finds two pictures: one of waffles, sliced fruits, and muffins and the other, a shapely red apple that glistens with droplets of water. She places the apple in the center of her collage.

Tanya licks her lips and says, "Who's going to help find me a burger?—it needs to have cheese, lettuce, tomato, pickles. . . ."

"Don't let's start on pickles," laughs Charlene.

Sara finds Tanya a four-layer chicken sandwich with everything she listed but the beef. "How about chicken?"

Tanya smiles broadly. She thanks Sara and proceeds to paste the sandwich next to the toddler. The sandwich turns out to be taller than the toddler. Then she takes the alphabet stamp set and black ink and prints the word "importance" going vertically down the right side of the page. She adds the words, "of a" at the bottom of the page, and then prints in vertical letters "men" going down the right side of the page. I am struck that she frames her collage with the phrase, "importance of a men" as she has just emphasized being independent and making it on her own. But Tanya is not finished yet, and by the time her collage is complete, a picture of a black girl in a white graduation cap and gown covers part of the word "importance" and a picture of a football player covers the letter M in men. Her viewers can no longer make out the meaning of her phrase, which she says does not concern her. "I had to have that graduation picture and there was no space left for it. And my boyfriend plays football and he needed to be there." (See Figure 4.1) Then she asks the group, "Why is it that famous people always go with other famous people? Why can't they ever go out with people like us?" The conversation (including Teresa and Celia) stays on celebrities for the rest of the class period as the girls continue cutting, pasting, taking off, and putting on their words and images.

This class session illustrates the way the PPPT girls typically engaged the media collage activity. This same flow of conversation occurred from group to group, moving seamlessly from debates about racial identity and representation, to food, to celebrity figures.[3] Typically, at least one girl would express difficulty or frustration about not finding herself represented in the magazines, and references to "style," either in terms of clothes, hairdo, or general look—what the girls called "attitude"—animated session after session.

The girls were engrossed with images of food and talked about food cravings and eating binges ("You won't believe how much I ate last night for dinner. . . . I went to Shoney's on Sunday morning, to the-all-you-can-eat breakfast buffet. I stuffed myself with a plate of sausages, pancakes, eggs, grits. My momma said I was going to make myself sick with too much food. It was too good."). At times they helped one another find their favorite foods, as "girlfriends do for each other." There was a tipsy silliness with which the girls expressed their desires for food. I wondered what role these images of and conversations about food were playing in the activity sessions. On one level, I could recall with great detail my own food cravings during each of my three pregnancies.[4] Perhaps this was the case with the girls, and the magazine images of food prompted them to express their distinct cravings. But, on another level, I was struck by the playfulness of these conversations about food and how they referenced a female world full of nourishment and delight. The girls relished one another's descriptions of mothers, aunts, and grandmothers preparing pies, biscuits, ham hocks and

Figure 4.1: Tanya's collage

collard greens, fried chicken, and vats of potato salad for church picnics and family reunions. On yet another level, I was struck by the eroticism of the food images some girls selected (for example, Tracey's picture of the red glistening apple and Vaquan's sleek, hour-glass-shaped flask full of orange juice that even the girls teased her about for, in their words, "looking sexy"). I wondered in what ways these images and the girls' reactions might be reflecting inner conflicts about their changing bodies, but particularly their passage into adult sexuality, conflicts that were also expressed in some of the girls' self-portraits. For example, readers will recall Clarise's poem lamenting her fast-moving bodily changes: first pubic hairs, then breasts, a period, and then sex; and Tara who expressed resentment toward people who gave her full body "looks," which indicated her conflicts about what others think of her.

On yet another level, I was struck by the contrast between the food items the girls selected and those they routinely (but secretly) brought into the classroom. Items like soda, chips, and candy bars were contraband that served as social glue between the girls. These food items were exchanged with both a playful and a more serious nose-thumbing at the powers that be. Nonetheless, it was not these everyday food items that showed up in the collages; rather, the collage food items were more "healthy" (fresh fruit rather than chips), more "sensuous" and "luxurious" (piles of pancakes with butter and syrup dripping down the sides), and undoubtedly more expensive and beyond the girls' daily reach. The point is that there was a quality about the food items and the girls' conversations about them that invited entry into multiple worlds—a female world of nourishment and sexuality and a consumer world of riches.[5]

But it was conversations about famous people—especially musicians— that tended to dominate discussion. Making these media collages were occasions when girls swapped their knowledge of the "stars," most especially a celebrity's lifestyle and troubles as reported by the press. Stories about redemption and respect—how a star overcame hardship or addiction or was able to rise against the odds—were told with special detail and enthusiasm. I wondered in what ways the girls' empathy for and/or harsh criticism of a celebrity reflected a girl's own self-appraisal or wishes for herself. A media star earned the girls' instant respect when she was able to "hold her head high" amid disparaging media attention—when the media "talked shit about her," as some girls put it.[6] Hard, protective individualist values and models of selfhood like those I described in the previous chapter—being tough and self-reliant, having a thick skin, and refusing to be "beaten down" by the press—were woven into these conversations about the celebrities. The PPPT girls held in highest esteem those celebrities who defined the meaning of "style" and "attitude" as an "I don't care what people think of me" stance toward the world.

After each girl completed her collage, she presented it to her viewers, providing an explanation for the images and words she had selected. What I have to say about the collages is based on both sets of conversations— those that took place during the making and those that took place during each girl's presentation. These collages, like the self-portraits, hold multiple meanings. But, by comparison to the self-portrait activity, there was more commonality and at times predictability in the girls' discussions and explanations of the collages. Put slightly differently, the media-based collage activity highlighted converging elements and continuities of meaning in the girls' social worlds, especially how they perceived themselves being "addressed by" and "answering to" these worlds. Still, like their self-portraits, the media collages convey an individual girl's creativity and agency.

In this activity the girls critically engaged and appropriated media images, not as passive consumers, but in active dialogue with how these images speak to their self-image and self-presentation. ("This is my style"; "This is me, an independent mother.") The girls' conversations reflect much that has been written about the power of advertising images to both create and respond to viewers' desires.[7] These images are said to be less about *reflecting* viewers' wants or wishes than they are about *addressing* the viewer. According to John Berger's classic analysis of advertising, *Ways of Seeing,* "We are now so accustomed to being addressed by these images that we scarcely notice their total impact" (1972: 130). Berger continues on to explain that advertising images offer the viewer "an image of himself [*sic*] made glamorous by the product, making the viewer 'envious of himself as he might be.' Yet what makes this self-which-he-might-be enviable? The envy of others" (132).

Judith Williamson (1978) explains that advertisements "hail" the viewer as someone who is already the person in the ad—someone who would naturally consume the product because of the kind of person she is. A girl's media collage, and her resonance with certain advertising images, could be understood in a similar way, as insight into her narrative of "self-which-I-might-be," "what I think might make me the envy of others," or "who I am because I consume (or wish to consume) this or that product."

As with the self-portrait activity, this media-based activity engaged the girls in a dialogue between self (Who am I?) and society (Who do others think I am?). These media collages extend this dialogue, drawing specifically on images and discourses that define or are associated with *social* identity (i.e., "I am a black, Mexican American or white girl and such girls are like this or that." "I am becoming a full grown, sexual woman and women are like this or that." "I am becoming a mother and mothers are like this or that"). As the debate about who "looked and didn't look black" in the dialogue at the start of this chapter suggests, images about racial identity and representation are not fixed; rather they are fluid and based on specific contexts. A girl's answer to the question, "Who am I as a black or

Mexican American or white girl?" is contingent. African American writer and anthropologist Zora Neal Hurston made this contingency ever so clear in her classic essay, "How It Feels to Be Colored Me." Her reply to such a question included the following statements: "Compared to what? As of when? Who is asking? In what context? For what purpose? With what interests and presuppositions?" (quoted in Johnson 1987: 178). But, as I will argue in this chapter, the girls' answers to the questions of who they are as mothers were much less fluid and contingent—indeed, they were idealized.

Self- and Identity-Making and Social Worlds

Money Talk and Money Talks

I'll start at the top of the page—money talks—I put this picture of money and these words because I like money. I want to have money so I can live in this house [pointing to the picture of a spacious, two story suburban house with a circular driveway in front] *and have this car* [pointing to a black Lincoln Navigator SUV], *because you need to have transportation. I picked out the phrase "very serious" and "important," because money is very serious, you need to have it in order to have these things. I have a diamond here because I am loved. And this is me and my style in the corner"* [pointing to a black woman with a pasley shirt and styled hair looking seductively into the camera]. (See Figure 4.2)

For Alisha, like many of her PPPT classmates, "money talks." She "likes" money; it is "serious" and "important." The vast majority of PPPT girls would seem to agree—the most prevalent image used in these collages is money (including credit cards) with food and cars being not even close seconds. Forty-five out of fifty girls made collages with images of money. (See Figures 4.3, 4.4, and 4.5)

If John Berger is correct, that advertising images work upon anxiety—anxieties about how we look, whether we are likable or desirable to others—then having money to purchase whatever is being sold is crucial. Berger writes:

The sum of everything is money, to get money is to overcome anxiety. Money is life. Not in the sense that without money you starve. . . . But in the sense that money is the token of, and the key to, every human capacity. The power to spend money is the power to live. (1972: 143)

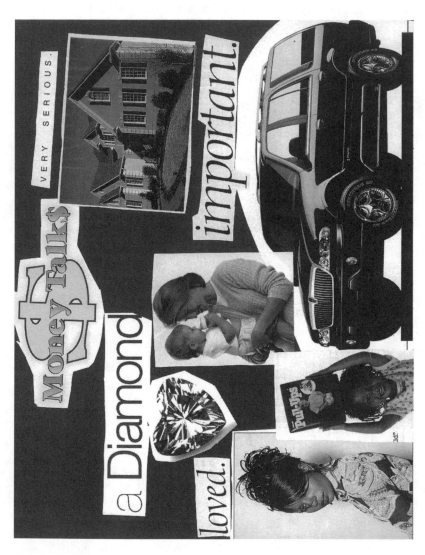

Figure 4.2: Alisha's collage

Figure 4.3: In Figures 4.3, 4.4, and 4.5 "Forty-five out of fifty girls made collages with images of money."

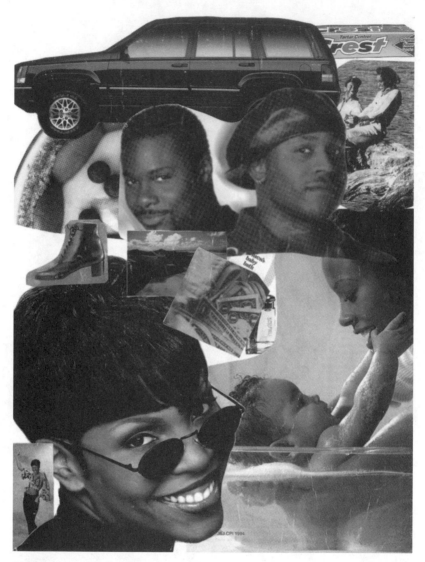

Figure 4.4

Figure 4.5

Figure 4.6: Charmine's collage

Charmine echoed this view of money when explaining her collage (see Figure 4.6):

At the top is my baby—she is My Greatest Creation [pointing to a picture of a baby and the words, greatest creation, clipped from a magazine]. And I am proud to be a Capricorn; I'm proud to be black, I'm dark and lovely with roots that are African [pointing to these words she has clipped out and placed on the collage]. And I have style, beauty, and I'm lovable [again pointing to these words clipped from a magazine]. But it's money that makes the difference—[pointing to the pictures of dollar bills, change, two credit cards, American Express and Visa] I mean *Millions* [said with great emphasis in her voice].

Charmine's explanation of her "Who am I?" collage, her narrative of self and identity, highlights the dialogue between self and society, the intermingling of personal and cultural meanings. Her greatest *creation* (her baby as an extension of herself) is at the top, the pinnacle. Underneath is her *self* ("I am proud to be a Capricorn" [birth sign], and *racial identity* ("I'm proud to be black; I'm dark and lovely with roots that are African"). A string of qualities regarding how she "carries herself" with style, beauty, and love fill out her collage, which above all, identifies money as "making all the difference." Not just enough money to survive, but "millions."

I was struck by the preponderance of phrases, images, and references to money in the PPPT girls' collages and wondered in what ways these images provided insight into the girls' engagement in consumer culture. I had been made acutely aware of the consumer *environment*s (local groceries, downtown clothing shops compared to stores in local malls) in which the girls were treated (and mistreated) according to their race, class, and gender. The PPPT girls routinely reported on (and reenacted through performance) their weekend shopping experiences as being fraught with tension. I heard about being thrown out of the mall for inappropriate dress, being falsely accused of shoplifting, and being asked to leave backpacks with a salesperson while "white girls strolled through the store with pocketbooks the size of suitcases." But what did these references to and images of money mean to the girls?[8]

According to Elizabeth Chin (2001), ethnographer and author of *Purchasing Power: Black Kids and American Consumer Culture,* we don't know enough about American children's distinctive race, class, and gender-based experiences of the consumer world. Chin spent two years documenting the consumption patterns of poor and working-class black youth in New Haven, patterns that highlight "intimate and complex terrains of obligation, reciprocity, need, and desire" (18). In part, these young people enter a consumer world with acute awareness of the economic "nuts and bolts of daily living." Unlike their middle-class counterparts who are "shielded from mysteries like rent, grocery budgets, and the cost of clothes," the youth in her study were savvy about "how much their needs cost the family and are expected at a young age to use their own money to buy socks, underwear, and other necessities" (5). Meanwhile, there were high demands and expectations for sharing, reciprocity, and mutual obligation placed on the three girls (and their families) whom she followed intensively. These demands hindered the range of and possibilities for the girls' consumptive activities; "whether eating, making purchases, asking for clothes, school supplies, toys, or treats," they were "fettered by material deprivation and social demands" (5–6). Yet, despite this, Chin shows how vibrantly and intensely the girls engaged with consumer culture, which resonates with the spirited way in which the PPPT girls engaged the media images. Equally important, Chin's study challenges popular, disparaging images of poor and working-class black youth as being overly immersed in consumer culture, stereotyped as "crazed and brand-addicted inner city youth willing to kill for the items they want" (3)—a stereotype that I would not want viewers to hold of the PPPT girls' collages.[9] I join Chin in wanting to change the terms of debate about consumerism from its focus on flawed, consumeristic *individuals,* and instead, turning attention to the gender-, class-, and race-based *conditions* within which young people engage the consumer world.

From this perspective, perhaps, the preponderance of images of money within the PPPT girls' collages illustrates not only their awareness of how much money it takes to have material comforts, but how out of reach this world is. People who have more can underemphasize the role that money and material comforts play in having a "good life."[10] At the same time, I was struck by the extent to which discussions about money and how much things cost were woven into everyday conversations at the PPPT (not just the collages). My reactions to the girls' preoccupation with money offers yet another layer of interpretation.

There was always at least one girl in the group who would initiate a conversation about money with the question, "How much did this or that cost?" Markers, paper, magazines, books, writing journals, folders, pens, handpainted-paper, tape, scissors, food stuffs, whatever I brought along, they wanted to know how much I had paid for it and whether they could take it home. The same held for some of my personal possessions: How much did my shoes cost, my earrings, my tape recorder, the video camera (I explained it wasn't mine)? They didn't ask if they could have these things, however. The girls' questions about money unnerved me; I worried that they might see me as a bearer of goods and/or as withholding goods (see chapter 6 for more discussion of this). Meanwhile, I noticed that the girls also asked these same questions of each other—"how much did your hair braiding cost, where did you buy that necklace, how much were those earrings, can I have them?"

But I was most surprised by the girls' reactions to what I had paid for things—it was often much less than what they had expected. They tended not to believe me—"Those shoes couldn't cost twenty dollars. I know those shoes are leather, how could they cost twenty dollars? I could buy those shoes. Where did you get those shoes?" It was as if the girls were surprised that a certain item they thought was beyond their reach was not. This happened so often that I began to wonder whether the girls' "money talk" was, among other things, a forum for them to figure out the value of things, including their own social value in relation to mine.

Neil Altman's (1995) discussion of the role of social class in public clinic work, described in his book, *The Analyst in the Inner City,* helped me untangle my feelings and better understand the girls' "money talk." Altman is interested in how class dynamics shape the psychoanalytic encounter, and his insights can be applied to ethnographic encounters as well. He refers to the work of Muriel Dimen (1993, 1994), who writes about how economically advantaged psychoanalysts, subject to envy and resentment by their less well-off clients, can experience anxieties and conflicts about their wealth, including guilt and a false sense of security. Because many professionals have nothing more tangible by way of capital than their credentials and expertise, some members of this class can feel anxious about holding on to their knowledge and expertise (Altman 1995: 81). Indeed, Barbarara Ehrenreich (1989) makes a strong case, in her book *Fear of Falling,* that personal conflict and insecurity are inextricably tied to and stem from middle-class efforts to maintain their (unearned) advantages within society. One's awareness that his or her "credentials" are born of exclusionary practices and not simply one's own "merit" can lead to torn feelings about middle-classness, and a gap between how one is perceived (as a bearer of status and power) and how one experiences her- or himself (as vulnerable). I certainly identify with these torn feelings and have written about them elsewhere.[11] Dimen (1994) puts it even more boldly, stating that middle-class professionals can experience a sense of "fraudulence and looming loss" (79). From this perspective, the girls' "money talk" and my discomfort about it reveals two distinct class-based "structures of feeling";[12] a distinct middle-class constellation of guilt, insecurity, and fears about "falling"[13] set next to a poor/working-class constellation of envy, resentment, exclusion, and fears about survival.

There is yet another layer of emotion to consider. In my work with the PPPT girls I was unequivocally positioned as a mother. And insofar as I was viewed as a maternal figure by the PPPT girls, their "money talk" may relate to feelings of exclusion in two senses—materially and maternally (see chapter 6 where I describe a fieldwork encounter that led me to see my maternal role in a new light). According to child psychoanalyst Melanie Klein (1995), a child's first sense of loss/separation from mother is felt as an exclusion and it is this feeling (and the anger and destructiveness toward mother that arise as a result) that must be repaired over the course of development. Perhaps part of what animated the girls' focus on money echoed back to earlier experiences of separation and loss in relation to their own mothers and was being replayed in our relationship. My point is that within this ethnographic context, the girls' "money talk" may reflect our respective class-based structures of feeling (my middle-class-based sense of guilt and fear of falling, and the girls' poor/working-class-based sense of envy and of exclusion), and may also be wrapped with deep seated and ambivalent feelings about maternal-child bonds (Klein 1975). I will discuss the nature of maternal-child bonds more in the next chapter, but here I want to stress the overlapping sources of anxiety (my own and the girls') regarding the salience of money.

Glamour and Style

Just as I was surprised by the consistent and recurring images of money, I was also taken with the consistency in consumer items the girls selected for their collages. Brand name items, cars, fashion, jewelry (diamonds mostly), and perfume topped the list. What I see linking these consumer items is their common reference to style and glamour (understood through a racial and class lens). The way the PPPT girls spoke of the images and words they selected sheds light on their definitions of and values about femininity. For the black girls, femininity seemed to incorporate three main things: strength (e.g., "strong, black woman"); alternative standards of beauty (e.g., style with an attitude); and respectability.

"Strong," "black," and "woman" were strung together in many of the girls' explanations of their collages, as if these were linked characteristics. Interestingly, "strongblackwoman" is a one-word phrase that Joan Morgan (1999: 72) describes as a "syndrome" from which many black women are unable to escape. She argues that this congealed identity is a burden; it places an unrealistic expectation upon black women that they will always appear unflappable, whatever the hardship or pain. Morgan worries that the "strongblackwoman" identity works to deny black women a complex psychology. Indeed, Morgan sees this image as a stereotype that has been turned into an acceptable identity at great cost to black women.

In describing how the images they selected represented themselves or their style, the girls articulated a definition of beauty that resists white standards. Much of the girls' conversation about hairstyles and fashion indicated that "looking good" meant projecting an attitude of self confidence and control. "Looking good" was less about adhering to an ideal type of beauty, and more about making "what you got work for you," including one's personality. How one "carries" oneself seemed more key to being beautiful, than having an ideal body type.[14]

The girls' explanations of the fashion images they selected emphasized respectability. Stylish fashion selections were often described as "sexy, but not too sexy." These "sexy, but not too sexy" outfits were marked by class distinctions. Rather than the understated "little black dress" denoting the classic style of the rich (Davis 1992) the girls chose more glamorous clothes—short red dresses; sleek and bust-revealing business suits; long body-clinging gowns, to name a few.

The girls' discussion of style and glamour reminded me of something British sociologist Beverly Skeggs (1997) wrote:

> Glamour . . . is a way of holding together sexuality and respectability, but it is difficult to achieve. . . . Glamour is the mechanism by which the marks of middle-class respectability are transposed onto the sexual body, a way in which recognition of value is achieved. (110)

Skeggs grounds her discussion of glamour in interviews she conducted with white working-class women, whom she claims seek to be glamorous because it "gives agency, strength and worth back to women and is not restricted to youth. They do glamour with style. Glamour is about a performance of femininity with strength" (111).

Performances of femininity are always deeply class- and race-based, reflections not only of one's beauty and taste, but of one's social position and value.[15] I see the girls' conversations about style, attitude, and deportment as being tied to their conflicts over social distinctions about who is and is not valued (which they are also trying to figure out through their money talk, for example, how much are things worth and can they get these things). Being glamorous, like having access to money, is a way to signal to others that one has value. It was not as if the girls seemed to expect that they would be valued or respected, rather they seemed to view their value as something to be achieved (through "attitude," style, respectability). The girls' references to struggles for respectability include their discussions about celebrities. In the conversation that opens this chapter Tanya asked, "Why is it that famous people always go out with other famous people? Why don't they ever go out with people like us?" Tanya's question was greeted with laughter by her classmates because everyone knows that this would be improbable. The difference between "famous people" and "people like us" is not simply about fame, beauty, taste, or style (because those can be "achieved" with money); it is about social position and respect. Indeed, it was a celebrity's ability to command respect against great odds, to be recognized and treated as valued despite whatever might have tarnished her or his reputation, that galvanized the girls' interest. The girls noted different strategies that celebrities used to garner respect—from "speaking her mind" to "holding her head up high" to seeking redemption through religion/spirituality. But the goal was the same—getting respect.

My point is that the girls' "Who am I?" media collages and explanations are about much more than their engagement in consumer worlds. These forms of self-representation also speak to the powerful role that money and commodities play in the girls' notions of femininity. Their media collages also provide a glimpse of the girls' insights and conflicts about social relations of respect that shape the self- and identity-making process.

Ideal Motherhood

In Alisha's "money talks" collage, there was one image she did not reference in her explanation to the class. It is a picture of a white, blond-haired woman holding a white baby.

"Tell us about this image," I asked.

"It is there because it is a look of love between a mother and her baby, like I feel for my baby." Alisha stops, then continues, "All I want is for my baby to be happy, to feel loved."

Alisha does not see herself as the mother in this image. Recall that she pointed to a black woman with a stylish hairstyle and said, "This is me and my style." Rather, this mother-child image is *addressing* her as a mother and the feeling she has, or ought to have, for her baby.

Tarisha's collage has three "look of love" images placed side-by-side. (See Figure 4.7) The first is an image of Victorian romance—a white man in a white linen suit wearing a top hat holds his beloved's face tenderly in his hands. The white woman, dressed in white lace and a bonnet, gazes up into her man's eyes (it is an image from the movie, *Little Women*, with

Figure 4.7: Tarisha's collage

media stars Winona Ryder and Daniel Day Lewis, although this was not mentioned by Tarisha in her explanation). The second is a picture of a white woman with a full head of long, red curls (who looks to be the film star Nicole Kidman) holding an infant in her arms, carefully protecting his or her head with her hand and gazing into the baby's face. Above these two images Tarisha pastes a picture of an elegant spacious pink-tiled bathroom adorned with gold hardware and floral curtains. There is an inset with a white woman helping a white child into the bathtub. Tarisha explains that all three images are "beautiful; they show being loved and living a whole new way of life. Like living in a mansion or something." Berger might suggest that the first two "look of love" images speak to personal transformation (romance, maternal love), and the third speaks to transformation of class relationships through a general atmosphere of assembled products that creates a sense that one is well-off. But what is striking to me is that these images are linked in Tarisha's mind, that the mansion and bathroom are settings in which love (both adult, romantic love and maternal love) can flourish.

In the top right corner of Tarisha's collage there is a picture of a black woman wearing a very short red dress. Tarisha points to it and says, "Here I am standing tall, tough. This is my style." At the top of the collage Tarisha has used the alphabet stamp set to print the phrase, "I want my baby 2 B Happy." Tarisha says (pointing to the picture of the black woman in the red dress), "This is me and these are the things I want for my baby. But more than anything else, I want my baby to be happy, to feel special. I want to make it feel loved." Again, the image, that Tarisha says is her, is the glamorous black woman wearing a short red dress, "standing tall, tough." Indeed, a not-mother figure is "who I am" for Tarisha (and for Alisha). But what do these other images—images shot through with whiteness—mean for Tarisha and Alisha?

One answer is that these white images of love reveal a belief (conscious or otherwise) that whiteness is enviable.[16] Perhaps, but this is not how I would interpret it. Rather, I see the girls drawing upon these images as part of a larger convergence of cultural symbols that tie the "good" life to a life without hardship. That these images also tied the good life to ideal motherhood and by extension to the ideal child is key.

Not all the PPPT girls selected white images of maternal-child love. Recall that Tracey found a light-skinned black woman wearing silk pajamas who is exchanging a playful and loving gaze with her baby. (See Figure 4.8) And there were abundant images of smiling black mothers holding smiling black babies

Figure 4.8: Tracey's collage

looking directly into the camera (more than half the collages contained such mother-child images). Both sets of images were explained in a patterned way—that a girl wished for her baby's happiness, that her baby would come to know how much it is loved. "Whatever people may tell her, I want my baby to know she was not a mistake, that she is loved," explained Louise as she described the mother-child image she had selected for her collage.

"Whatever people may tell her" (and "whatever I may tell myself") is the internal dialogue, underlying the appeal and promise of these magazine/ advertising images. In part, the PPPT girls' images and statements about maternal love are their way of talking back to dominant cultural discourses about teenage pregnancy. To those who would say their babies were "unwanted," "unplanned," or a "mistake" (including critical voices in their own heads), the girls' replies were unwavering—their soon-to-be-born babies are worthy and valuable. In this way, these images of maternal love are to motherhood what the images of glamour are to womanhood, a performance of femininity with strength, respectability, and value.

There is power and strength in the steadfast, unconditional love that "good" mothers provide children, especially children who must rise above hardship. "Being there" for their babies through life's inevitable struggles— maternal protection—was the most prevalent quality indexed by the PPPT girls in their discussions about motherhood. "Being there" was part of a constellation of qualities, including "facing the consequences of" their pregnancies and "being responsible for," and "not letting down," and "starting life over with" their babies. Shadra and Michelle respectively echoed the sentiments of many of the PPPT girls:

> I don't ever want my child to feel as if the world is coming down on her because that's just how the world does everybody. And that's something that she will learn to be true as she gets older. I would give her the world if I could and the moon and the stars too, if I could. I want her to know she will always have someone to talk to, someone who will always be there for her.

> I wish the best for my baby and that I will always be with him. I mostly wish an easier life for my baby and that he will know that he is loved.

The girls' explanations of their maternal love images and their discussions about motherhood reveal the complicated connections between material conditions and maternal love. On one level, the girls' images may be speaking to their fears about not being able to love/care for their children through material goods. On another level, these images may be speaking to the girls' own personal longings for the ideal maternal caregiver, someone who will "be there" against all odds, what some feminist critics have called the "myth of maternal omnipotence" (Chodorow and Contratto 1982). I have written elsewhere about the tenacious hold of this myth (Luttrell 1997), but my work with the PPPT girls has made me even more aware of its grip.

Briefly put, the myth of maternal omnipotence has to do with a false perception of mothers, a view that the sole reason for a mother's existence is to gratify her children's wants and needs *and* that she has the power to do so. But these perceptions don't simply exist in the world as notions swirling around our heads. Rather, deeply held personal feelings of love, hate, dependency, and resentment toward our early caregivers (predominantly women) get fused with and fuel such cultural perceptions and beliefs. This illusion about mother love (and its power), this false perception of a mother's command of her child's life and development, is problematic in at least three ways. First, it sets up social expectations about maternal practices, that mothers have "natural" instincts or propensities for caregiving and self-sacrifice. Second, it ignores the extent to which social forces and the environment shape the conditions under which children are raised and develop. And third, it masks a mother's own subjectivity, her distinct range of feelings, motivations, needs, and wants as a person. The myth of maternal omnipotence holds up a standard for mothering and maternal-child bonds that is impossible to achieve.

Elements of this myth are infused throughout the girls' art forms and in their informal conversations about their hopes for their babies. I am especially struck by their all-encompassing wishes for an ideal world for their soon-to-be-born babies, how the girls' vision of maternal love is not simply about the provision of goods, but about the creation of a more perfect world, at best the "world, moon, and stars" but at the least, an "easier life." This idealized view of mother-child relationships is child-centered, a view that dominates both psychological theory and popular discourse about the nature of mother-child bonds, so it should not surprise us that this view comes across in the girls' collages. At the same time, the girls' emphasis on maternal love also speaks to their class-based expectations that life is a struggle ("the world comes down on people and that's just how the world does everybody") and that maternal love is a powerful antidote (hardship can be survived if someone is "there for you"). On still another level, the black girls may be answering to what Patricia Hill Collins (1990) calls racial "controlling images" of the "black matriarchy," where black women are simultaneously exalted for their sacrifices and support of black families and disparaged for their undue control over black men and children (another version of the "strongblackwoman" image and the myth of maternal omnipotence).

But what seems especially pernicious about the idealization of maternal love is how it is tied to and draws upon the cherished American value of individualism and self-reliance—that individuals (i.e., mothers) rather than collective entities (i.e., communities, the state) should be able to provide for their children's needs (as well as other dependents like the elderly). This cultural emphasis on individual self-reliance, which feminist psychoanalyst Jessica Benjamin (1988) argues includes "contempt for the needy and dependent" and a rejection of "social forms of providing nurturance," rests upon yet another set of tenacious cultural beliefs and personal meanings—gender polarities. These polarities, according to Benjamin "pit freedom against nurturance: either we differentiate or remain dependent; either we stand alone or are weak; either we relinquish autonomy or renounce the need for love" (171–172). These polarities are gendered insofar as freedom and autonomy get idealized and culturally associated with men and masculinity, while the capacities for nurturance and dependency are split off, denigrated, and culturally associated with women and femininity. I suggest that these maternal love images are especially hard for the girls themselves to unpack, which becomes clearer if we compare the girls' discussion of maternal love with their discussion of heterosexual adult love.

Heterosexual Romance

While most of the girls drew on idealized images of maternal love, less than a third of the collages contained images of heterosexual romance. I was surprised that there were as few images of heterosexual romance as there were, especially given contemporary discussions about teenage girls' preoccupation with romance. There were images of black couples playing ball in a field; walking arm and arm under a tree; water skiing together; sitting on the floor embracing each other; snuggled together on a couch watching television, and so forth. In explaining these images, most girls talked about "having a man in my life." Charlene drew laughter and nods of agreement from her viewers when she explained, "I want a man in my life. I'm not saying he has to be a husband or anything, but I'm looking for a man."

Tracey selected a picture of a black couple that she said showed the kind of relationship she hoped for. The image proved to be controversial, sparking debate among the girls as to whether the image represented love or whether it was a scene about domestic violence. The girls constructed several stories to explain what was going on in the picture, which depicts a man and a woman sitting across from each other. The man's knee is bent and he is holding the woman's arm, which she has lifted to her forehead. The picture is not in color, but in brownish hues, making it all the more ominous, or romantic, depending upon your viewpoint. (See Figure 4.8) Tracey listened attentively to her classmates spin different tales about this man's violent behavior, "He hits her up the side of her head when he goes off. . . . No, no, no, he's the type that comes home and if he sees that everything's calm and quiet, he has to make trouble, so he starts hitting her." "She's holding her head after being hit, and he is trying to say he's sorry." Tracey finally put an end to the discussion by saying that even if the man had just hit his girlfriend and he was apologizing, promising that he'd never do it again, in that case, it was still a "picture of love." Her statement generated further debate among the girls as to whether the picture could be about "love" if it involved violence or abuse. In the end, Tracey said she was keeping the picture on her collage; her classmates could see what they wanted in her picture. For her, it still symbolized "love and happiness."

I found it interesting that these images of heterosexual romance were so often accompanied by stories like the one above. It was as if the images called upon the girls to create a narrative about characters, events, things that had preceded this or that interaction (e.g., "The couple is on their honeymoon, water skiing"; "The man has just asked the woman to marry him," "He has just hit her and is begging her forgiveness," and so forth). And I was surprised by how much these stories articulated both a sense of danger or violence, as well as being a wellspring of fantasies about the "man of my dreams."

The girls' discussions of the images of heterosexual romance they had selected, as well as their commentary on celebrities' successful and failed romances, reveal their tacit knowledge of what makes a typical or successful romantic relationship. Through these discussions, the girls showed their knowledge of the scripts and scenarios within the world of heterosexual romance. For example, while making her collage, Ebony found an article about Wesley Snipes, which sparked the following conversation.

"Look here, what he says. He says that everybody wants his time and energy, and they always want his money. Ohh, . . . and then he says, 'good sex is hard to come by,' 'good sex can make you happy; you come away feeling happy'."[17]

"You know he dates white women," Shannon announced.

"Give me that, he doesn't say that," Tara grabbed the article from Ebony.

"It says he dates white women?"

The girls start talking all at once about "famous people" and the things they can say and do, who they can date, and how much easier it is for celebrities to cross the color line in romance than it is for people they know.

Meanwhile, the script most often discussed by the PPPT girls had to do with men and women who were "players"—who "knew how to play the game and not get hurt." The idea was not to let on that you liked a man because you would soon find out that he was "playing you"—that he had a string of girls and you were just one among many. The girls seemed to especially enjoy telling stories about how a girlfriend, or in some instances, they themselves, had "played" someone "at his own game." Sociologist Greg Dimitriadis found the same script among youth in a small Midwestern city where he ran a weekly program in a community center for African American youth. The program focused on engaging young people in discussions about popular culture, "African American vernacular culture (generally) and hip hop or rap music (specifically)" (Dimitriadis 2001a: 32). Through these discussions, Dimitriadis learned about, among other things, a "local ethic" that borrowed on themes in Southern rap music; this ethic included "playing, respect, friendship, and community" (46). Dimitriadis describes the world of heterosexual romance that he observed as being a site of "intense anxiety" for both young men and women who worried about getting hurt and losing a sense of self in relationships. "In the face of uncertainty and contingency, loss of autonomy and hurt, these young people drew upon an ethic of invulnerability and mutual manipulation" (45).

Anthropologist Dorothy Holland and her co-authors (1998) offer another way to understand the girls' images and talk about heterosexual romance as conveying their knowledge of the "figured world of romance," within which girls fashion a sense of self and learn the "rules" that govern male-female relationships, love, and sex. In the figured world of romance there are scripts about romantic encounters, conduct, and motivations, including different "types" of men and women and their place in a hierarchy (Holland and Eisenhart 1990). For example, a "hunk" (an attractive man) would be less likely to date a "dog" (an unattractive woman); and if he did, he could more likely expect sexual favors from her than from a girl who is attractive or has as much prestige as he. Similarly, a "jerk" (an insensitive or stupid man) doesn't know how to show a woman that he appreciates her or that she is unique, and thus is unsuccessful in his romantic relationships. The same elements of the figured world of romance noted by Holland and Eisenhart—attractiveness, prestige, how to know one is valued by one's partner—were evident in the PPPT girls' conversations and especially in their stories about "playing and being played."

Not everyone referenced having a man as part of her collage, but it was striking how often the black girls referenced their love of black men.[18] Meanwhile, the girls did not speak about their own romances much in the classroom setting. There were times when a girl would refuse to answer her classmates' questions about a boyfriend for fear that this information might get used against her.[19] As Malika replied:

> I'm not saying anything. Last time I told my girlfriends about how much I like Malcom—he's my baby's daddy—they were all over him. Yeah, that's what I say, don't be talking about your man because that will be the end of it.

But what struck me most about these stories of romantic love is how much less idealized, more elaborated, more grounded in personal experience and expertise they were compared to those regarding maternal love. The girls reflected on the world of romance with cynicism ("I know what that guy is after") and doubt ("They're happy now, but that will end in no time at all") and at times resistance, as with the picture some girls refused to see as "romantic" because of what they saw as its violent edges. But the images of maternal love were discussed less critically. It was as if these images spoke for themselves, as if maternal love was a more "natural" and intrinsically motivating activity, whereas heterosexual love was more storied and social. The motivations connected to heterosexual love were understood to be complex and mutually reinforcing (even if dangerous, unequal, or cause for pain). These relationships were understood to provide something for both the man and the woman (e.g., the validation that one is attractive or has prestige or value or can "play the game"). But the more or less unspoken motivations connected to maternal love were not mutual. To make a child know she is special, to realize that one is not alone in the world, that there is someone who will always "be there," is a one-sided version of the meaning of maternal love. This is the child's side, the side that does not acknowledge the subjectivity of the mother who is doing the loving or "being there." It is a love so ideal that it cannot be fully realized by any *real* mother (or person). And if this reality is set aside, if mothers are seen as omnipotent, fearsome, and/or perfect, then the possibility for experiencing mutuality in the relationship is cut off. Compared to the more elaborated cultural scripts and scenarios defining the "rules of the game" for heterosexual romance (including skepticism), the cultural script for maternal-child love seems underdeveloped, cast in oversimplified and idealized terms—the perfect mother and the "special" baby. Without the means for social instruction and peer group culture that would prepare girls to see themselves as *subjects* in the figured world of motherhood (i.e., people who have mixed feelings, intentions, and goals, including maternal ambivalence), it is all the easier for them to accept myths of maternal omnipotence and idealized notions of motherhood that dominate the culture.[20]

Another way of seeing the distinctive scripts and scenarios for these two worlds—heterosexual romance and motherhood—is that both are sites of anxiety. But the strategies for managing anxiety are different; in the world of heterosexual romance, the way one protects oneself against loss and disappointment is to be invulnerable and skeptical, wary of all versions of "the game." In the world of motherhood, one protects oneself against loss and disappointment by splitting the mother (and baby) into two types: the ideal and the denigrated.

The girls' collages shed light on how they are being addressed by and answering to different social worlds that are anxiety-ridden and evoke different responses. There is the world of consumer culture that promises social respect but is based upon social inequities (especially racial discrimination in the case of the black PPPT girls) to which the girls must answer; there is the world of womanhood divided by class and race to which the girls answer with strength and respectability expressed through glamour; there is the anxiety-provoking lure of heterosexual romance to which the girls answer with varied strategies of self-protection; and there is the soon-to-be-experienced world of motherhood and the attendant worries about maternal protection and provision, to which the girls answer through idealization.

At the same time, each girl's collage takes us inside her own world, confirming her unique mark, creativity, and agency amid what critics consider a barrage of deadening media images.

Answering Questions that Are Not Their Own

Adolescent Female Sexuality

Remember Kaela from the previous chapter, who portrayed herself at age seven on her way to the candy store. Kaela engaged in the "Who am I?" collage activity with the same energetic fashion. After pasting a constellation of common consumer items (car, perfume, money, and mansion-like house), she added a picture of a *grand*mother and baby caught in a look of love. Kaela explained that her mother was getting more and more excited about having a grandchild; Kaela said her baby "was sure to be loved." She used the alphabet stamp set to print the words "I love Black Men." Then Kaela pasted the word virgin? (cut from a magazine) at the center top of the page. (See Figure 4.9) Without missing a beat, one girl asked her why she

Figure 4.9: Kaela's collage

had the question mark after the word virgin: "You are pregnant, aren't you? I mean you are showing, there's no mistaking it." Before Kaela could respond, another girl said she could understand why someone might have questions about whether or not she was still a virgin: "What about girls who are raped or sexually abused?" A heated debate ensued and there was no consensus about what makes a girl a virgin, what makes her "pure" in the eyes of others or in her own eyes. Kaela then announced to the group that she wished she was still a virgin, and that, if she had it to do over again, she would wait to have sex. At least two other girls nodded in agreement, until Tara interrupted, "Well, how long would you wait before you had sex?" "How old do you think a girl should be before she has sex?" Before Kaela could answer, another lively discussion erupted with some girls arguing for abstinence before marriage and others saying this wasn't practical because their boyfriends "wouldn't stand for it." In this discussion, there were no girls who acknowledged their own desires for sexual activity.[21]

The girls' discussion reflects what Michelle Fine (1988) calls the "blanketing" of female sexual subjectivity—the muting and suppression of a discourse of female sexual desire. Fine points out that female desire and pleasure is not openly discussed; the prevailing framework for discussing sex "allows girls one primary decision—to say yes or no to a question not necessarily their own" (34). This results in a process of subjectivity—called splitting—through which girls' bodies and sexualities get divided along an artificially constructed set of opposites: a set of opposites that Jessica Benjamin refers to as splits between "subject and object, good and bad, doer and done-to" (1988: 222). We can see the girls struggling to answer a question not necessarily their own when Tara asks, "How long would you wait?" The question is not, "What is your pleasure," but "When will you say yes or no?" By framing and embracing the question in this divided, yes or no way, it precludes the necessity for girls to deal with contradictory tendencies within themselves about what they desire.

What does it mean to be a virgin? Is Kaela a pregnant girl trying to answer to her social world where she must account for her sexual activity in ways not required of boys? Or of some girls? As Zora Neal Hurston (1928) would ask, "Compared to what? As of when? Who is asking? In what context? For what purpose? With what interests and presuppositions?" The contemporary context of a *missing* discourse of female desire and pleasure makes it especially difficult for girls to answer what it means to be a virgin. And it is not as if the PPPT girls can find a voice or fashion a self-representation that is independent of the varied and competing discourses that define teenage sexuality, including the sexual double standard by which boys and girls continue to be judged according to different criteria and face different consequences for their sexual activity. Rather, the girls must find a voice by taking a stance toward these discourses.

From this perspective, Kaela is taking up her own *questioning* stance toward sex and female desire. Indeed, when speaking about sex the PPPT girls took up many different stances, including three stances identified by Greenburg et al. (1993) in their work on the effect of media images of teenage girls' views about sexuality—"uninterested, intrigued, and resistant" (180). I will elaborate on this further in the next chapter, but here I want to emphasize Kaela's agency, her answer, which is to question the *meaning* of virginity, and to consider, even if tentatively, how she defines her own desires.

Racial Socialization

Sara's collage was made up completely of words and phrases she clipped out of the magazines; it contained no media images, it did not engage consumer culture, nor did it present a life-as-I-might-want, full of luxury items.

When I met Sara she was fifteen and held a job at a local fast food chain. She liked having a job because she could use her wages to buy clothes, see movies, and go partying, all of which she otherwise would have been unable to enjoy.[22] She moved between living with her grandmother, who was a retired nurse's assistant, and her mother, whose employment was not stable. Sara was an eager participant in the sessions and attended class more regularly than most. She had earned the reputation of being a good student because she turned her assignments in on time and with accuracy.

Sara kept cutting out words and phrases, making a pile in front of her. It wasn't until the next session that she started to winnow through her pile, placing the following constellation of words and phrases onto her piece of construction paper: (See Figure 4.10)

Smart; Tone your thighs with squats; one on one
As Good As New
Cool Down
Love to Spare; Power Up
Bright Lights, Big Mouth
Take Control
Dance fever; God's Gift; Beautiful
Wise Wisdom
This was how she explained the meaning of her collage:

Figure 4.10: Sara's collage

I was told to cool down when me and my teacher were fussing. This is how it started. I was in Ms. Little's room when I was supposed to be in Ms. Pepper's room and Ms. Little came into the room and started yelling at me. I started yelling at her (I don't let anybody yell at me). She told me that I needed to cool down and go to my right class. I was mad and angry. I wanted to hit her and just leave school—not see her face anymore. But I got through it by talking to my grandmother and then talking to Ms. Little and my grandmother in a conference. When I get angry it is hard for me to hold myself back but I got to learn to deal with things better and not get so angry. So that's who I am.

Many of the words/phrases included in her collage had to do with what she needed to do to "get through it" (i.e., her feelings of anger). "One on one" referred to her grandmother's advice: "It isn't good to bottle up your emotions, but you should find a way to express yourself one on one. She says you don't want to give people ammunition to say you are acting colored."

She said both Ms. Little and her grandmother told her to "cool down," to "not let people get the better of you, you got to take control of yourself." Sara explained that during the conference she had complained that Ms. Little was "too hard on" and sometimes "spoke down to" her and the other girls. Ms. Little acknowledged that maybe sometimes she is harsh, but this is "for the girls' own good" because they need to "toughen up" if they are going to survive in an even harsher world outside, a view of the world that Sara and her grandmother easily embrace. Ms. Little says her philosophy of "tough love" rests on "never forgetting who you are and where you come from." Sara explained that "Bright Lights, Big Mouth" was how her teachers and her grandmother see her, that she is smart but "can't keep her big mouth shut."

"As Good as New" refers to her body, that after giving birth, she plans to "tone my thighs" and get in shape. "Love to Spare" and "Power Up" represent Sara's emotional capacities—her abundant and intense love for herself and her baby. "God's Gift" refers to Sara's soon-to-be-born baby, whom Sara hopes will be able to enjoy life without "a care in the world." She put the phrase "Dance Fever" on the collage to represent one of life's greatest pleasures, dancing. "Beautiful, wise, and wisdom" denote the qualities she admires in herself that she hopes to pass down to her child.

Sara's collage references several themes that are threaded throughout the girls' self-representations: class-based understandings about life's hardships and the value of toughness and a thick-skinned self; a performance of femininity with strength and maternal love; and racial identification and affiliation. Sara's explanation of her collage also takes us inside a world of black womanhood where racial socialization is a point of tension and connection, where important black women in Sara's life hope to guide her through the maze of her feelings and the realities of her world.

Sara's description of this world reminded me of two forms of resistance, what Robinson and Ward (1991) have called "resistance for survival" and "resistance for liberation," strategies that black adolescent females adopt in their struggles against life's hardships and negative judgments. The first strategy, "resistance for survival," is "oriented toward quick fixes that offer short term solutions" (Ward 1996: 60), such as "mouthing off" when mistreated by authorities. The second strategy "offers confirmation of positive self conceptions as well as strengthening connections to the broader African American community" (60). Sara's experience of racial socialization illustrates both.

By suggesting that she wants Sara to avoid "acting colored," Sara's grandmother is drawing on the same stereotypical conception of blackness that she is preparing Sara to reject. This is part of a mixed message embedded in racial codes of conduct that require black children to answer to a question not necessarily their own. Writing about her own experience of these mixed messages, Karla Holloway (1995), tells a story about a mother who admonishes her child about not behaving well in public by saying, "Act your age, not your color." Holloway writes that "Those words, whispered with an intensity only a black child understands, initiate a public behavior firmly attached to a conviction that our places in line are easily jeopardized" (4). I would add that those words are part of a process of subjectivity through which black children's sense of selfhood gets divided along artificially constructed opposites that associate badness with blackness and goodness with whiteness.

Meanwhile, mixed into their warning to Sara, both her teacher and her grandmother affirm Sara's intelligence, her quick wit and "bright lights," as crucial abilities that Sara holds to deal with the world around her. These two black elders acknowledge the existence and reality of life's hardships and racial divisions against which Sara must fight. By encouraging Sara to identify and name her anger and to confront issues one-on-one, these two women are promoting a strategy of liberation.

Racial Selfhood and Identity

Celia, a white girl, "went missing" like Alice, whom I mentioned in the previous chapter. Both opted for the "homebound" program—Celia in her eighth month of pregnancy and Alice in her fifth. Celia's collage presents a dialogue she is having between herself and her social world, and how she must answer to questions that are not necessarily her own.

When I first met Celia she was already having complications with her pregnancy—she was in her fifth month. Celia was living with her parents and two sisters, both of whom had also gotten pregnant as teenagers. Celia described her parents as "hard working" and as "Christians." Her father works as a mechanic and her mother works as a supermarket clerk. Celia was quiet during most of the sessions.

At the center of her collage Celia pasted the word "American," which she had cut out of a magazine. At the top, in larger bold black letters she placed the word, GOOD. Into the o's of "good" Celia added her own details—a smiling face and a frowning face, indicating, "How I feel somedays happy, sometimes sad." To the left of the word, GOOD, she pasted colorful, different-sized letters to spell NICE. She artfully constructed the word, "nice," including a border, which took her the better part of the session. The next day Celia wrote in smaller, red marker letters the phrase, "Fair Person" at the very top of her collage. She added several other phrases— "treats everyone equal," is "against violence," is a "friendly person!" and a "good friend." She used markers to make a pastel colored banner around the phrase, "treats everyone equal." (See Figure 4.11)

Celia spoke quietly and softly as she explained her collage to her classmates, saying, "This is who I am. This is what people who know me would say about me." The room grew quiet and I sensed tension in the room (my own? Celia's? Celia's classmates'?). I wasn't sure how to interpret this because Celia was friendly with Alisha, a black classmate with whom she rode the bus to school, and she was often included by the other girls in informal conversation and planning for out-of-school activities. It seemed to me at the time as if the girls were reluctant or unwilling to enter Celia's framing of her self and identity—they were not "having it," so to speak.[23] Breaking the silence, I asked Celia, "I notice you have a banner around 'treats everyone equal'; can you tell us about this?" she replied:

> Well, to me, everyone is human and it doesn't matter if you are black or white. You shouldn't look at people and say, "Oh I don't like them," you should be nice to everyone. I believe everyone should be considered for who they are as a human being and not for the color of their skin. Underneath, everyone is good. So I try to treat everyone equal. I'm not prejudiced.

Tanya offered her opinion, "Well, people don't treat each other equal and that's how the world is. Subject closed." Everyone started talking at once, gathering up their belongings because the class session was over.

I planned to begin the next session by asking Celia more questions about her collage. When she did not arrive in class I wondered whether and

Figure 4.11: Celia's collage

how to broach the topic again. I needn't have worried because Tanya remarked, "Celia's not here, and I had a question for her." "Yeah, I had a question too, say, what do you mean you are *American*?" (said with an angry intonation). The girls started talking all at once and it was hard to make out what anyone was saying. The conversation quickly turned to food and who was wanting a hamburger.[24]

Celia's collage raises questions, some of which I have inadequate information to answer. My focus in this section is on Celia's agency. Like Kaela and Sara, I see Celia trying to answer a question that may not be her own—in Kaela's case it is about the meaning of virginity and mixed feelings about her sexual desires, in Sara's case it is the split meanings of racial codes of conduct, and in Celia's case it is about the complicated meaning of whiteness.

I see Celia trying to answer to her social world as a white girl living in a racially divided town, a white girl who does not want to be seen as prejudiced. I suspect that the question she thinks is being asked of her as a white person is, "Are you or are you not prejudiced?" This question does not leave much room for considering the multitude of feelings and experiences she might have about her racial subjectivity and "difference" as a white girl who is far from well-off and feels far from advantaged; as the single white pregnant girl in her class (just as Alice had been); as a white Christian girl who attends a small, racially mixed Christian evangelical congregation; as a white girl who dated a black youth (who is not her baby's father, but "could just as easily be" according to Celia) and kept this information from her parents. Celia clearly considers the address "American" as unproblematic, a view her classmates do not share with her. From her black classmates' perspective, Celia's claims to being American were annoying, if not offensive.

What does it mean to be American? Zora Neal Hurston (1928) would surely challenge this structure of address, as did some of the PPPT girls in the discussion. "Compared to what? As of when?[25] Who is asking? In what context? For what purpose? With what interests and presuppositions?"

Ruth Frankenberg (1993) argues that color and power evasiveness is the dominant language of race in the United States today. For many people, to be caught in the "act of seeing race" is to be caught being "prejudiced." Frankenberg argues that color-blind discourses, like the one Celia draws upon, hold mixed messages. In some cases, color differences are denied—the "I don't see color, I only see human beings" version. In this version, seeing color in people is not a good thing to do, it can even be offensive. In other cases, color differences are noticed but do (or should) not mean anything. As Celia states, "I believe everyone should be considered for who they are as a human being and not for the color of their skin."

Celia draws upon other discourses of race as well; there are Christian overtones in her statements, the language of essential goodness in people ("Underneath, everyone is good") and the golden rule of being "nice to everyone." There is a liberal humanist overtone, the belief in "human sameness to which 'race' is added as a secondary characteristic" (Frankenberg 1993: 148), as in Celia's remark, "underneath, everyone is the same." There is also Celia's emphasis on American cultural beliefs in equality, fairness, affinity/friendship, and independence.

But, in each instance, Celia is trying to craft a racial identity, without directly acknowledging her privileged place in the racial hierarchy. This is, according to Frankenberg, the appeal of color-evasive and power-evasive ways of thinking through race. These discourses focus on *individuals* and their samenesses and/or differences that should not matter, rather than on social, institutional, or political forces that create and sustain inequality. Frankenberg sees Americans as being trapped within an "essentialist racism" discourse that dates back 500 years, when "race was made into a difference and simultaneously into a rationale for racial inequality. It is in ongoing response to that moment that movements and individuals—for and against the empowerment of people of color—continue to articulate analyses of difference and sameness with respect to race" (1993: 139). The challenge for Celia (and for Americans in general) is to create an acceptable balance between her "entrapment" in essentialist racism and her conscious engagement with it (140). The same trap existed for the black PPPT girls when they struggled over racial representation, arguing over who could and couldn't claim a "black" identity.

In this chapter I make three related points. First, when asked to answer the question, "Who am I?" the girls crafted responses that engaged multiple social worlds in which they saw themselves as actors—the consumer world, the world of womanhood and motherhood, and heterosexual romance. Each of these worlds is anxiety-ridden and peopled by "types" who have scripted responses to the contingencies and divisions within each world. The "stylish" or "glamorous" independent woman, the idealized mother and the "special" baby, the "players" and romantic couples, all of whom searched, in one way or another, for respect and an enviable position in the world. Second, what the girls had to say about their collages to one another reveals their knowledge of difference, what I am calling their body-smarts, that is full of both pain and wisdom. This knowledge is about how one's body matters, what it should look like, where it can go, how it will be addressed and received, how it will resist or assent to being labeled as this or that. This knowledge arises from the girls' engagement in different social worlds. Mostly the girls' body-smarts emphasize their increasing awareness that how they are being addressed by their social world is at odds with how they see or would like to see themselves. This awareness can be hurtful, creating a sense of private loss, and it can be liberating, opening up possibilities for change. Finally, each girl's collage also beckons us to recognize her creative agency in answering to her world, especially answering questions that may not be her own, about love, sexuality, racial identification, and motherhood.

CHAPTER 5

Showing and Telling Pregnancy Stories

Scene I: At the Clinic

Nurse: Miss Gray? Have a seat right here. *(girl sits down on top of a table)*

Nurse: *(pulling up the girl's sleeve)* Okay, first I want to take your blood pressure. Okay? Fine. All right, now I want to ask you some questions. Have you been having sex?

Misty Gray: No, I have not.

Nurse: Okay, Now why don't you go in that room for your checkup and return back to this room when you're done. We need you to give us a urine sample. Here *(handing the girl a plastic cup and handi-wipe packet)*, take this into the bathroom and be sure to wipe yourself clean.

Misty Gray: *(her hand shakes as she takes the items)* Okay. *(Misty Gray exits, then returns to the nurses station)*

Misty Gray: I'm back.

Nurse: Okay. Miss Gray, this test has come back and it says that you're pregnant.

Misty Gray: What? No, how . . . that can't be. How can I tell my mom this?

Nurse: I can help you if you want me to.

Misty Gray: No, that's okay . . . I can handle this myself.

This was the opening scene to an improvisational skit about what the PPPT girls called a "pregnancy story." It was performed and videotaped at the PPPT in 1992. Like most of the girls' performances I recorded and transcribed,[1] it is difficult to convey the drama of these stories and the engagement of the audience. Readers cannot sense the twinkle in Misty's eyes when she tells the nurse she has not had sex or the despair in her voice when she asks, "How can I tell my mom this?" Spontaneous audience responses—applause, laughter, and gestures of approval or disapproval—also get lost in the translation.

In this chapter I discuss what we can learn from the girls' improvisations about the self- and identity-making process, especially in terms of the girls' alternative notions of agency and selfhood. My analysis draws from a tradition of narrative analysis that focuses on storytellers' *representations*—the content and themes in a narrative—and storytellers' *enactments*—patterns in the telling, including how characters are positioned in relation to one another as a way to accomplish certain effects.[2] In this case, I was interested in the girls' representations of the world of pregnancy and motherhood—the content of their dramas—and in their enactments, whether a character positioned herself as a victim, giving over to other characters the power to initiate action, or whether she positioned herself as having agency and assuming control over events.

The improvisational activities grew out my awareness that the girls enjoyed performing and were receptive audiences for one another's storytelling (see chapter 6 for more discussion of this). Their performances reminded me of sociologist Erving Goffman's observation that, "What talkers undertake to do is not to provide information to a recipient but to present dramas to an audience. Indeed, it seems that we spend most of our time not engaged in giving information but in giving shows" (quoted in James 2000: 183).

Much of the girls' informal conversation with me and with one another was performative, as they presented life events as dramas. It was in this context that I introduced a research activity, a theatrical exercise called "freeze."[3] The exercise worked like this: Girls would gather into "teams" and choose an event or dramatic moment that they would act out. The girls had ten minutes to decide upon a scene and develop their "characters." During the performance, a teammate or an audience member could call out "freeze," at which point, the girl could stop or redirect the scene. One of my reasons for using the freeze activity was to open up the performances, so that multiple, even contradictory perspectives or possibilities could get expressed.[4] I was purposively vague about how the girls could use the freeze and explained that they could choose not to freeze the action—it was up to them.

There were three ways in which the girls made use of the freeze game. All three were the girls' inventions, as I had not provided specific examples. In the first instance, a girl would stop the action and ask a character to explain herself or defend her actions (e.g., "How can you talk that way to your mother?" "Why are you taking your boyfriend at his word?"). Freezes were also used by a girl to interrupt a scene (often at a provocative moment) by saying, "This is not how it should be." The girl who had called out freeze would then take the place of a character, offering her corrective version. For example, in one scene between a "nurse" and a "girl," just when the nurse character started berating the girl for having unprotected sex, a team member called out "freeze." In this case Tara said, "I won't have that. Let me show how to treat someone with respect." A third way the girls used the freeze was to offer their own stories. For example, in many clinic scenes, like the one that opens this chapter, a girl character would deny that she was having sex when asked by the nurse. And in response, audience members would give their own version, much like Charlene, who said: "When I went for my check up I suspected I might be pregnant but I had only had sex once. When the nurse asked me, 'have you been having sex,' I said 'no' because it wasn't like I was really having sex."

Without my direction or prompting, teams of PPPT girls would return (again and again) to reenact the same two scenes: a "clinic" scene between a girl and nurse and a "home" scene in which a girl told her mother that she was pregnant. These two scenes routinely featured a cast of female "characters"—the sensitive or denigrating nurse; the quiet/passive or tough/active girl; and a much wider range of mother types. Sometimes, but not often, an improvisation included a scene with a girl and her boyfriend, most commonly referred to as "my baby's daddy." There were no scenes that included a girl's own father.[5]

The girls' performances engaged larger public discourses about the problem of teenage sexuality, pregnancy, and motherhood, particularly in terms of negative stereotypes.[6] The girls would argue about whether a character was portrayed in a stereotypic way, saying, "Is that how you want people to think about pregnant teenagers, as drug addicts who don't care about their baby's health?" asked Kendra, after viewing a skit that featured a nurse and a girl who was challenging the nurse's medical advice. Because the subject of "teenage pregnancy" is almost invariably framed as a social problem, and, as I argued in part I, because much of the discourse draws on complex images of "wrong" or "wronged" girls, it is not surprising that scenarios and characters in the skits drew upon and sometimes sought ways to redress these images.

There were times when I wondered whether the girls' performances served as a means for them to work out difficult feelings. Through these performances, the girls could temporarily suspend reality and switch roles. They might either pretend to subject another to damaging treatment they themselves might have received or they might reenact the scene in a more positive way. Perhaps the girls were attempting to gain a sense of mastery or self-healing through their play acting. This is how a therapist might see it. But my focus was on the common themes that recurred across the improvisations and the type of conflicts that were presented. I took note of how these conflicts were framed and how they were resolved (or not). For example, a persistent conflict in these skits had to do with establishing paternity. Resolutions were typically prompted by a girl announcing that she was going to get a blood test to verify her claim. I also paid particular attention to social positioning in the performances, including how a girl character might attempt to save "face" in a difficult situation. Goffman (1963) would see these face-saving strategies as ways the girls were managing their "stigma," their tainted identities. But my analysis goes beyond this in two ways. First, I argue that the positioning of characters provides crucial insight into the girls' complicated feelings about and unconventional notions of selfhood and agency. Goffman's theory assumes a particular notion of selfhood, an autonomous individual who sees him- or herself as making choices and as able to manage information about him- or herself.[7] Goffman's theory also assumes that a person, in this case a PPPT girl, holds the same beliefs and values about her "situation" as the rest of society, which, as I have already argued, is not the case among the girls. The girls' performances make this very clear, illustrating how they wrestle with multiple positions—as victims of stereotypes and mistreatment, as vulnerable to men's deceit, as daughters who fear disappointment and loss, and as decision makers who have not chosen the conditions under which they must take action.

While I was usually an audience member, there were times when I was recruited by the girls to play the "nurse" or "mother" character and once to play the "girl," an instance I will discuss later in this chapter. Taking up these different roles made me even more acutely aware that these performances belie easy interpretation and analysis. What might trigger a feeling or response from the speaker/actress was quite distinct from how different listeners/audience members engaged and responded. The lesson I learned from playing a character is that there is an irresolvable and visceral tension between personal and public self-representations, between the experience of storytelling and that of analysis.

Who Am I as Pregnant?

The storyline of Misty's pregnancy begins in the context of medicalization. Each clinic scene firmly establishes the nurse as "in charge," a technician regulating blood pressure, weight gain, urine samples, and hygiene ("Be sure to wipe yourself clean"). Nurse characters made clever use of props to establish their regulatory role. These included make-believe blood pressure cuffs, imaginary stethoscopes for amplifying the baby's heartbeat, clipboards with patient information sheets, and a cloth for covering the bottom half of a girl's body as she lies waiting to be examined. The nurse's actions and words, as in real life medical interactions, served to separate the girl's "self" from her body.[8]

The characters in the skits drew upon dominant medical metaphors in which the body is understood to be a distinct entity, going through changes, doing things, and sending "signals" to which a girl must pay attention as part of her pregnancy.[9] Questions about sexual activity ("Have you been having sex?") followed this same medicalized pattern, as if sex and pregnancy were things happening or "done" to the body and not actions girls take. Indeed, it was "the test" that served to confirm or disconfirm a pregnancy regardless of what a girl said or knew about her body ("It says that you're pregnant"). Similarly, it was a "blood test" that was routinely requested from boyfriends who denied their paternity. These medical tests were understood to be flawless and authoritative, whereas women and men were understood to be either mistaken or deceitful.

In one sense, these clinic scenes shed light on the girls' unexamined or "naturalized" view of pregnancy as a "medical" state of being in need of management. Girl characters were consistently portrayed as compliant patients who were being instructed in how to view their changing bodies. There were no scenes, for example, where a girl described and a nurse listened to her perceptions or sensations of bodily changes brought about by pregnancy. It was always the nurse who did the talking about what to expect and how one would feel, to which girl characters listened. But when asked to "account" for their sexual lives as part of this clinic ritual, girl characters took up both self-punitive and self-affirming stances.

Defending the Sexual Self

Misty, like many girl characters asked by nurses about whether they were having sex, denied it. At times, a girl character would quietly admit that she *was* sexually active by laughing uncomfortably, saying, "Well maybe a little." And on a few occasions, girl characters answered back to the nurse in a parody, exaggerating their sexual activity, "You bet, I have had sex so many times with so many guys I wouldn't know who the father is" (such retorts were filled with wild laughter or bravado and were well received by audience members). Being compelled to defend their sexual reputations against nurses' insinuation that they were "promiscuous" or "ignorant" was at the heart of the drama in many of these clinic scenes.

Nurse characters were portrayed as divided types: either "good" (i.e., sensitive) or "bad" (i.e., denigrating). "Good" nurses expressed concern and showed a girl kindness. For example, one nurse character said, "You look tired, here, come sit down, put up your feet and let me get you a drink of water. Was it a long bus ride?" Other sensitive nurses provided a girl with important advice or inspiration, often based on personal experience. For example, one nurse character tried to console her crying patient: "I was a teenage mother and I know it is hard. You can't hang with your friends, you can't fit into your favorite clothes, people tease you or make you feel ashamed. But you can hold your head up high and go on about your business."[10] "Good" nurses, like the one portrayed in Misty's story, offered their help or support, which was routinely declined in favor of self-reliance ("I can handle this myself" or "I need to face this one alone").[11]

"Bad" nurses, on the other hand, were portrayed far more often. Sometimes a nurse would lecture a girl about the importance of birth control as if she were ignorant. The girls described these scenes as "nurses talking down" to a patient, often citing their own experiences of this. Other times a nurse would be cold or distant as if the girl were "just one more person bothering her." Performances of nurse mistreatment were so routine and some were so unsettling to me that I found myself asking, "Is this how you are treated at the clinic?" Typically, a girl would respond by laughing and saying, "I'm just playing, most of them is nice, but sometimes . . ."

Girl characters who withdrew into silence in the face of a nurse's verbal abuse left their audiences on edge. I would experience relief (and it seemed that other audience members felt the same) when a girl would "freeze" the action during a nurse's verbal abuse. As if to rescue these victimized patients, the new girl character would be recast as "tough" or the nurse as kind or at least respectful. But, most often, girl characters answered these attacks by acting tough or offering comic retorts that showed they had "thick skin" and were unfazed. I saw these performances as yet another example of the girls' "hard, protective" individualism:

> Nurse: You've been having sex and not protecting yourself and now look at the mess you are in.
> Girl: Who are you calling a mess?

The subtleties of the girls' performances were stunning. A nurse character could produce a dismissive "look" that stopped even the most "in-your-face" girl character in her tracks. There were girl characters who acted "tough," stiffening their bodies or returning a "look" with a cold stare that could not be mistaken as anything but indignation.

Then there were two scenes in which a girl character "went crazy on" a nurse who had been insulting:

> Nurse: How many guys have you had sex with? Have you ever used protection? You haven't ever used protection, have you? I' ll bet you don't even know what protection is. I can see I am wasting my time on you.
> Girl: *(standing up face-to-face with the nurse spitting each word out loudly)* Don't you talk to me in that "I'm better than you" in your voice. And don't try to tell me what I have and haven't done. You don't know me, you don't know who I am.

> Nurse: *(looking up from her clip board, giving the girl a "look," eyebrows raised)* Come this way. *(said in an annoyed tone of voice)*
> Girl: Don't look at me like that. Haven't you ever seen a girl before? Haven't you ever seen a pregnant girl before? Who do you think you are sitting in judgment of me? *(A string of "cuss" words followed, and audience members stood up applauding and yelling their support)*

These two performances exemplify what Karla Holloway (1995; quoting novelist Lorene Cary) has called "turning it out" (and also as "acting colored," a problematic expression I discussed in the previous chapter). Writing about the defenses African American women must develop in order to maintain bodily dignity in the face of racial stereotypes and mistreatment (especially among medical providers), Holloway worries that these acts of resistance "can mean handing over to our adversary our version of the stereotype that motivates their disrespect to us—just to prove to them that they could no better handle the stereotype than they can determine and control our character. No one wins in that situation, but usually we feel better" (31). While audiences reacted to each girl's "turning it out" with shouts of approval and applause, the pain evoked by these two scenes was palpable. Tracey reflected quietly after watching the first skit: "It looks funny to watch except for how much it happens—I mean how many times I seen people and been treated like that."[12]

The girls' "tough" characters and these incidents of "turning it out" deepened my grasp of the girls' philosophy of "hard, protective individualism" seen through a racial lens. These "bad" nurse and "tough" girl scenes shed light on how the girls coped with private feelings through these public negotiations. They skillfully used humor to deflect their feelings; they presented themselves as tough, thick skinned, and invulnerable to pain; they used silence as a sign of their indignation. But the following incident spurred me to think more about how social distinctions (class and race) link up with private feelings, notions of selfhood, and strategies of resistance.

It was in the third year of my research, and Grace asked if I would play "a pregnant girl at the clinic." Stella must have registered surprise or worry on my face because she said, "You can do it, just look over at me if you need some good lines." I grabbed the props (a hospital robe and a magazine) and sat impatiently jiggling my leg as if I had been waiting a long time to be seen. Shantae, who was playing the nurse, walked up with her clipboard and gruffly announced my name, "Wendy Luttrell." I stood up, feeling a bit shaken hearing my name called out so publicly and in such an authoritative tone. We moved to a space set up with a long table and two chairs. The "nurse" ordered me to lie down and roll up my sleeve. She forcefully pulled at my arm and tightly wrapped the make believe blood pressure rope around it until it pinched. Before I could even say, "Stop—that hurts," the "nurse" said, "It has to be tight for it to work." Then, without missing a beat, she started firing off the standard series of questions about sexual conduct. "How many times have you had sex? You haven't been using protection have you? How many men have you been with anyway? You probably can't count how many." Her voice grew louder and harsher and I heard someone in the audience gasp. I was unable to speak, even though I kept opening my mouth to try. Tears began to fill up in my eyes and I could hear Grace say, "Wow, she's good, she's pretending to cry." With tremendous relief, I heard Stella yell, "freeze." As I stood up, tears spilled down my cheeks. I looked out at my audience who was applauding, complimenting me on my outstanding "acting job." I gathered up enough composure to say, "Well I wasn't acting, I felt scared and ashamed. Nurse Shantae really intimidated me." My confession drew laughter at first, and then a moment of silence before Stella said, "Well that may be how you feel but you can't ever let on that you feel that way."

There are many things I learned from this exchange—This test? This invitation to enter the girls' world? This initiation of sorts? This enactment of hostility? Subjecting my own performance to the interpretive practice I applied to the girls', I recognize that my social positioning in the play is as victim. The "bad" nurse is doing things *to* my body that I am passively accepting by not speaking up (in the moment I remember feeling as if my body were separate from "me," as I have often felt in the doctor's office). I also play the compliant patient, and Nurse Shantae is just "doing her job" (even if rudely). I am "rescued" by Stella who calls "freeze," which I took as a show of kindness, whether it was intended to be or not. I try to "save face" with my audience, who I believe must be wondering why a grown woman has been moved to tears by a young girl pretending she is a mean nurse. My "saving face" strategy is to admit to my vulnerability, which, given my social position in the larger world, I have the luxury of doing.

This is one "accurate" rendering of what happened. But there are others, and this is where my analysis goes beyond Goffman's. I found myself *surprised* by my own feelings. Among many things, I felt caught "off guard," and yet relieved in some way that I was still in one piece. Because I admired so many girls' "tough" and "in-your-face" performances, I was embarrassed by my inability to do the same. Moreover, I felt keenly aware of my expectation, born of privilege, that I should be treated kindly and respectfully by the nurse. Was this part of my initiation into the girls' social world—being disabused of such notions? Was this the reason Nurse Shantae had pulled so hard on my arm—an attempt to "toughen me up"? And was Stella's advice, "You may feel that way, but you can't ever let on," also part of the lesson about selfhood being imparted?

But perhaps Stella's advice was also an acknowledgment that she *does* feel vulnerable in a way she can't "let on." If viewed in psychodynamic terms, we might speculate that a nurse's abusive, punishing treatment is standing in for a girl's own sense of shame or blame, and that a girl's "toughness" against nurse's attacks protects her from her own feelings. These processes of projection and splitting are protective mechanisms against hurtful or unbearable feelings or feeling out of control of one's life. But, in so doing, feelings of vulnerability or grief are censored, and thus cannot be grappled with. Perhaps it was because my performance brought these disavowed feelings to the surface in a safe way (I was acting it, not they) that it was so well received by the audience.

Meanwhile, there is an especially Southern convention of interpersonal racial dynamics and anxieties in which "good" whites (i.e., not prejudiced against or discriminatory against blacks, but all the same, often paternalistic) are split off from "bad" whites (i.e., prejudiced, discriminatory, or violent toward blacks), and "good" blacks (i.e., accommodating to white privilege and standards) are set against "bad" blacks (i.e., rebellious or hostile to white people, their privilege, and standards). These sets of splits and projections occur on both sides of the racial fault line and may be implicated in the clinic drama. For example, how much of my reaction is based on my fear of the "bad," black nurse's hostility coupled with my desire to be seen as a "good" white person? And how much of the girls' applause was related to their delight in seeing a white woman authority figure being made an object of contempt and intimidation? Meanwhile, my rescuer Stella's reaction had been quite distinct from Shantae's as the hostile nurse's, yet up to this point I had been blind to these differences among individual girls.

I also felt hurt that some girls thought I had been "acting" and did not see me for my "real" self—the person I imagined myself to be. And in this moment that "real" person was ever so complicated, ever so tangled up in my multiple positions (gender, race, class, age, authority) and in my conscious and unconscious needs, desires, and identifications. These clinic scenes speak to many things, including the ways in which the girls were "speaking back to" and "turning out" racial stereotypes. But because of my own participation, I realize the extent to which the characters being played in these scenes also speak to the links between social divisions and psychodynamic forces in the self- and identity-making process. There is a complicated web of emotions and social distinctions that constitute selfhood, whether it is thick-skinned and "hard," or vulnerable and "soft." It is this web of emotions that has yet to be given full and careful consideration in theories about self and identity formation.

Defending the Moral Self

Nurse characters, whether cast as sensitive or denigrating, questioned the girls about their decisions. One strategy used by many girl characters was to take the moral high ground. Character after character, who, in answering back to a nurse about her "situation," talked about having a baby as an opportunity to wipe the slate clean.

> Nurse: So what are you going to do about your situation? You are too young to be having a baby.
> Girl: I didn't plan to have a baby right now; I don't know anybody who had a plan. But it has given me a chance to change some things like my friends and all the partying I used to do. Having a baby is letting me start over and focus on getting my life together.

Charmine called, "freeze," and offered her own version:

> Yeah, I used to run the streets with my friends smoking, drinking, and obviously having sex. In a way, getting pregnant is the best thing that ever happened to me. I now have somebody who has to depend on me to get my life together, and I don't want to let him or her down.

Many of the PPPT girls echoed this sentiment, in everyday conversations and in their performances. As Marisa explained:

> I know I can't be thinking only of myself now. The good thing about being pregnant is that it has made me change some bad habits, including eating better and taking vitamins, getting more sleep.

Nicole talked about "cleaning [herself] up" and how getting pregnant gave her "more reason to finish school, to work hard, and keep on track."

Through these performances, the girls seemed to be answering dominant discourses about teenage pregnancy—turning what is framed as a problem into an opportunity. These performances also reaffirmed many one-on-one conversations I had with the girls about how their pregnancies were serving as a pathway to maturity, which, as I discussed in part I, may be part of a working-class definition of motherhood.

But I was most struck by the language the nurse and girl characters used to talk about a girl's "situation," and what this meant about a girl's sense of self and agency. It was common in the clinic scenes for a nurse to ask a girl what she thought she was going to do about her pregnancy. This recurring question implied, at least from my vantage point, that the girl had "choices"—adoption, abortion, or "keeping the baby." But I took note of the fact that the word *choice* was not used—rather, the girls drew on a lexicon of words and phrases that had to do with decision making, but not options or choices. I expected, for example, that there would be a range of responses from girl characters to a nurse's query about what she would do about her "situation." I found it striking that among the hundred improvisations, only one performance featured an "adoption story" (during which a girl called "freeze" and changed the girl character's decision to "give her baby away," saying, "I know it will be hard, but I need to raise this baby; it's too much a part of me."). Only two performances openly explored abortion as a decision.

In the first skit about an abortion decision, the girl character answered the nurse's probing questions like a broken record:

Nurse: What are you going to do?
Girl: Have an abortion. I am too young to raise a child.
Nurse: Are you sure about this, that this is what you want? *(the nurse raises her voice)*
Girl: I am too young to raise a child.
Nurse: You need to think this over more, sleep on it. Tomorrow you may feel different, advised the nurse. Besides, what will your

mother think if you do this? What about your aunts? Your minis-
ter? What will they say about this? How will you face them after-
ward? *(The nurse is yelling at the girl at this point)*
Girl: I am too young to raise a child.

An audience member called out "freeze" at this point—"You keep saying
the same thing over and over." Other girls in the room nodded their heads
in agreement.

"But I *am* [her emphasis] too young to raise a child and that's all I have
to say," said Charlene, who was playing the girl, and she walked away from
the "stage" area.

Charlene looked frustrated and upset, and I avoided probing further
about what she said in front of everyone. Later, when we were alone, I asked
Charlene how she felt about the skit. "I could never have an abortion, but I
thought about it, I thought about it a lot. Some days I can't get it off my
mind. There are times I wonder, . . . [long pause] but I don't believe in
abortion, abortion is killing, and that is . . . no that's just something I
couldn't do [her voice trailing off]."

In the other abortion-decision skit, the girl character answered the
nurse's question, "What are you going to do?" with three words, "Have an
abortion."

Nurse: That's not acceptable. If you are going to be laying up there
with a boy then you can have a baby.
Girl: *(hangs her head in silence)*
Nurse: You will never be able to live with yourself if you have this
abortion. Your mother didn't kill you, did she? Why would you
want to kill your baby? You know you are doing wrong here. I can
see it in your face, in the way you are hanging your head.

Informal discussions about abortion, to which I had been privy or part
of, were not so emotionally charged (for me at least). I was accustomed to
the PPPT girls stating matter of factly that they wouldn't have an abortion
(information about which I did not ask, but which was routinely offered by
the girls). There were girls who had said it was against their religion and
others who said having an abortion was not a decision they would make,
but they were not against other women making that decision. Meanwhile, I
was not asked for my own views about abortion, perhaps because I had
purposefully avoided the topic, feeling it might put the girls (or me?) on
the spot. So when I heard what I considered to be vehement anti-abortion
rhetoric being spoken by the nurse character, I was taken aback. Surprising

myself, I called out "freeze." I asked the girl character what was going through her mind as the nurse was speaking.

"Nothing," she replied.

"No feelings or thoughts?" I asked.

"Well, I don't like people raising their voice to me."

The girls started talking at once.

"The nurse wasn't raising her voice, she was speaking her mind."

"Yeah, but she shouldn't be doing that, she's not the girl's mother."

"But that is her belief and she has a right to express it."

Rhonda playing the nurse character, interrupted the conversation and said calmly, "This is what I believe, that it is wrong to kill your own baby and abortion is killing."

This exchange put me in touch with how much I had been listening to the PPPT girls through the political rhetoric of the abortion debate, and my own "pro-choice" position. The terms of this debate, according to Kristin Luker (1996), pit woman against fetus, woman against patriarchal state, but also woman against woman:

> Pro-choice and pro-life activists live in different worlds, and the scope of their lives, as both adults and children, fortified them in their belief that their views on abortion are the more correct, more moral and more reasonable. When added to this is the fact that should "the other side" win, one group of women will see the very devaluation of their lives and life resources, it is not surprising that the abortion debate has generated so much heat and so little light. (215)

As I attempted to move outside the parameters of the abortion rhetoric, and to listen to what these two "abortion" skits were saying, I realized that they were about killing, about violence, and not about the abortion debate. Abortion *is* understood by women as violence, as feminist psychologist Carol Gilligan (1982) reminds us in *In a Different Voice*. Indeed, "The occurrence of the dilemma itself precludes nonviolent resolution" (94). The choice is not between violence and nonviolence, but between one form of violence and another. Barbara Johnson (1987), in writing about the rhetoric of abortion, neatly sums up Gilligan's argument in a way that best characterizes the logic of decision making I heard in these pregnancy narratives:

> Female logic, as she [Gilligan] defines it, is a way of rethinking the logic of choice in a situation in which none of the choices are good:

> "Believe that even in my deliberateness I was not deliberate": be-
> lieve that the agent is not entirely autonomous, believe that I have
> not chosen the conditions under which I must choose. (191)

It strikes me that the drama and anxiety of these clinic scenes are part of the logic of decision making, and that the girls' responses defy conventional notions of autonomy and agency. Put slightly differently, the question the girls see themselves answering is not their own. The question being posed is, "What choices do you have in your situation and what decision will you make?" But the question the girls are grappling with is, "How will I live with a 'decision' that is not deliberate?" Let me explain. Conventional notions of pregnancy and motherhood pit self against body; woman against fetus; and mother against child. These notions split something that is whole into parts. These split notions of the pregnant self imbue both medical and legal discourses. Legal scholar Patricia Williams (1991) writes: "I don't believe that a fetus is a separate person from the moment of conception; how could it be? It is interconnected, flesh-and-blood-bonded, completely a part of a woman's body. Why try to carve one from the other?" (184).

Williams provides a compelling example about split notions of pregnant selfhood in the law. The legal case that piqued Williams's interest concerned a pregnant woman from Washington, D.C., "who was put into prison by a judge to keep her off the streets and out of drug-temptation's ways, ostensibly in order to *protect* her fetus" (184). The litigation that followed turned out to rest on the issue of the inadequate living conditions for prisoners, whether pregnant or not. Prisons do not provide sufficient exercise, health care, and nutrition, especially for prenatal nurture. Williams says that in the case:

> the "idea" of the child (the fetus) becomes more important than
> the actual Child (who will be reclassified as an adult in the flick of
> an eye in order to send him back to prison on his own terms), or
> the actual condition of the woman of whose body the real fetus is
> a part. . . . The idea of the child is pitted against the woman; her
> body, and its need for decent health care, is suppressed in favor
> of a conceptual entity that is innocent, ideal, and all potential.
> (184–185)

I see the girls' answers to nurses about their "situations" as illustrations of this paradoxical notion of selfhood. On one hand, the scenes stress that a girl's agency lies not in how she separates herself from her baby or how she sees herself as autonomous from another, but rather, how she is connected to and responsible for others. But, at the same time, these same scenes pit the "idea" of the child as innocent and ideal against the "real" pregnant self who lacks "real" choices. These scenes suggest that the girls' understanding of their own agency—of what it means to take control of oneself and one's surroundings—is far more complicated than is granted by dominant definitions. For the PPPT girls' "agency" has more to do with "connection," "responsibility," and "taking the consequences" than with "intentions" and "wills."

Who Am I as a Daughter? Who Is My Mother?

Scene 2: At the Kitchen Table

> Misty: This is very hard for me to tell you.
> Misty's mother: How come Misty?
> Misty: You sure you won't get mad?
> Misty's mother: No I won't get mad.
> Misty: Well, you're going to be having a grandchild.
> Misty's mother: A who? A what? *(long silence)* You're kidding me. Say that again.
> Misty: A grandchild.
> Misty's mother: A grand what?
> Misty: Child.
> Misty's mother: By who?
> Misty: You know . . .
> Misty's mother: No, no, no, girl. Who is having the baby?
> Misty: Me.
> Misty's mother: You? By who?
> Misty: Oh man . . . I forgot his name. *(the characters and audience break out into laughter)*
> Misty: I'll get serious.
> Misty's mother: What is his name so I can call over there. . . . Does his mother know?
> Misty: No, she don't. . . .
> Misty's mother: Well did you go over to his house? What did he say? And don't play with me, I want to know.
> Misty: Um, my baby's father said it isn't his.

Scene 3: At the Baby's Father's House

> Misty's mother: *(knocks on the door and Enrico's mother opens the door)* I don't know you and you don't know me but my daughter is

supposed to be pregnant by your son and I would appreciate it if you would call him here so we could get this straight.

Enrico's mother: Enrico, come here. *(He enters the room)* This woman here says that her daugher is pregnant by you. Do you . . . do you remember this?

Enrico: Nah, Nu uh. It's not mine.

Misty: You're a liar. *(The girl playing Misty laughs and turns to the audience saying she is trying to get serious)*

Misty's mother: Wait, wait, wait. . . . First of all . . .

Enrico's mother: No you wait, I see it like this. I've seen this woman *(pointing to Misty)*, this female in my house on more than one occasion. And the first time I seen her she was here with my son's friend. The second time I seen her she was in here by herself, and the third time I seen her she was in here with my son. So you talk about this being my son's child I think you should have your daughter taken to the health department because she's been having hmmmnahmmmmmnahmmmmna with more than my son.

Misty's mother: She says that it is his child. He might not say it's his but when the baby comes and whatever she decides to do, she will have a blood test taken.

Enrico's mother: *(turning to Enrico)* Yes, and if it is you, you will get a job or some whatever and pay for this child.

Misty's mother: Child support will be paid and . . .

Misty: And what do I get to say about this?

Misty's mother: And you shut up.

Enrico's mother: Yeah. If it wasn't for you all we wouldn't be going through this!

(The scene continues and Enrico accuses Misty of sleeping with his friend; he refuses to acknowledge that the baby is his or to take any financial responsibility)

Scene 4: Driving Home in the Car

Misty's mother: I just want you to think about this real good, the possibility of what you're going to do. Because it's your pregnancy and you need to go ahead and let me know what you're going to do.

Misty: Are you going to help me?

Misty's mother: Am I going to help you? This is your decision.

Misty: I did not make this decision.

Misty's mother: *(pretending to put on the car brakes)* You did not make what decision?

Misty: Let's go on. . . . Let's get on with life.

I asked Keisha, one of the performers of the Misty skit, what she hoped to convey to her audience. She said the play was meant to be a "warning" to young women.[13]

"The play shows how boys say it is not their baby and make it a problem for the girl and her reputation," Keisha explained.

Shondra, another performer added:

> Your baby's father needs to be there for you and the baby, but that's not what is happening. Girls believe guys who tell them, "if you get pregnant I'll be right by your side." Then when they do get pregnant the guy accuses the girl of lying, or being a whore. And you can't get help from social services if you don't give them the baby's father's name.

For Keisha and Shondra, the play serves two warnings to girls about the conflicts they will face if they become pregnant. The first warning is, How are you, as a pregnant girl, going to defend yourself and your reputation?; and the second is, How will you secure the necessary resources for raising a child? (which includes establishing paternity). Both warnings were made repeatedly throughout the hundred skits I observed. And characters managed the anxiety arising from these difficulties in patterned ways.

Warding off accusations made by boyfriends that they had been "sleeping or messing around" with other boys characterized confrontations between a pregnant girl and her baby's father, often positioned like Misty—as victims of their boyfriends' deceit. Girl characters were either "rescued" by girlfriends who would corroborate a girl's story, or protected by a mother who demanded financial support for her daughter. At first glance, these typical responses support a view of the pregnant girl as having been "wronged." But this oversimplifies the complex emotions attached to "being wronged," including the girls' own sense of agency and ambivalence.

Throughout the mother-daughter scenes, girl characters moved between different positions, from seeking self-reliance and independence, to seeking interconnectedness and responsibility, to seeking recognition from their mothers. The final scene of Misty's story best illustrates these complex negotiations. Misty's mother, drawing on a vocabulary of selfhood that stresses personal agency as responsibility, asks what her daughter is going to do about being pregnant. She is reminding Misty that it is *her* pregnancy and she alone must make her decision. Meanwhile, Misty is asking her mother to understand her decision as not her own, as not of her own choosing. And she makes an ambiguous plea for her help (help in making the decision or help caring for the baby? Or both?). Misty's mother (comically) balks at this suggestion. Nonetheless, a different notion of self-hood has been given voice—a notion that dependence, connection, and especially ambivalence are not "good" or "bad," they just "are."

I don't mean ambivalence in the colloquial sense; that a girl is mixed in her feelings, that she feels a bit positive and a bit negative and somehow can't make up her mind. I mean ambivalence in the psychological sense that we all carry contradictory impulses and emotions toward the same person. My use of the notion of ambivalence here borrows from the work of psychoanalyst Melanie Klein (1975, 1989) whose views I will describe very briefly.

According to Klein, a normal part of human growth and development is to work toward the unification or integration of opposing feelings of love and hate. Ambivalence, for Klein, is not a problem; rather, the problem is to manage the anxiety that ambivalent feelings provoke. Split emotions (love and hate) are understood to be a given in all significant relationships, but the predominance of one over the other shifts and is never fully or permanently integrated.[14] Meanwhile, particular experiences of loss and change (Klein features mourning), among which pregnancy and motherhood certainly qualify, may shake up the balance between love and hate so that these emotions become more intense in such a way that magnifies feelings of anxiety.

According to Klein there are stages, or "positions," between which people move over the course of development. Initially, a baby experiences her or his mother as undifferentiated from her- or himself. But as a baby becomes aware that mother is a separate entity, the child must find ways to cope with uncertainty, especially the reality that the mother can be both nurturing and withholding, satisfying and frustrating, of the baby's needs and desires. In order to manage these conflicting experiences and attendant emotions, the baby separates the loving (good) from the hateful (bad) sides of the mother. This mode of organizing experience enables the infant to protect the nurturing from the endangering aspects of the caregiver. According to the Kleinian system, this splitting process is an important psychological protection used in the course of everyday life. It is a psychodynamic shield that enables an individual to cope with or manage opposing realities, to deal with contradictory feelings or tendencies within the self and/or toward others. Over the course of development, the more extreme versions of splitting (good-bad; idealized-denigrated) give way to greater integration. The impetus of development, then, is for the child to integrate, as much as possible, the split sides of the mother, coming to view her as a full and complete person. This is a gradual recognition, that the loved and hated mother are one and the same.

According to this view, we might see the girls' mother-daughter skits as highlighting their growing recognition that "mothers" (even if not their own mother) can hold conflicting emotions. It is important to stress here that some of the PPPT girls were not living with their mothers; indeed there was a huge range in the quality of mother-daughter relationships. Nonetheless, and despite the girls' actual experiences with their mothers, the skits consistently represented mother characters as more "real" than nurse characters. Whereas the nurse characters were presented as opposing types (good or bad), mother characters were presented as holding multiple feelings and positions. Meanwhile, when contrasted to the girls' depictions of themselves as mothers in their media collages, which represented only one side of motherhood—the idealized, omnipotent mother (the side of motherhood that the culture promotes)—the mother-daughter skits convey a more complicated image of maternal-child bonds.

Throughout the scenes, daughter characters assumed that a mother character would have her own, most often strong, reaction to the news; and a daughter character sought ways to dispel or temper whatever might be coming her way—"This is very hard for me to tell you"; "I have something to tell you that is going to make you upset"; "I need to tell you something but you have to sit down and take a deep breath"; and Misty's classic line, "You are going to have a grandchild" (not "I am going to have a baby"). Mother characters' reactions varied considerably, from Misty's mother comic *disbelief*, "A what? By who?"; to *denial*, "Go on, no, I'm not hearing this"; to *blame*, "I told you if you started hanging around that boy this would happen"; to *disappointment*, "I raised two daughters and managed to get them out of high school and now you go and do this"; to *rejection*, "That's it, you leave my house now, you are no child of mine"; to *violence* (one mother character started hitting her daughter). Most scenes continued the conversation between mother and daughter, oftentimes focusing on how resources were going to be secured—"You are going to have to get a job"; "I'm not going to be taking care of the baby"; "You will stay in school and I will take care of the baby, and there won't be no argument about it." Mother characters persistently insisted that their daughters make their *own* decisions (like Misty's mother) despite whatever reaction they themselves had. It was also common for mother characters to become their daughters' advocates vis-à-vis men (even while they might be blaming their daughters), especially when it came to securing resources for raising the child.

Unlike the tough "in-your-face" girl characters at the clinic, daughter characters were cast as respectful (perhaps because harboring angry feelings toward one's mother is too painful, or perhaps because it is not anger but sorrowful identification with one's mother that the girl characters are expressing). It was rare for a daughter character to talk back; but the two exceptions are telling. One daughter character retorted to her mother's blaming remarks, "Like mother, like daughter," at which point the mother character pretended to slap the girl character across her face. Another time, the daughter character raised her voice and shouted, "What are you yelling about, you made the same mistake," to which the mother hung her head.

It could be argued that the good/bad nurse scenes were "stand-ins" for scenes with mothers, in other words, that it was "safer" for a girl to express her anger toward the nurse characters than toward her mother, upon whom she must depend.[15] But I think it is more complicated than this. The mother-daughter scenes were presented as if they were a test of relationship. The girls seemed worried or fearful about whether their mothers (and they, themselves) would pass the "test." Equally important, these scenes recognized the power of mothers' (and their own) feelings, including feelings of vulnerability and dependency, rejection and a sense of betrayal, disappointment and loss, all of which might be evoked by this relational "test."

In responding to this test, both mothers and daughters moved between knowing and not knowing, between expressing a desire for, and being averse to knowledge about, each other's feelings. For example, in response to one performance in which the mother character placed her hands over her ears as the daughter character told her that she was pregnant, Cheri called out "freeze" and said:

> My mom was in denial too [using the same gesture as was just performed in the play by putting her hands over her ears]. I didn't tell her for four months and she never said a word, like it wasn't true if we didn't talk about it. I finally told my teacher because she asked me to stay after class. She said she was worried about me, she could tell something was wrong and that I shouldn't give up on myself. I told her, and she said, "I was too young when I had my first child. But it didn't stop me, it doesn't have to stop you."

After telling her teacher, Cheri went home to tell her mother who surprised her by saying, "I knew it all along; I was just wondering when you were going to tell me yourself." In many of the skits, and in the personal stories shared as a result, girls told of ways they felt both drawn to and wanting to avoid their mothers. Other girls insisted that others (a mother, a sister, or a friend) knew they were pregnant before they did. Marisa called out "freeze" during a mother-daughter skit, saying:

People started asking me if I was pregnant even before I knew. They said they saw it in my face; my face was getting fuller, and in the eyes, people say they can see you're pregnant in the eyes. I still wonder how my mother knew before I knew.

The same was true for Stella, who described her mother "begging me to tell her when I started having sex. But I didn't, and somehow my mom knew I was pregnant. She took me to the doctor. I thought she would be much more upset than she was. I just don't understand how she knew." The girls told about mothers who were in denial and mothers who knew before their daughters knew they were pregnant—both sides of knowing—just as they themselves knew and did not know about their own pregnancies. Both mothers and daughters used similar strategies, for example, when a girl put off going to the clinic or didn't tell anyone until asked and when a mother didn't ask questions for fear of getting an answer she didn't want to hear.[16]

A second strategy was to exaggerate a sense of happiness and acceptance attributed to mothers in the face of a girl's fears. Monica's account is a case in point:

> I went to get birth control pills at the clinic and they told me I was two months pregnant and I couldn't believe it. I was worried sick about telling my mom. I didn't want to have to tell her; I knew she would be upset. I waited another month before I finally told her. She looked devastated, but she didn't cry in front of me. Later that night I could hear her crying and crying in her room. But now she feels great about the baby—she's the apple of her eye.

I found it striking that so many girls spoke with deep sadness about having disappointed their mothers at the same time as being insistently confident that their mothers would eventually come to cherish the grandchild.[17] Alisha's reflection on her personal experience is an especially poignant example of how she was managing her feelings of sorrow. After watching a skit where the mother was cast as rejecting, Alisha told the following story:

> I couldn't tell my mother. I told my friends first, gave myself three pregnancy tests at home, then finally went to the clinic. I think I was in denial about being pregnant. My friends kept saying to me, are you pregnant? You know how people get into your business, people talk but nobody could believe that I would get pregnant. I am so quiet. I am not the type who gets pregnant. After a few days, I wrote my mother a letter and left it on the ironing board and went on to

school. I didn't go home straight away because I didn't want to see her—she works second shift and leaves the house when I get home from school. I didn't want to get hit—not that my mom hits me, but you never know. So I arrived at around 4:00 and my dad was there but didn't say anything to me [her dad is out of work on disability]. Later he comes into my room and tells me how everyone makes mistakes. He was much more supportive than I ever imagined. My mom came home late and she didn't talk to me for two days. She finally talked to me on the weekend. She was upset, angry—it devastated her.

"What did the letter say?" Teresa asked.

I started by talking about how I love her and am grateful for all that she has done for me. I wanted to explain to her why I was being anti-social around the family. I told her that I was growing up and that she keeps treating me like I am still a child—like I am five or ten. Then I said I am not a child anymore, that she needs to understand that people change. People make mistakes. That I was pregnant, that I was sorry, that I knew I had made a mistake but now I was going to have to take the consequences.

"What did your mother say?" Teresa asked.
"That I had a hard road ahead; that I would have to make my own peace like she'd have to make hers."
Alisha sounded defensive as she explained that she is "not the type of girl who gets pregnant," as if she is in dialogue with those who would accuse her of being so. Alisha spoke with sorrow when talking about her mother, how she regrets disappointing her mother. When she described her mother as being "devastated," she said it with a forceful certainty, as if she had taken on her mother's feelings as her own. Nonetheless, Alisha believes change and mistakes are a natural part of life ("people change, people make mistakes"), perhaps reiterating her identification with her father's philosophy of life as filled with hardship and mistakes. At the same time she desperately seeks recognition from her mother, she wants her mother to acknowledge that she is growing up and no longer a child.

I suggest that the power of mother-daughter feelings—struggles between knowing and not knowing, managing divided emotions (i.e., sorrow and joy), and efforts toward mutual recognition or at least a making of peace—are key to the girls' self- and identity-making process. Perhaps this is why the girls returned to mother-daughter scenes again and again, as a way to revisit and redo these conflicts in a safe or more manageable way.

Selfhood, Agency, and Development

In the previous chapter I argued that theories of development are lopsided in that they take a child's perspective. The story of separation and individuation is told as a process of separating from a nurturing (i.e., good) or hostile (i.e., bad) maternal figure or "holding" environment where personal needs and interests are set aside in favor of the child's (Klein is no exception to this). Historically speaking, this ideology of motherhood is tied to the ideology of childhood.

> The ideology of motherhood as the ideal of femininity coincides with the institutionalization of childhood during the eighteenth and nineteenth centuries. As representations of the child's vulnerability and need for nurturing and protection became more prominent, motherhood became an "instinct," a "natural" role and form of human connection, as well as a practice. (Hirsch 1989: 14)

Crucially, the price of this ideology was its detrimental effects on women who were able to enact the ideal, those who could not afford to live up to it, and those who were excluded from it altogether (as were slave women). Marianne Hirsch argues that it was at this historical juncture that a "maternal voice" was suppressed in literature and in psychology, when mothers were no longer viewed as subjects in their own right, but, were now seen as objects to be idealized and/or rejected. She quotes feminist scholar Evelyn Fox Keller as saying, "Few of us ever get to know the real mother, her real power, or the limits of her power. Instead she survives as a specter alternately overwhelming and inconsequential" (Hirsch 1989: 167). Indeed, one important project of feminism has been to expose and challenge the ideology of motherhood, a project that has not yet been achieved. Twenty years ago Nancy Chodorow and Susan Contratto (1982) argued that feminist writing falls into the same ideological trap—depicting mothers' power as either fearful or as powerless—both of which engender anger on the part of the child. But these depictions persist.

This same trap characterizes the conventional wisdom about the lives and conflicts of adolescent girls. There is a vast literature on this topic, including the cultural prescription and expectation that adolescent girls will be at war with their mothers. It is understood that an adolescent girl will not only try to separate, but will seek to disidentify from the figure and the story of her mother in an effort to become her own woman. But in the girls' "pregnancy stories," the mother-daughter plot was presented with much more complexity. Their scenes are more like dramas about seeking connection and recognition and managing feelings of vulnerability and loss, than needing-to-separate and dis-identify stories.[18]

Marianne Hirsch (1989) argues that there is one tradition among feminism that does present motherhood (and by extension, daughterhood) as more complex—"the tradition of black American women writers of the 1960's, 70's, and 80's" (176). Her book provides several examples, concluding with Toni Morrison's (1988) *Beloved* as an exemplary text. In this novel, Morrison presents Sethe with a maternal voice that is both despairing about and resistant to the impossible conditions under which she, as an African American and a slave woman, conceived and cared for her children. We sense the unbearable pain and anger this engenders for Sethe's daughter, who speaks this pain and anger from her grave. Hirsch argues that this account of mother-daughter relationships presents a feminist antidote to lopsided accounts of development, and I sensed the same to be true in the girls' skits where, the power of daughters' and mothers' feelings were being given voice.[19] Rather than being split off, as either *against* or *for* the other, the girls' skits spoke "with two voices" (Hirsch 1989: 199), with some mothers being presented as complicated subjects in their own right, and some daughters struggling to hold opposing feelings at once.

The girls' skits speak to an alternative version of selfhood and agency, which I believe provides the drama of their tales. In these dramas, the individual agent (a girl) is not entirely autonomous; she is aware that she must confront conditions—stigma, racial stereotypes, mistreatment, subordination—*and* search for ways to be creative and maintain her dignity at the same time. Moreover, the pregnant self must struggle to integrate the "idea" of the child, the actual child, and one's own body and self of which the child is a part. The pregnant self must answer to these conditions and questions, which are not necessarily one's own. "Did you want to have a baby? Is it your decision to become a young mother?"

I return to Alisha as a case in point. After telling her own pregnancy story, in a conversation with me alone, Alisha sought to clarify her regrets about her pregnancy: "I wasn't in love with my boyfriend, I mean we love each other, but we weren't in love. I don't regret getting pregnant, I regret having sex when I did. It should be special and it wasn't." Here Alisha's regrets seem to be more about her less-than-ideal experience in the world of romance (i.e., having sex that was not special) than they are about her impending motherhood. This framing of her regrets is well matched with the ideology of motherhood, where it is quite acceptable to regret having sex (especially given the missing discourse of desire for young women) but it is not acceptable to hold regrets toward one's baby. After a long silence where she looks like she is concentrating hard on what she is going to say, she ends our conversation saying: "If you asked me, 'Did you want to have a baby?' I would say no. But since it happens, and if you are having sex you have to know that it could happen. You have to know that there are consequences."

"Believe that even in my deliberateness I was not deliberate" is what Alisha seems to be saying to all those who would ask, "Did you want to have a baby?" She has read her social audience correctly because this *is* the prevailing question asked of pregnant teenagers; it is seemingly the only question being asked. I worry that her social audience may not be able to hear or tolerate the complexity of Alisha's answer.

Finally, it strikes me that, in spite of the girls' fears about telling their mothers, it is their mothers from whom the girls not only seek recognition and connection, but have any hope and even expectation of getting it. This is one of the reasons why I think that the nurse-girl scenes are played out in more divided, "good" and "bad" terms, which is precisely how the culture at large has framed the girls' "situation"—as a situation in which they are "good" or "bad" and have made or must make "good" or "bad" decisions. Through these nurse-girl scenes we see how little hope or expectation the girls have of getting the support and recognition they so urgently need and deserve.

Re-representing Youth Worlds, Identities, and Relationships

Part II has focused on the (oftentimes painful) gap between how the girls saw themselves and how they thought they were seen by others. This knowledge—the girls' body-smarts—was brought into clearer focus through the self-representation activities designed for this research. By inviting the girls to represent themselves to themselves and one another in a group setting, where they benefited from one another's critical eyes and reflected on shared experiences and knowledge, we get a glimpse of their multifaceted social and inner worlds, and the nuances of their self- and identity-making process. I want to summarize key points about this process and its relevance for educators.

The girls' self-representations shed light on how they are being addressed by and answering to their social worlds that are anxiety-ridden and full of hardships. Two related processes of self-making—identificatory struggles and splitting—stand out as means through which the girls learn to place themselves in a gender, race, and class hierarchy and to manage their conflicting feelings. As I have argued, the girls describe their worlds as being peopled with different "types"—people who engage specific scripts (sometimes resisting and sometimes assenting to whatever these scripts might be); who hold certain places within a hierarchy; and who have affiliations with some but not other types of people. Types of people are also divided between those who are "good" (idealized by the culture) and those who are "bad" (denigrated by the culture). The girls' depictions of the worlds of heterosexual romance and motherhood provide two clear examples.

In the uncertain world of heterosexual romance, with its sexual double standard, there were distinct "types" of men, including the "players" who don't commit to any one girl. Women who played the game were divided among those who did and did not have to defend their sexual reputations. The types of women with whom most of the PPPT girls identified were the "sexy but not too sexy" and the "tough" and "in-your-face" women who were invulnerable to pain. This "type" was careful not to entrust her feelings to men. Importantly, "types" of women in this world were not just different, they were either idealized or denigrated. "Good" girls, who are careful to conceal their sexual desires so as to avoid getting a "bad reputation," were pitted against the "bad" girls, who acted publically on their desires, "showing" their sexuality in unbecoming ways. "Good" girl types were further divided between those who denied their own sexual desire and those who fell victim to others' desires, who were taken advantage of by men. These are the "wronged" girls who stand apart from girls who are "wrong"/"bad" because they willingly acknowledge and act upon their sexual desires. And from still another angle, there was the association of sexual feelings with the "body," which is split off from "self" and "mind,"[1] including the framing of girls' sexual agency as a simple yes-or-no decision.

Both ways of splitting—the either-or framing of sexual agency and the separation of mind and self from body—can provide girls a safeguard against conflicts about sexuality in adolescence. These processes serve as a self-protective shield against social demands such as the barrage of sexual imagery that eroticizes young girls or the sexual double standard. These processes also enable girls to reconcile possible personal desires with social demands. But there is a cost that was expressed in the girls' self-representations, particularly in their portraits of and discussions about childhood, which spoke to their sense of loss and pain about no longer feeling "pure," "cute," "small," and "innocent."

What strikes me as especially important is how the girls' insights into the world of heterosexual romance (in the cultural dramas they presented) speak to a much more complicated set of issues than is usually entertained either by researchers or by educators of youth.[2] For the most part, research on adolescent sexuality has looked at rates of sexual intercourse, pregnancy, contraceptive use, and safe sex practices, narrowly defining adolescent sexuality as initiation into sexual intercourse. This research has tended to equate sex with deviance, not development. But the PPPT girls' self-representations clearly show that adolescent sexuality is far more encompassing than the timing of sexual intercourse. It is not only about sexual practices, but also about what young people know and believe about sex, what they think is natural, proper, or desirable, and in what ways they think they are and are not measuring up to sexual norms. Sexuality and its links to social relationships of power, but particularly the imbalance of power between men and women, were hinted at in the PPPT girls' conversations (see chapter 4). And the links between sexuality, identity, and self-understandings, including whether one is "good" or "bad," was of particular concern to the girls. And yet, these multivaried and complex meanings, ideas, and values that constitute sexuality are eclipsed in schools and, where it exists in sex education. Developmentally speaking, rather than focusing on the "whole person" and how sexual feelings and actions get incorporated into adolescent identities and relationships, sex education is highly fragmented, often focusing solely on health-related behaviors and risks. Sociologically speaking, by not directly addressing the contradictory pressure girls face about how to act as women, sex education mistakes as "personal" what is also a deeply cultural and social conflict regarding gender, race, and class relations of power. This does a disservice to youth, but especially to girls.

As the PPPT girls' self-representations illustrate, the question posed to young women is one that is not necessarily their own, saying yes or no to desires they may not have yet even discovered or declared for themselves. Framing female sexuality in terms of either-or; who is and who is not a virgin; or how long one should wait to "give in" to another's sexual demands does not help girls confront either the developmental or the social task ahead of them. Rather than having sexual feelings split off—denied, banished, or punished—adolescent girls need opportunities to contemplate these mixed sexual feelings, desires, and behaviors and move toward integrating their sexual desires into their identities. Insofar as girls are discouraged from actively thinking about and expressing the power of their sexual feelings, they are left unprepared to cope with a key task of adolescent identity and development—reconciling personal desires with social demands.

Research and education on adolescent sexuality and identity needs to foster integration rather than splitting. This means first disentangling sexuality from pregnancy and deviance. Second, it means being as concerned about the costs of denying sexuality for adolescent development as we are about the costs of early childbearing. Third, it means promoting a more personally reflexive approach to sex education that encourages young women and men to ask themselves: "How do I know what I want or desire sexually"; and, "In what contexts can I act on my own feelings?"

The girls' self-representations referencing the world of pregnancy and motherhood offer yet another example of identificatory struggles and splitting in self- and identity-making. The girls' portrayals of the *public* world of pregnancy and motherhood were peopled by two opposing "types" of women: those who were idealized/"good" and those who were blaming or scornful "bad." The *interpersonal* world of pregnancy and motherhood was peopled with mothers and daughters who were more complicated and complete. The drama of this world was marked by its characters' sense of agency—mothers and daughters' efforts to affect their environments, to seek recognition for their *own* feelings, and to search for some kind of fit (no matter how imperfect) between their own feelings (including the feelings a girl might have for her soon-to-born baby) and those of another.

The overall drama of the girls' self-representations highlight the pivotal role that the ideology of motherhood plays in shaping understandings of the self- and identity-making process. This ideology, which includes equating women with nurturance and self-sacrifice, pitting "good" against "bad" maternal figures, and squelching mothers' own subjectivities, has a tenacious hold on individuals. It imbues philosophies of childrearing in which it is the child who is seen as the "subject" of development whose needs are to be met by the maternal "object." Regrettably, this ideology of motherhood holds sway on many levels within the educational system—from school's continued invisible dependence on individual mothers' work in preparing children for the school day (Luttrell 1997); to the gendering of teaching as a "women's" profession; to the suppression of a maternal voice among teachers (Grumet 1988); to the "educated motherhood" curricula (Burdell 1998, Luttrell 1996, McDade 1992) that asks mothers (young and old) to put aside their own needs and interests in favor of their children—the philosophy reflected in, "If you don't do it for yourself, do it for your child."

In an even bigger sense, the ideology of motherhood limits an understanding of intersubjective relatedness—how we learn to recognize and appreciate another's subjectivity. It keeps researchers and educators from asking the following crucial questions about development:

> How does a child develop into a person, who, as a parent, is able to recognize her or his own child? What are the internal processes, the psychic landmarks, of such development? Where is the theory that tracks the development of the child's responsiveness, empathy, and concern, and not just the parent's sufficiency or failure? (Benjamin 1995: 32)

In light of the grip of the ideology of motherhood and an underdeveloped theory of development, I think the PPPT girls' self-representations are especially provocative. As I argued in chapter 4, the girls held complex views and feelings about the world of heterosexual romance (including cynicism and ambivalence). But they held idealized and lopsided views about the world of motherhood, especially when drawing from media images and popular culture. Their cultural and emotional scripts for maternal-child love in the "Who am I?" media collages were split (i.e., the perfect or imperfect mother and the "special" or unwanted baby). On the other hand, the girls' self-portraits and role plays told a different story. Expressions of fear about "holding hatred toward their babies" (see chapter 3) and signs of recognition that mothers hold their own strong and conflicting view and feelings when faced with the news of their daughters' pregnancies (chapter 5) could be said to illustrate a more complete picture of motherhood, including some acknowledgment of maternal ambivalence on the part of the PPPT girls.

In a culture that glorifies and idealizes the maternal role when it is self-sacrificing and demonizes those individuals who don't measure up, being able to acknowledge and tolerate maternal conflicts and ambivalence should be viewed as an *achievement* (Parker 1995).[3] As I have argued, what is missing in current thinking about childrearing and child development is an understanding of mothers' own contradictory needs, wishes, and desires, all of which create anxiety, and from which mothers seek relief. Feminist scholar and analyst Roszika Parker (1995) suggests that we should consider mothers' development as being parallel to babies' development:

> Then we can see that the mother's achievement of ambivalence—the awareness of her co-existing love and hate for the baby—can promote a sense of concern and responsibility towards, and differentiation of self from, the baby. Maternal ambivalence signifies the mother's capacity to know herself and to tolerate traits in herself she may consider less than admirable—and to hold a more complete image of her baby. (17)

Rather than denying the reality of maternal conflicts and ambivalence that so many of the PPPT girls expressed, educators and concerned adults could encourage pregnant girls to explore and express their mixed feelings. For it is facing these mixed feelings that lead to growth and development, and they should be tapped rather than ignored in the schooling of pregnant girls.

I would argue that one of the most important educational interventions that adults could offer pregnant girls is encouragement to develop and hold more complete images of themselves and their soon-to-born babies. This means helping girls face and wrestle with the ways they see themselves and think they are seen by others. This is where the self-representation activities and the framework for analyzing them that I propose in this book can prove most fruitful.

Finally, the girls' self-representations speak to the crucial role that adults play (as teachers, parents, youth workers, researchers) in influencing the girls' body-smarts. Readers may recall Sara's media collage, which illustrated how her teacher and her grandmother (chapter 4) passed on to Sara a knowledge of her difference that was both helpful and hurtful. Sara's story is not idiosyncratic or uncommon, as too many students in urban high schools will report. Even the best-intentioned adults can unwittingly play a dual role. Adults can be perpetrators of pain when we collude with racial, gender, and class codes of conduct and neglect to examine our own assumptions about this or that "type" of student. Adults can also be fonts of wisdom when we challenge unspoken assumptions, resist such codes of conduct, and name injustices when we see them. In light of a barrage of media images and popular discourse that cast urban youth of color in a negative light, adults who are willing and equipped to connect with and confront young people's body-smarts cannot be underestimated. Admittedly this is a daunting task for many adults, especially for the disproportionate numbers of white teachers who do not share the same racial, class, or gender background as their students and have limited time and support, for engaging their students' knowledge of difference and lack a repertoire for doing so. But this is a necessary task if schooling is to help young people make and revise themselves in their own images rather than turning their self-definitions over to others.

PART III

NOTES TO AND FROM THE FIELD

CHAPTER 6

Entering Girls' Worlds

In this chapter I reflect on my research process. I have organized it into three parallel and related parts that include ethnographic *doing, knowing,* and *telling.* I will explain how I arrived at viewing ethnographic research as a "social art form,"[1] an exercise in abiding curiosity, careful listening, painstaking observation, sustained attention, emotional engagement, missed opportunities, and the search for self-knowledge. I write about three key interpersonal encounters to illustrate my analytic approach and the dilemmas I faced trying to enter the PPPT girls' worlds. Above all I want to make a case for what I have called "activist" ethnography (Luttrell 1997: 121) that, among other things, enables researchers and those who are the subjects of research to change how they see themselves and are seen by others.

Ethnographic Doing

In retrospect I realize the extent to which I strayed from my original research design. Despite the fact that I routinely encourage ethnographers-in-training to maintain a sense of openness and flexibility, to trust their instincts, and to allow for surprises in fieldwork, this lesson is harder to practice than it is to preach. I learned from doing this project that a key habit of mind for the ethnographer is being able to be patient and accepting of surprises and conflicts in the field.

I began the project wanting to learn about how the PPPT girls experienced the cultural phenomenon and social problem of "teenage pregnancy," especially in the school setting. This interest paralleled my previous study where I sought to understand how black and white working-class women experienced the cultural phenomenon and social problem of "low literacy" and what a high school diploma meant to them (Luttrell 1997). When I had asked the women to tell me about their school experiences in my previous work, they had responded with what I called a "narrative urgency" to tell me about what had happened in the past, especially events in childhood, to explain life in the present (Luttrell 1997). My open-ended question, "Tell me what you remember about being in school," was most often met with the comment, "You want to know about my childhood? I could write a book about that." Among many things, these life stories were about how the women had *learned* to take on a subordinate position, and the powerful role they understood school to have played in this instruction.

I (naively) assumed the PPPT girls would have a storehouse of life stories to share with me, that they would narrate their pasts in light of the present as the older women had. But I quickly learned otherwise. The girls did not claim that they could "write a book" about all the things that made them who they are today. I was surprised when I began my formal taping sessions that several girls said they didn't know where to start or what to say. Their relationship to childhood events, often told in bits and pieces, were not unified or linked as the older women's retrospective accounts had been. The PPPT girls did not draw lessons from this or that childhood event (consciously at least) as the older women had.

I shouldn't have been surprised that the girls' life stories would be emergent and disconnected. As adolescents, their "life story"—the "This is who I am and how I got that way" version—was evolving. Developmentally speaking, adolescence is understood to be a stage of life during which young people solidify their self-understandings and social identities. Other scholars have written about working with adolescents and found the same thing. Karin Martin (1996), for example, describes her young interviewees as describing their lives as being an "out of control roller coaster ride."[2] I especially like the way Chris Mann (1998), who collected life histories from working-class British girls, puts it: "their lives are not remembered in tranquility in the calm waters of late maturity but described in the full flood of experience, riding the rapids of tumultuous feelings" (82).[3]

The girls' reaction to being interviewed was set in stark contrast to how readily most of them exchanged vivid and compelling accounts with me, their classmates, and teachers about things happening in their present everyday lives—from shopping trips to hallway fights to disputes with boyfriends. It seemed they enjoyed *performing*, using their bodies and the space around them as if they preferred to "show" rather than "tell" about their lives. Much of the girls' informal conversation with me and with one another was performative, where a girl took up and play-acted a character in a life drama (such as a fight with a girlfriend or a weekend shopping trip). These everyday shows, as sociologist Erving Goffman (cited in chapter 5) would call them, used the historical present tense and invoked direct speech. A girl would stand up beside her desk, making full use of a range of gestures, punctuating her narrative with body language for added emphasis, adopting different voice tones for different roles, pulling her audience along with her every move. There was a lively narrative drive in these performances that was unmatched by any formal interview conversation.

Once I recognized that the girls' form of storytelling—their way of understanding themselves in terms of their biographies—was performative, I began noticing recurring patterns and themes. There were patterns in the objects of popular culture the girls used to communicate with one another and me.[4] I referred to several of these objects/symbols in parts I and II. For instance, the girls imitated Oprah Winfrey's style as a way to ask questions and to express multiple perspectives on the hardships they faced and the decisions they were making as pregnant teenagers. Their use of the talk show style was one way they conveyed their own sense of being an object of public interest as well as public scrutiny. Their wide-ranging (often comical) "answers" to the probing questions "Oprah" asked about how they were going to manage being a young mother ("Oh, I'm not worried, my mother is going to raise the baby" [said with an ironic tone and followed by laughter]) seemed to play off their perceptions of what others imagined, as well as their own doubts or worries.[5]

There were also patterns in how the girls made use of their bodies and the space around them, for example, performing the pregnant body as if it were not their own or stuffing backpacks under their shirts to make their bodies "show" more than they already did. Often a girl would surprise herself as she performed, getting carried away by the intensity of the acting. I came to realize that the girls tended to "disclose more of themselves as characters in a story than as participants in a discussion" (Paley 1986: 128), especially when describing the events of their lives. Then, when the girls discussed the merits of this or that pregnancy story skit—should the character be a drug addict, a victim of sexual abuse, an "honors" student?—it became clear that they were wrestling not only with dominant discourses about "teenage pregnancy," but also with how much they wanted to disclose about themselves. Mostly what struck me was how immediate, how bodily and physically exuberant, how expressively improvisational and emotional these performances were.

It was in this context (and perhaps my own delight in the girls' energy and playfulness) that I began to think differently about engaging the girls;

not as "informants" or "interviewees" who had "stories" to tell, but as improvisational actors whose performances held rich and multiple clues to the girls' self- and identity-making process.[6] Thus, I designed the role-play activity (described in chapter 5) as one way to tap into the girls' experience of pregnancy. This activity provided what ethnographer Barbara Myerhoff (1992) called "opportunities for appearing."[7] I agree with Myerhoff that among other things, storytelling (and this case performance) is "an indispensable ingredient of being itself, for unless we exist in the eyes of others, we may come to doubt even our own existence" (233). The girls made inventive use of these "opportunities for appearing," performing imagined "others" *and* performing themselves as they are, as they wish they might be, and as they think others imagine them to be.

Then, in this same spirit, I engaged the girls' use of teen magazines and designed another opportunity for appearing by asking them to make collages answering the question "Who am I?" Turning to yet another genre of self-representation, I engaged the girls as "book artists"—as illustrators and authors—asking them to make self-portraits and write about their (self)images.

The more I stayed out of their way, the more the girls would talk and free associate while doing these self-representation activities. For me, this meant giving up my more immediate desire to ask questions, make sense of, or put order into the girls' creative expression or their conversations. It took almost the entire first semester of the schoolyear for the girls and me to establish some kind of trust. I tried not to interrupt an individual girl's comments or an informal group conversation, but I did enter into a dialogue if I was explicitly brought in by the girls. When a girl asked for my affirmation or to comment on her self-representation while she was working on it, I did so, starting by asking her to tell me what she liked and disliked most about it. When a girl announced she was "finished" making her collage or self-portrait, that's when my formal questioning began. (See the Appendix for my list of questions.)

Other sorts of ethnographic data would have been informative and opened up ways to understand the girls' identities and self-making. For example, I might have spent time hanging out with the girls at their homes or going on shopping trips and this would have yielded a fuller picture. But it was important to me that the self-representation activities I designed took place in the context of school because I want educators to be able to adapt such activities to classroom settings.[8] My approach to ethnographic inquiry has always sought to integrate knowledge and action in my research practice. This meant designing research activities that would facilitate personal growth for the girls and serve as models for educational practice.[9]

In designing each activity, I took the lead from the girls themselves. Role playing was part of the girls' informal interactions, a way they communicated with one another so I drew upon this form first. The teen magazines used for the collages were routinely circulating among the girls, often being read "undercover" when one was supposed to be reading or copying notes from the board.[10] The book-making project was the most traditionally school-based in the sense that it drew on creative language arts activities (illustration and writing) and the more conventional, art class exercise of self-portraiture.[11]

By tape recording the girls' conversations during the self-representation activities I could trace patterns in the associations girls made, their identifications with characters, images, and texts, and their dilemmas about representation, especially perceived gaps between what "others" see and how they see themselves. This data gathering made it possible for me to examine carefully how the girls wrestled with issues related to body image, self-understanding, and social identity, and to trace the different ways in which their efforts were infused with ideas and assumptions about race, gender, and class. Equally important, like some other innovative uses of visual representations in qualitative research,[12] the girls' artwork served as a way to engage them in critical discussion about their lives. As they made and performed multiple self-representations, the girls self-consciously identified with, used, assented, or resisted stereotypes about "the pregnant teen." I saw my role and my questions as a means of drawing out, as fully as I could, the breadth and scope of the girls' perspectives.

Each self-representation activity served as its own window on a girl's set of interests, curiosities, and patterned feelings. This was enhanced by *my* interest in the girls' "play"—their free associations and imagery, as well as their "work"—their written texts and role plays. My ethnographic approach parallels a certain clinical approach, what psychoanalyst Adam Phillips (1998) calls "restoring the artist" in clients. He distinguishes between "analysis as a corrective emotional experience" and analysis that seeks to explore that "part of the person that makes interest despite, or whatever, the early environment" (12). He sees the role of the analyst as bringing an attitude of abiding curiosity about whatever these interests might be. Likewise, my aim in the ethnographic encounter was to attend to the artistic forms the girls already were making, and to probe their emotional experiences by "restoring the artist" in them. I brought a "free-floating" and sustained attention to whatever the girls were already making, including their pregnancies. This attitude of curiosity stands in direct conflict with an attitude of judgment (whether aesthetic or moral) or dismissal (seeing the girls' perceptions and productions as unimportant). This attitude searches for understanding rather than assessment or blame. By inviting observation and curiosity, I also hoped to legitimate the girls' own inquisitiveness about themselves and others, including me and the project.

One of the biggest challenges I had to overcome was the girls' view of me as a teacher to be tested—would I allow them to eat food during class, could they use the phone to check up on their babies or make plans with their boyfriends—all of which were against school rules. Being a researcher in a public school setting made it difficult, if not impossible at times, to work outside and/or against my adult status and authority position. Building a sense of trust, rapport, and relationship over time and being treated as a person in my own right—those times when the girls would ask me about my own children, compliment me on my earrings or outfit, or ask for my opinion on this or that personal dilemma—these were all ways we established mutual interest, despite the obvious power differences. But it was in those moments when I engaged in and was engaged by the girls' "play," especially the times I was asked to perform in a skit as the nurse, mother, and as the pregnant girl character, that the girls and I came to know each other, and I came to know myself in new ways.

There are a great deal of data that I gathered from this project that are not presented directly but nevertheless inform my analysis. For example, the one-to-one interview data and the journal entries I collected from the participants guide my interpretations, especially in terms of knowing more about the girls' social context and what was on their minds at different times throughout the academic year. I have chosen to discuss and present in this book the material that was meant for public viewing and for which I had data on the groups' discussions and debates about the perils of representation. The way I have decided to "curate" this material, the way I have presented it here for readers, is organized around these materials as windows onto the girls' identity and self-making, their personal conflicts, and the dilemmas of representation that they wrestled with.

Ethnographic Knowing

There is no psychoanalysis or anthropology apart from the interpersonal encounter, an encounter that draws unavoidably on the investigators' power of empathy as well as observation. (Chodorow 1999: 134–135)

In this section I talk about how my interpersonal encounters with the girls sharpened or blunted my powers of empathy[13] and observation. I believe that at the end of the ethnographic day, what we are able to know de-

pends upon ongoing attention to interpersonal encounters and how well
we know ourselves in our ethnographic relationships.[14]

The Gift

In chapter 4, I wrote about my reactions to the girls' preoccupation with
money, especially their routine questions about how much things cost and
whether they could take home whatever items I might have brought
(markers, paper, magazines, food stuffs, and so forth). Their questions unsettled me. They made me keenly aware of my resources and that I was seen
by the girls as a bearer of goods, that I might distribute or withhold at will.
I worried about disappointing the girls when they asked for things I did not
give them. I was unused to such direct questioning about money and possessions ("How much did that cost?" "Can I have that?"). My mother had
raised me to be "well-mannered," which, for her included not asking how
much something cost and excluded asking whether I could have something
that wasn't "mine." In my mother's world, if it was not "on sale" she didn't
buy it. Getting a bargain was as important as getting the item itself; and
paying "full price" for something was like throwing money away. Her
"money-wise" ways were in part driven by need and in part a matter of
principle. Her efforts to achieve middle-class status shaped everyday life as
she carefully managed family resources to make sure that her children had
whatever was necessary (from clothes to music lessons to neighborhoods
selected for the best public schools every time it was necessary for us to
move, which was quite often). My parents' upward mobility meant that
money was a preoccupation, but, a closeted one. So when I encountered
such directness about money it tapped into my own anxieties about
"middle-classness," while also raising questions for me about what money
and possessions meant for the girls.

At the same time, I experienced my "middle-classness" in a much different way with the PPPT girls than with the white and black working-class
women with whom I had previously worked (Luttrell 1997). In that research I was the same age or younger than the women participants. I was
positioned either as a daughter, asking questions of and attentively listening to elders speak about their childhood experiences of school, family, and
work or as a "cousin" exchanging life stories.[15] It was not uncommon for
the women and I to exchange gifts and resources. For example, many
women gave me baby gifts when my second and third children were born;
others offered to babysit for my oldest child and often showered her with
treats when I would bring her to an interview. I offered financial assistance—a loan to a woman to get a new pair of glasses, to pay for another's

medical treatment, and to fix another's car. Only once was this assistance accepted. These exchanges did not feel emotionally charged (for me at least).

But with the PPPT girls, I was unmistakably positioned as a mother. My maternal position was imposed from the "outside"—everything from being associated with the PPPT's "educated motherhood curriculum" to the girls' questions about my children, my mothering, or in what ways I might or might not agree with their mothers in a dispute. I also experienced my position as a mother from the "inside" as I struggled to come to terms with the stark contrast between my own adolescent daughter's social world and the PPPT girls' worlds. I was often caught up in feelings of guilt and despair about the inequities that divided my own children from "other people's children."[16] I believe that balancing these maternal positions heightened my sense of guilt and my desire to attend to what I perceived were the PPPT girls' needs. The following encounter made me begin to think about my emotional participation (not just my position) as a mother in a more integrated way; not just as an impediment (something getting in the way of my research relationships), but as an opportunity for developing more interpretive power, particularly regarding the dynamic relationship among social inequality, social distinctions, and personal meanings.

In my second year at the PPPT, the girls and I were discussing their favorite reading materials, when Brandi said she liked reading autobiographies of "strong, black women who came up during segregation." Indeed, throughout the girls' self-representations, identification as a "strongblackwoman" (Morgan 1999) was a recurring theme. I asked Brandi whether she was familiar with Anne Moody's book, *Coming of Age in Mississippi*. Brandi said no, but she would like to read it. On her next trip to the library she intended to ask the librarian to help her find a copy of it. Her reference to the librarian touched off an angry discussion among the girls about how "mean" and "disrespectful" the librarian was.

"Every time I go in she gives me a look, like I don't belong there," explained Tskaie.

Later I mentioned the girls' complaints to their teacher, Ms. Nelson, who said she thought the girls were right, that the librarian held an "attitude" toward them, especially when the girls came in as a group to do an assignment. As a result, Ms. Nelson had stopped sending the girls to the library.

That weekend, while browsing at the local bookshop, I came across multiple copies of Moody's book and eagerly scooped six of them off the bargain table. As my mother's daughter, I felt proud of my bargain hunting and, in retrospect, good about myself for being able to bring this resource to the girls, but especially Brandi, of whom I was particularly fond. Initially withdrawn from the project activities and me, Brandi had recently begun to participate, and to confide in me about everyday concerns, including her "up and down" moods.

On Monday, I arrived at the PPPT, my arms full of books, to find six girls gathered outside Ms. Nelson's classroom talking about movies they had seen that weekend. As I approached, I realized that Brandi was not among them, and that I was, in fact, one book short. How had I miscounted? Then I recognized Alisa (who had recently given birth) among the girls; she had unexpectedly returned to school, which accounted for my mistake.

The girls' ritual questions filled the hallway: "Where did you get the books? How much did they cost? Can we have one? Can we take it home?" I said, yes, the books were for them, but that since I hadn't realized Alisa was returning to school, we were one book short.

"We'll wait until Wednesday when I bring another copy for Brandi before you each get one," I explained.

Tskaie took a copy from my arms, explaining that she knew about this author from her friend who was reading it for her "honors class"; "I'm going to sit on the bus reading it just like her, the big star student." She begged to take it home with her, "Please, Ms. Wendy. Besides, Brandi has a clinic appointment and won't be back today. You can bring her one on Wednesday." This seemed reasonable (I felt relieved to hear that Brandi was out for the day); and, I didn't want to disappoint Tskaie or cause her to be angry with me.

Alisa took a book, "I'm going to give this to my mother, she loves reading these kind of stories."

The girls spent a few minutes looking through their books, speculating about what sort of person Ann Moody might be now, when Brandi entered the classroom.

Before I could say a word, Tskaie said in a teasing voice, "Ms. Wendy brought us these books, but she didn't get one for you."

Brandi looked rattled and I sensed her disappointment or worse yet, her anger with me. I meanwhile felt angry with Tskaie, feeling as if I had been manipulated into playing a role I didn't want to play (a mother responding to a demanding child). My dismay with Tskaie's comment must have registered on my face because Alisa jumped in to correct the record.

"She didn't expect me back so soon; here, take mine, I didn't want it in the first place—it isn't the sort of book I like to read anyway." Brandi refused to take the book.

Hoping to put things right, I confirmed, saying "Alisa's right, I didn't expect her back. You can count on me to bring in the book on Wednesday." This did not satisfy Brandi, she looked away when I spoke. Whatever else I had done, I had not said the right thing. Meanwhile, I was upset with myself for having agreed to Tskaie's request against my better judgment, something I am prone to do in order to please others or avoid conflict. And now, despite my good intentions, the very person whom I had meant to please was upset with me. It was hard for me to shake myself out of these feelings.

What I knew about Brandi's circumstances evoked my concern and sympathy (and, in retrospect, also a view of her as needy). Brandi is the oldest of four children whose home life was described to me by PPPT teachers as "impossible." Brandi's mother has a history of drug abuse and has been unable to care for her children consistently. Brandi's uncle also lives in the house and uses drugs. Brandi's ten-year-old sister "does the family wash by hand in the kitchen sink" (as one teacher described). Brandi prepares the meals, takes the younger children to the clinic when they are sick, and helps them with their homework. According to Ms. Nelson, there is no clock, no phone, no cable for the television so the children don't know what time it is. The children appear to be isolated, with no extended family members or neighbors involved in their lives. Brandi routinely arrives at school late and often does not have her homework completed.

Ms. Washington and Ms. Nelson disagreed about what to do regarding Brandi's situation. Viewing her as "strong-willed, independent, and smart," Ms. Washington (the counselor) favored letting Brandi take care of things herself. She argued that Brandi had run away from the foster home in which she had been placed by social services two years earlier and returned to her mother. Brandi had "made her own choice" to stay with her mother so there must be a good reason. Ms. Nelson favored taking some kind of action, although she was not sure what. She said she understood why Brandi had chosen to stay with her mother, out of both love and obligation to her siblings, but now that Brandi was expecting her own child, Ms. Nelson felt something must be done, for Brandi's baby's sake. Knowing all this about Brandi's situation made me feel especially to blame for having let Brandi down. At the same time, I felt annoyed that she was being so seemingly unforgiving about the incident, as if I had intended to hurt her feelings. I was feeling torn between an ideal perception of myself as a "giving" ethnographer and my less-than-ideal feelings of hostility and frustration toward the recipients of my "gifts."

Writing up my field notes, I described Tskaie's comment as akin to sibling rivalry and a teasing game over scarce resources. I described my own defensive reaction, including my feeling of having been accused of being neglectful. While this certainly described my emotional experience, was it Tskaie's? And what about Brandi's? I recalled having witnessed many versions of this teasing game over the course of my time at the PPPT. The girls often playfully engaged one another in dramas over goods and resources, this was simply the first time I noticed how much I had been pulled in to it emotionally.

I began to consider more carefully my own reactions to these games. For example, it was often the case that a former PPPT student would bring her baby to "show off" (as Ms. Washington put it). I met many PPPT graduates this way, as they stopped by with their babies (now toddlers) to update the teachers on their lives. During these visits, someone would inevitably start to tease the child about a bottle, or blanket, or teddy bear that she or he might be holding. The game went like this: someone would take the object away, saying "Can I have this bottle?" Or "This bottle is mine, I am taking this bottle, what is a big girl/boy like you doing with a bottle?" The person's tone of voice would be lighthearted, her words often accompanied with a smile or laughter. Each young child would have her or his own response (running behind a mother's legs, grabbing back for the object, or starting to cry) and eventually the object would be returned with great fanfare, including hugs, kisses, and the refrain, "I'm just playing with you." Mothers' reactions were fairly consistent, in one case, encouraging the child to defend her- or himself—"Don't let that girl take your bottle," in another case saying, "don't whine, just go get it," and in another case demanding, "You're not going to let her take your blanket, are you?" While these games did not seem mean-spirited or threatening, there were occasions when a child would cry and I would feel anxious for her or him. When this happened I would ask, "Why are you teasing the baby that way?" to which I would get the same response, "Oh, we're just playing, it doesn't mean nothing."

Why was there such a gap between my own feelings and the girls' responses to this teasing game? My emotional experience of this game seemed more riddled with anxiety, while theirs seemed conspicuously absent of it. What denied feelings or fears might be contributing to our respective reactions?[17] It made me think about Valerie Walkerdine's (1997) discussion about the psychic costs of growing up poor, including how little we know about "patterns of defenses produced in family practices which are about avoiding anxiety and living in a very dangerous world" (37). Perhaps the game served to build up a child's psychological defenses against anxieties about making do, and was a means to "toughen" a child up, as Kusserow (1999) might argue. Perhaps the teasing game was what Jean Briggs (1998) might call "morality play," a means to enculturate children into cultural values and prescriptions, in this case, prescriptions about fending for one's self.[18] Perhaps Tskaie's tease was a part of these patterned defenses that evoked in Brandi feelings of loss and vulnerability, feelings she didn't wish to acknowledge. I also wondered whether Alisa's willingness to give her book to Brandi as something "she didn't want in the first place," was yet another learned response to guard against disappointment or dilute a sense of entitlement, or whether she was trying to reassure me that she wasn't giving up anything that mattered to her. In any case, I began to view Brandi's behavior as a response to feelings of loss, disappointment, or exclusion rather than an accusation against me.

In the next class session Brandi's feelings came into clearer view. Tskaie was using the video camera to "interview" her classmates, "Oprah style."

"What is the most difficult part about being a teenage mother?"

"Pushing it out," Brandi called out laughing.

Alisa said, "Be serious, it is caring for your baby, going to school, working, being tired, too tired to think."

Shanika added, "Having enough money to raise it, getting the things it needs."

"What is the most important decision you have made so far as a pregnant teenager?"

Brandi motioned to be first, "I'm not going to have any more babies."

"Do you mean right now or in the future?" asked Tskaie. Her question touched off a lengthy debate among the girls about whether they would have more babies.

As we rewound the tape to view it I noticed the wide-eyed, smiling faces of each of the "interviewees." The camera swept from Brandi, to Shanika, to Alisa, back to Brandi who put her hand across her face and in the process flashed her middle finger in my direction. A few girls gasp, "Oooo, Ms. Wendy, look at Brandi."

I turned to her and said, "So you're angry with me?"

Brandi looked straight into my eyes, "I wanted that book for my own self, not everyone else."

This encounter pointed out my own unexamined assumptions about Brandi's "neediness" and my desire to "help." If I was to genuinely try to enter Brandi's world, I would have to see her as an individual, with "her own self" wishes, wants, and wills, not as someone whose needs I could fulfill. Flipping me the finger seemed fitting for my lack of recognition. At the same time, what happened emotionally between us was a two-way communicative process. My maternal wish to attend to Brandi's needs (and its unconscious opposite, my unacceptable feelings of resentment) converged with Brandi's own mixed feelings about love and hate, dependence, vulnerability, and maternal care, and this mix contributed to our mutual misrecognition. Put slightly differently, in this web of emotional engagement, some of the feelings had primarily to do with Brandi and her inner relational world and conflicts (including her mental representations of self-other) and some had to do with my own inner relational world. Insofar as I was the adult researcher and she was the child researched, it was my responsibility to figure things out. And one of the demands of this structural role was to ask myself hard questions about my self-definition as the "good" ethnographer/mother, and my feelings about this identity.

One lesson I take from this encounter is that class- and family-based patterns of protecting working-class and poor children against hardship, to which Walkerdine (1997) refers, are bound up in complex maternal-child relationships that engender mixed feelings of love, hate, dependence, and gratitude (on the part of the positioned "child" and on the part of the positioned "mother"). These feelings enter into cross-class and cross-race relationships between girls and women (especially since class and race are so often conflated), particularly those relationships related to care and power—teacher-student; nurse-patient; therapist-client; social worker–client; and researcher-researched. These relationships require closer scrutiny if we are to understand the emotional politics of class, race, and gender in America.[19]

Not Crossing the Color Line

Clarise is showing off Polaroid pictures of her newborn, and says, "He is light skinned with good hair." Shadra tells of her friend who has confided that she is worried about her baby: "She was born with light skin but it keeps getting darker. I've heard that this happens. But I tell her, don't worry, it looks like she has good hair." Kendra adds, "I want my baby to have light skin like his daddy, not dark like me." What does it mean to Kendra that she is "dark" and wishes something different for her baby? And what role do I, as a white woman, have in conversations with black girls about "light-skin" and "good hair"? I hold myself back from asking questions about this because it feels too raw to touch.

Later that same day the girls are reminiscing about childhood hairstyles in reaction to Shadra's self-portrait, and Kendra remarks (see chapter 3 where I first report on this conversation):

> I remember how my momma would set me on the porch every morning before school combing and braiding my hair, for hours it seemed. I'd say, "Let me go, I'm going to be late for school." But she would be running her fingers through my head saying how tight and curly and BEAUTIFUL my hair was. She'd put ribbons, bows, beads, barrettes, pulling and yanking at my head and when she got finished I looked so cute—"cuter than those white girls," she'd tell me.

Unlike the first conversation, in which I was not part, Kendra turns to me and says, "No offense, Ms. Wendy, but that's what my momma would say." I feel relieved, grateful even, for the chance to say, "no offense taken."

Kenneth Clark's (1963) infamous "doll" experiment, illustrating black children's white preference, shook up both black and white Americans' views about the complexities of the color line. In my work with the PPPT girls I was often confronted with the ironies and contradictions that permeate the color line, for example, Kendra, who wants her baby to have light skin (not "dark like me") is the same girl who honors her mother's tender instructions about black pride and beauty. I was struck time and again by this profound combination of (self)denigration and (self)love that I observed throughout my work with the PPPT girls.[20]

I see Kendra's complex self-knowledge as evidence of her body-smarts, that is, her painful and prideful perception of gender difference (who is, and is not, a desirable girl) understood through the lens of her racial education that is "colorist" or "colorphobic" and from which she has learned about her racial inferiority. This colorist education is not limited to African Americans. When white Americans express a preference for blonde hair and blue-eyes, we don't think twice; but when African Americans express this, it gets called white preference and self-hate.[21] Yet, and still, I did not cross the color line to ask about or discuss what I felt was racially charged in this painful side of the girls' body-smarts. That I avoided this side of the line is no doubt a consequence of my white privilege as well as a personal desire to avoid racial conflict. But I also view my reluctance to probe as illustrative of a human conflict, shared by white and black Americans alike, between knowing and not knowing, thinking and not thinking about powerful emotional experiences that involve social distinctions. This ambivalence is embedded in the ethnographic encounter between me and the girls, and in student-teacher relationships, a point to which I will return in chapter 7.

Mixed Emotions in Fieldwork

I returned home from the PPPT program after hearing Tara talk about her mother's death and how she couldn't cry at the funeral (reported in chapter 3):

"She [her mother] told me not to cry at the funeral, so I didn't. I didn't cry except on my birthday. I can't cry."

"Why can't you cry?" demanded Shadra.

Tonya avoids answering and says, "My half-sister cries all the time and my half-brother, well, he's crazy."

"But you might feel better if you could cry," offers Kaela.

"Yeah that's what my counselor says. But I need to get on with my life. I can't be crying all the time . . . you can't spend your life feeling sorry for yourself," Tara replies.

Hearing Tara talk about being asked not to cry, being unable to cry, and her need to move on with her life, put me painfully in mind of my own ways of coping with loss. And on such a day when faced with a girl's grief, I found it hard to muster up the ethnographer in me. Instead of writing field notes, I cried.

There is a growing interest in more closely examining the emotions of the researcher,[22] although this topic is sometimes greeted with accusations of "navel gazing" or "narcissism" on the researcher's part, as in the popular joke about the ethnographer who, speaking with her informant, says, "Enough about me, tell me what you think about me." I like the way anthropologist Ruth Behar (1996) puts it: "Emotion has only recently gotten a foot inside the academy and we still don't know whether to give it a seminar room, a lecture hall, or just a closet we can air out now and then" (16).

To study others' emotions, as a symbolic interactionist, an ethnographer or experimental psychologist; to heal another's emotional wounds as psychiatrist or psychoanalyst; to write a memoir about one's own inner turmoil or to craft a story that reveals a character's structure of feelings—all of these endeavors are well regarded within the academy. But to speak of the "observer's" own emotions and feelings and how these connect up (or don't connect up) with the "observed" is still highly suspect, whether one is concerned about science or authorship.

For Behar, the fieldwork method is "oxymoronic":

> Participant observation is split at the root: act as a participant,
> but don't forget to keep your eyes open. . . . [When your fieldwork
> is over] dust yourself off, go to your desk, and write down what
> you saw and heard. Relate it to something you've read by Marx,
> Weber, Gramsci or Geertz, and you are on your way to doing an-
> thropology. (5)[23]

This is how I often felt after an emotion-packed day at the PPPT, that I was
split at my roots. On some days I would try to dust myself off so I could
write what I had seen and heard and relate it to theories about social and
psychodynamic forces, but this often felt "hollow at the heart."

In retrospect I can see that my work with the PPPT girls was about
finding a way to sustain two distinct (often cast as opposing) ways of
ethnographic knowing. One is the way of "dusting off," detachment, and
analysis, and the other is the way of being an emotional participant in what
one is seeing.[24] I believe ethnographic knowing is about embracing both
ways. This is what makes ethnographic knowing an exemplary kind of
knowing; it takes personal subjectivity into account in making and assessing knowledge claims of any complexity. My emotional engagements with
Tara and her grief, Tskaie's tease, and Brandi's response, brought me closer
to an understanding of the complex web of emotions that are bound up in
race-, class-, and gender-based relations, and where the girls and I intersect
in this web. I see Tara having learned to disavow feelings of loss and sorrow
as part of her version of hard, protective individualism, her tough stance
toward life. Tara's hard, protective stance strikes me as enabling her to confront the economic insecurity, discrimination, and unspeakable loss (including her father's and mother's early deaths) she has faced and which
puts specific demands upon her management of grief. Tara's path of survival takes its toll, including alienation, resistance, and splitting off of parts
of herself, all of which were expressed in her art forms. I, on the other
hand, had been raised to minimize feelings of loss and disappointment—
"There's no use crying over spilled milk," and, if you try hard enough you
can "make lemonade out of lemons." I intuitively gleaned from the adults
around me that feelings of loss can hold you back. Just as Tara's denial of
feelings helps her survive in a world of hardship, my amending of feelings
prepared me for upward mobility, including the losses that must be sustained when one leaves behind family and friends, what sociologists Seely
et al. (1956) have called surviving "psychic death."[25] Its emotional costs include guilt and anxiety.

I needed both ethnographic "ways of knowing" to sort this out. I
needed to have analytic distance, and to be present, able to acknowledge

powerful emotions. Both ways of knowing guided my analysis of how personal strategies for managing loss can be tied to social, structural forces of inequality. It seems to me that Behar (1996) splits apart these two ways of knowing in fieldwork, valuing one over the other. I prefer to view fieldwork as a means to uphold, not reconcile, the tension between the two.

Epistemological Tensions in Ethnographic Knowing

I realize that there is an irresolvable epistemological tension in these two ways of ethnographic knowing—analytic distance and emotional participation. I don't seek a resolution in my work; rather, I see the rhythm of moving between these two as generative, especially when it comes to negotiating fieldwork relationships. I believe that one's ability to "know" another, especially his or her unbearable or unpleasant thoughts and feelings, is dependent upon what the "self" (in this case the researcher) is able or willing to take in, face, or "contain" of his or her subjects' emotions.[26] For example, insofar as a researcher cuts off or changes the topic when an interviewee expresses strong emotions, the "knowing" is less full than it could be.[27] Likewise, my ability to be present with Tara's sorrow depended upon my emotional participation and self-knowledge about grief and sorrow.

At the same time what I could "know" about a PPPT girl depended upon her ability to tell about herself at any given time. This put yet another epistemological demand upon me as the researcher, what in colloquial terms is referred to as "reading between the lines." Looking for what is unsaid or "unsayable," paying attention to breaks in a narrative, and tracing the specific ways in which a conversation was being co-constructed were integral features of my researcher stance and methodology. Nonetheless, in any given research relationship, there may be experiences that cannot be told. Annie Rogers and a team of doctoral students (2002) at the Harvard Graduate School of Education have developed research methods that attend to such complexities; "engaging the unsayable"[28] is a method that begins with an acknowledged loss, the notion that stories are conveyed to an audience as partial or paraphrased versions of a whole story that is beyond our access as readers." Rogers and her colleagues caution that "what is said and what remains unsaid and perhaps unsayable depends upon what can be held in memory and reimagined as a story to tell, which further depends upon the listener's moment by moment responses." Rogers et al. also pay close attention to moments in an interview where a subject/narrator may be ready to speak about an experience and where she may resist doing so. Disruptions or halts in speech, dangling sentences, places where a narrator changes direction or lowers her voice serve as "clues to missing stories from which we can gauge the incompleteness of the stories we hear and inter-pret" (24).[29]

Over the course of my work I encountered incomplete stories, includ-ing eclipsed accounts of violence, abuse, material deprivation, and urgent need. I wrote about one such example in chapter 3. Readers will recall Kaela's self-portrait—her picture of herself as a child on the way to the candy store. As I went back through Kaela's writing and the transcription of the class conversation, I noted a break in the story she had begun to tell about her picture. But when I asked her about what had happened—"Did you go to the store; Are you going to put that part in your piece?"—Kaela responded, "There's a lot that has happened at that candy store but I don't want to say."

Kaela's picture of herself as a child referenced an experience about which she was not yet ready to tell. Perhaps the story had not yet taken shape for Kaela or the reality of its impact was too hard to say. Just because researchers may be ready to listen does not ensure that participants are ready or interested in or willing to speak, and this creates yet another set of researcher anxieties.

Ethnographic Defenses

Ruth Behar, drawing upon George Devereaux's work about the connection between research methods and researcher anxieties, writes:

> Because there is no clear and easy route by which to confront the self who observes, most professional observers develop defenses, namely "methods" that "reduce anxiety and enable us to function efficiently." . . . [in] situations in which we feel complicitous with structures of power, or helpless to release another from suffering, or at a loss as to whether to act or to observe. (1996: 6)

As this chapter charts, my fieldwork was anxiety-ridden. I think it is fair to say that the creative arts activities and my "restoring the artist" approach was my way of reducing a host of anxieties. It helped soothe my feelings of powerlessness in the face of the girls' hardships and suffering and gave me a way to respond to powerful emotions (both the girls' and my own). Bring-ing creative activities into an otherwise restrictive school day enabled me to feel empowered, even if minimally, to subvert the educational practices that limited the girls' everyday learning. And, the art-making activities, but especially the book-making project, which produced such beautiful, pre-cious, and artful objects that the girls cherished and that were so well received by others, enabled me to "give back" to the girls in a concrete and immediate way.

Perhaps most important, the creative arts activities permitted me to be present with and more fully attentive to the girls than I might otherwise have been. Engaging the girls as "artists" nurtured our relationship in ways I could not have predicted. It freed me from a certain rigidity I held about research protocol and staying "on task." It allowed me to overcome my own shyness and my reticence as a white woman working with girls of color, worried about how I might be received. And, in a few cases, like the time I was recruited to role play the "girl" at the clinic, I was transported to some other place and time. It is in this way that my methodological approach is most closely aligned with that of Pierre Bourdieu (1996), who writes that the (social) distance between interviewer and interviewee need not get in the way of "true comprehension." He suggests that the interview that arrives at true comprehension "can be considered a sort of spiritual exercise, aiming to attain, through *forgetfulness of self,* a true transformation of the view we take of others in the ordinary circumstances of life" (24) (my emphasis). The creative activities allowed me to forget myself long enough to take another view. Similarly, as I have argued, the creative activities provided the distance for some girls to take another view of themselves and others.

This is how I arrived at viewing ethnography as a social art form, a way of moving back and forth between art and science, spontaneity and discipline, aesthetic and social awareness. But I could not have claimed this had it not been for the work of anthropologist Karen McCarthy Brown (1991) who inspired me with her words:

> Ethnographic research, is a form of human relationship. When the lines long drawn in anthropology between participant-observer and informant break down, then the only truth is the one in between; and anthropology becomes closer to a social art form, open to both aesthetic and moral judgment. This situation is riskier, but it does bring intellectual labor and life into closer relation. (12)

Ethnographic Telling

The final challenge in fieldwork is to write about what one has seen, heard, experienced, and learned. For many ethnographers, myself included, this last phase of authorship is the most problematic. It is when the ethnographer strives to "bring the ethnographic moment back, to resurrect it, to

communicate the distance, which too quickly starts to feel like an abyss, between what we saw and heard and our inability, finally, to do justice to it in
our representations" (Behar 1996:9). This effort to *do justice* to what we
have learned can never be complete.

The "Double Crisis" of Representation

Many anthropologists, sociologists, historians, and educational researchers
have written about the problems of representation; what anthropologists
Ruth Behar and Deborah Gordon (1995) view is a "double crisis in the field
of anthropology." It is a double crisis because it has two roots: one in the
postmodern turn and critique of the realist tradition in ethnographic writing, and the other in the critique of white, middle-class feminist versions of
women's experiences that women of color, working-class women, and les-
bians have made so effectively.

In the double crisis of representation, ethnographers are said to face
three dilemmas in writing their texts. The first has to do with authority and
authorial style: On what basis does the researcher/author claim knowledge
about her or his subjects? Who speaks for whom and from what perspective? The second has to do with the "culture concept." Insofar as an ethnographer aims to portray a group's "culture," that is, members' shared beliefs,
values, and understandings, the ethnographer runs the risk of reducing the
complexity and variability that abound among members of any group. Especially troubling are efforts to convey the "essence" or "core traits" of a
group, which all too often has the effect of "othering" or "exoticizing" the
group being studied. The third is the question of appropriation: How and
where do researchers draw the line in using their subjects' voices and life
experiences for their own purposes as authors? Who benefits from the research, in what ways, and according to what rules of fairness or relations of
power?[30]

Working with the PPPT girls in this project has led me to see the crisis of
representation as not only a problem for the "researcher," but also a problem
for the "researched." In this book I have argued that the girls struggled with
the same three dilemmas: Who has the right to speak with authority about
their identities—as students; as sexual beings; as teenage mothers? How
"cultural" or shared is the experience of teenage pregnancy, and how can an
individual girl convey her personal worries, ambivalences and felt inadequacies without playing into stereotypes? Who benefits and who loses if she
doesn't "author" herself in her own image? Indeed, these are all questions
that lie at the heart of the self- and identity-making process.

The girls' struggles with self-representation highlight both the subjective and objective nature of the self- and identity-making process. What strikes me most is how their self-representations were both "created" through personal feelings and "found" in cultural forms, especially dominant discourses about the pregnant teen. Realizing the "created and found" nature of their self-representations is, in my mind, the transformative side of the representational crisis. We could view the girls' self-representations as things they created imaginatively through familiar or "found" objects of culture and into which they invested feelings about themselves, including feelings about their self-worth and social distinction. And in some cases, these creations also served to carry a girl into a new awareness, for example, Michelle's realization that she held unwanted feelings of hatred toward her baby or Twana's surprise at her own projected image of bodily tandem— the two-in-one embodiment—that characterizes pregnancy. The girls' self-representations proved to be an ideal means to explore the interdependence of these two dynamics—the created and found (i.e., the psychodynamic and the cultural). To overlook these links, whether for the researcher or for the researched, is to miss an essential piece of how social research is produced, and how it can be a vehicle for change.

In addition, the links between psychodynamic processes and social structures of power and inequality are not well-enough understood in ethnographic doing, knowing, and telling.[31] The interdependence of these processes is missing in the way we think about education, a point I will develop in the next chapter.

All this being said, as guardian of the PPPT girls' self-representations, I am curating their art work and retelling their stories in ways they might not. In muddling my way through the presentation of the girls' self-representations, I have been guided by three related considerations—*relationship, responsibility,* and *risk.*

My relationship with the girls began with a protective sense of responsibility on my part and an invitation to reciprocity. It was their initial cautious curiosity, and playful engagement, with one another and with me, a stranger, that surprised me over and over again. The girls' willingness to accept my invitation to open up and express themselves—what Annie Rogers (1993) would call their "practice of ordinary courage"—allowed me to do the same. Our mutual sense of trust deepened over time, not always evenly or easily, and was marked by the risks the girls and I were willing to take. The more I listened to the girls' stories, the more I realized my own stake in what they were telling me about the punitive and blaming discourses surrounding sexuality, pregnancy and motherhood. I had gotten pregnant while in graduate school and had felt the sting of judgment—my own and others—about whether I would be viewed as a "serious" scholar because I had not delayed child-bearing as had so many women faculty role models. I had also divorced when my children were quite young and still felt scarred by the scrutiny of legal and mental health professionals that were part of a custody battle. There is no doubt in my mind that the girls' stories spoke to my own history and opened up new ways for me to make sense of my past.

There is also no doubt that my whiteness shaped what I saw, said, and did. I know that at first I was acutely aware of being the only white person at the PPPT, but that this awareness faded over the course of my time there. I also know that I felt hostility from some of the black teachers, while others took me into their confidence because, among other things, they appreciated my bearing witness to "how bad things really are." And many of the girls took me into their confidence because I was an outsider to their community and thus, unlikely to "get into their business." Meanwhile, my whiteness and privilege were confounded by my research status, my ability to come and go without being subject to the same rigid rules of school, including not having to give grades or assess the girls' learning. In part, I am in a position to re-represent the girls' worlds, identities, and relationships in ways that they and their teachers can not, because I am white.

Some would say that a white scholar has no business re-representing the lives of black youth. Taken to its extreme, this stance suggests that outsiders cannot understand and will inevitably distort the experiences of any group they study of which they are not part. I disagree. That being said, there are deep emotionally charged feelings about my project—a white woman researcher talking about black girls' worlds. I have encountered a range of these emotions including my own fears that I would offend or be misunderstood, while presenting this research to audiences including African Americans. I have encountered two reactions, which upon reflection strike me as being key to the emotional side of the limits of representation, what we might call the emotional politics of ethnography.

After I had given a presentation to a small audience of researchers conducting a study of urban youth, one of three African American women in the audience said that she had not learned anything new from my talk. As a black woman she already knew that black women have complex and individual psychologies, and that they can't let their feelings be known, including to themselves. This might be new information for me as a white person, but it wasn't news to her. She saw my work as having an implicit white audience and to be addressing racist assumptions, including my own. After all, why should the girls' creativity be such a surprise? Doesn't this surprise tacitly assume racial stereotypes that would suggest otherwise? I responded by saying that she was right, my work both engages and exposes stereotypes (including my own). I explained that I saw my research challenging racial stereotypes in two ways: first, by arguing that there is a dynamic relationship between social processes (including racism) and an individual's psychological complexity that, is denied in dominant representations of urban, black pregnant girls; and second, that there is a need to bring to light the creativity, imagination and astuteness of a group of girls who have routinely been cast in deficit terms. In the most simple, but profound terms, I argued that the goal of my research, and hers is to provide an alternative, but still complicated picture of a disparaged and maligned group to *people who hold power and who have influence in changing lives.* Insofar as those people are white and hold racist assumptions, then all researchers (whether white or black) must speak to these assumptions in order to dispel them. She thanked me for my response.

Two weeks later, at a large public southeastern university, I gave a talk and an African American woman spoke up during the question period and said she felt uncomfortable with my presentation because she felt it exposed her and other black women to white people (in an audience of about twenty-five, there were three people of color, herself included). She wasn't sure what she thought about this but she would prefer to hear these things from a black scholar. Nonetheless, she appreciated my efforts just the same.

I see these two distinct reactions as sharing one thing in common. Both audience members are acknowledging the social and psychological demands of ethnographic telling. In social terms, despite whatever accuracy or sensitivity I might convey about the subjects of my research, neither I nor my audience can break out of the social structure of which we are part. Toni Morrison (1992) puts it this way:

> For both black and white American writers [we could add researchers], in a wholly racialized society, there is no escape from racially inflected language, and the work writers [researchers] do to unhobble the imagination from the demands of that language is complicated, interesting, and definitive. (12–13)

In psychological terms, despite our shared human need for knowledge, especially knowledge of emotional experience, there is also a tendency to avoid meaning. This is because emotional knowledge (which includes the pain of being both recognized and misrecognized by others) brings realizations that are hard to tolerate. I believe there are converging political and psychological conflicts that lie at the heart of ethnographic representation, conflicts about the desire to know and not to know.

Toward that end, to be *responsible* to the girls, to myself, and to my audience means not simply debunking myths and stereotypes about pregnant teens, but building alternative visions. I agree with Valerie Walkerdine (1997) who writes:

> Social Science research has been central in the management of populations and so we have a responsibility in taking apart those truths to construct narratives of our own, no matter how difficult that might be. The sure march of science will not stop while we are deconstructing! (76)

The girls' self-representations—their unique efforts to construct themselves in their own image—provide such an alternative vision. And it would seem that it is my responsibility to offer a framework of interpretation and action, understood not as yet another fixed "truth" but as a means for understanding and facilitating the process of becoming and being made.

CHAPTER 7

Split at the Root:
Rethinking Educational Practice

This book began with reflections on my first week at the Piedmont Program for Pregnant Teens. I introduced three themes that I argue lie at the heart of the PPPT girls' schooling experiences—the institutional force of discipline and punishment; the power of personal feelings; and the search for respect and respectability. These three themes emerged from and found expression across the girls' self-representations. Through each form of self-representation the girls creatively answered to their social worlds and wrestled (consciously and unconsciously) with conflicting emotions regarding their transition from girlhood to motherhood. Their answers to the question, "How does it feel to be a problem?" were persistently fraught with references to self-worth, value, respectability, and a desire to control their surroundings.

In these initial reflections I also introduced the girls and Ms. Nelson and Ms. Washington, respectively a teacher and a counselor in the program. While these two women were crucial players in setting the stage, for the most part they dropped out of the rest of the book as I turned my attention to the girls' self-representations. In this final chapter, I wish to speak to educators, like Ms. Nelson and Ms. Washington, who are charged with the education of girls, like the PPPT girls, and who find themselves imprisoned in an educational system that does not meet their own or their students' needs.

In the previous chapter I wrote about how ethnographers can feel *split at the root*—divided between their need for analytic distance from, and emotional engagement with, the subjects of their research. I think this metaphor is equally well suited to educators. For at its core, education is an anxiety-provoking enterprise; and educators, like ethnographers, develop methods and practices that serve to allay the fears and worries created by our culture and by the (culturally constructed) educational system itself. Teachers, like ethnographers, must find a way to sustain two distinct (cast as opposing) ways of knowing. One educational researcher, Richard Elmore, goes so far as to say that U.S. high schools are "probably either a close third or tied for second as the most pathological social institutions in our society after public health hospitals and prisons" (2002). In coping with the demands and difficulties created by educational institutions (including stressful interpersonal relations) teachers, like ethnographers, can find themselves feeling split at the root, torn between what has been posed as two distinct ways of knowing, for understanding their students' lives and learning. Indeed, part of the pathology of the contemporary educational institution (its reigning discourses, policies, research and practice) is that it tends to pit two ways of knowing against each other—*objectivity and evidence* against *emotional participation and artful engagement.*

Current educational discussion about accountability is a good example. State mandated accountability systems that focus on performance-based measures (of students but not of teachers) are the key means by which we gauge what is going on for students in schools. This objective, evidence-based way of knowing is not the only way, nor is it necessarily the best way of understanding how and what students are learning. As a result, educators often overlook or don't examine other forms of knowing, including teachers' own sense of responsibility for, and emotional participation and artful engagement with, their lowest-performing students. There is no expansive, inclusive discussion about how to gauge the quality of students' lives, learning, and relationships in school. Nor are there sufficient opportunities for educators to investigate and talk about exemplary institutional practices.

The three themes I identified at the beginning of this chapter—the force of institutional discipline and punishment; the power of personal feelings; and the search for respect and respectability—are missing from the current accountability discussion. These themes do not figure into current measures of educational quality, especially for students who have been marginalized, identified as "at risk," or labeled as "special needs." That said, I also suspect that these same three issues permeate teachers' everyday lives and teaching in schools. In this final chapter, I want to expand the discussion about how to gauge the quality of life, teaching, and learning in schools, and to consider two alternative approaches to educational practice. The two approaches—restoring the artist and resuscitating the notion of play—parallel those I mentioned in the previous chapter about ethnographic practice. My hope is to open up discussion about how to better prepare teachers to manage the anxiety-ridden world of schooling.

Education, Culture, Identity—and Anxiety

Many critics have argued persuasively that schools are sites of social reproduction; despite education's promise of social mobility, most students leave school holding the same place in the social hierarchy as they did when they entered.[1] Much ethnographic work in school settings has skillfully examined how educational discourses, institutional practices, and everyday classroom interactions work together in ways that protect privilege, reproduce inequality, and maintain the status quo.[2] Equally important, in my view, is that schools are sites of profound anxiety for students, teachers, and parents, all of whom worry about fitting in, being judged, and measuring up to their respective roles. The varied ways that these anxieties are institutionally created and individually felt is part of the process of social reproduction that should not be ignored.

Educational discourses provide students, teachers, and parents the means to gauge their success in their respective roles. These discourses influence what we take to be true or right or good about ourselves and identities as learners or teachers. There are specific educational discourses that direct our thinking about what it means to be a "problem"—and that characterize students as "slow" and "fast," "bright" and "dull," "promising" and "unpromising," or in regards to the PPPT girls, "regular" or "special needs" students. Teachers are directed by these discourses to think in certain ways about what it means to teach or what can be expected from "problem" students. What is troubling about these ways of assessing students is that they focus our attention on assessing *individuals,* comparing one student's or teacher's performance to that of another's in a "normative" group. This comparative information (useful as it might be) does not tell us what we need to know about the quality of life, learning, and teaching in schools. Indeed, these discourses serve to *justify* rather than *explain* differences in learning and achievement.

In the course of everyday schooling interactions, deep-seated personal feelings are easily evoked about ourselves and our identities. Feelings about power and powerlessness, fears of failure or rejection, jealousy, envy, and resentment toward those who are favored are all examples.[3] As organizations, schools seek to contain, or relieve its members from, the anxieties that accompany such powerful personal feelings. And, as individuals we do the same, hoping to avoid whatever pain or suffering is involved in not measuring up to school demands and standards.

British sociologist and feminist Jenny Shaw (1995) goes so far as to say that managing anxiety is an organizing principle of educational institutions and practices (33–34). To make her case Shaw draws upon the work, in the 1950s, of Isabel Menzies Lyth and her colleagues, who examined how hospitals and the work of nursing provoked anxiety, especially deep-seated personal feelings associated with grief and loss. In Lyth's view, for nurses to effectively do their jobs, they needed to be protected from feelings of helplessness in the face of death. From the organizational perspective, nurses needed institutional supports for dealing with deep attachments to patients who die under their care as well as from the resultant contact with grieving relatives. Put somewhat differently, for hospitals to function, nurses needed to be shielded from their proximity to suffering. Unfortunately some of the organizational responses for example rotating nurses meant to contain anxiety, created yet other problems, such as feelings of alienation.

Shaw applies this way of thinking about organizational responses to anxiety, to the institution of education, and its arrangements, especially the work of teachers.[4] She argues that schools must find ways to help teachers cope with the power of their own feelings, that are aroused as part of the school day. Schools use the same sort of organizational strategies as those found in hospitals, including depersonalizing routines and practices to help teachers distance themselves from the psychological demands of their jobs. Moreover, Shaw claims that individual teachers use the same sort of psychic defenses against attachments to students—splitting, projection, and the denial of responsibility—that Lyth found among nurses.

There are two especially important parallels between how nurses and teachers respond to their workplaces. One is to invest (usually male) authorities with superior powers, while diminishing their own sense of competence. The other is to find ways of distancing themselves from those in their care, including a denial of the power they hold over their patients' or students' lives. Moreover, the parallel hierarchical structure of hospitals and schools enhances the likelihood that "individuals will feel anxiety about whether they are up to the job, and similarly, the more likely they are to view both their superiors and inferiors within that structure . . . in terms of their external position" (Lyth quoted in Shaw, 1995: 39), not for who these individuals might be in their own right. The effects of this institutional structure on individuals are profound, leading to feelings of invisibility, inauthenticity, and alienation. The cost of this disaffection in schools is at best unaddressed for and at worst denied in current assessments of educational quality.

There were abundant expressions of structurally created and individually felt anxiety at the PPPT, starting with the graffiti that caught my eye the first day I arrived. *PPPT only hides you. Be proud stay with the regular team* and *Don't be ashamed of your kids cause you weren't ashamed of having sex.* These remarks speak to a range of student feelings about a strategy designed by schools to deal with pregnant girls who challenge educational norms. From an institutional perspective, separating pregnant girls from the "regular" classroom is one way to allay fears about whether such girls fit in or can measure up. This separation may also protect girls from undue hostility from their peers or from overly rigid school requirements. But this *gendered* singling out of pregnant girls as having "special needs" (parenting boys are not viewed as such) is an example of an institutional strategy that contributes to the very problem it is meant to solve. When schools respond to pregnant and parenting girls by drawing upon traditional gender roles (i.e., that women are culturally assigned the responsibility for children) and gender stereotyped curricular goals (e.g., educated motherhood), then inequalities between men and women are reproduced.

The PPPT girls developed their own individual strategies to cope with their feelings of anxiety created in them by school. But they shared in common one strategy. The girls held the joint perception that they had lost or were denied the "student" side of their selves, perceptions they often attributed to teachers, whom they blamed for harboring negative feelings toward them. On some level, it didn't matter whether a teacher had "given up" on a girl's education, or whether a teacher had tried to inspire a girl to "go on ahead." The fact that the girls perceived their student lives as having been compromised—that school had split their student self from their pregnant self—limited their sense of possibility.

The PPPT teachers had their own worries, stemming from a variety of conditions, not the least of which included isolation, wholly inadequate resources for teaching, and racial, class and gendered structures of authority from which they could not escape. Even the most mundane task—photocopying, making a phone call, using a computer—required permission to secure access. Equally disheartening were the teachers' feelings of frustration about being helpless in the face of the girls' hardships. Their proximity to the girls' difficulties was draining. Ms. Nelson's words summed this all up: "It is not easy being a teacher in this system; it has really tired me out."

But, in the end, it is the closing of the PPPT program, even with all its problems, that is most troubling. The slow demise of the program, over eighteen years, reflects a much larger trend toward the erosion of comprehensive public educational services. The current political climate of post-welfare "reform" and the federal No Child Left Behind Act mandating more state-level achievement testing as the single means to assess what is going on in schools and in student learning, has stifled public debate about what counts as quality in education. High stakes performance tests that document differences in student achievement simply do not provide enough insight into varied students' experiences of school, their understandings of academic subject matter, or their evolving selves and identities. We need more comprehensive ways to gauge educational progress that are both instructionally supportive and geared toward assessing the full range of children's capabilities. Equally important, we need to be evaluating the effects that inadequate basic social provisions have upon children who do not thrive in school; this aspect of educational assessment is rarely acknowledged or discussed.[5]

I realize that I am writing against a tide of educational reform strategies. But I do so because I am convinced these strategies, especially high stakes testing, are not only unfair and harmful, but are deadening, for students and teachers alike. I am also certain that no small-scale changes or quick fixes will redress educational inequities or heal the social injuries that are caused in school settings. Most important, I am also writing against what I view as a vanishing sense of social responsibility and commitment to children's entitlement to nurturance, including education. Parents today talk about being "lucky" if their child is well served in school, rather than assuming that their child is entitled to a quality public education. Nothing short of a total restructuring of social services, including public health, housing, and education, seems likely to alter current realities, especially in our urban centers. Nonetheless, and against all odds, students and teachers show up each day in schools, some more alive and interested in the school world than others. It is to these steadfast participants in educational settings and learning relationships that I offer the following thoughts on educational practice.

Restoring the Artist

In the best instances, school programs like the PPPT cast pregnancy as an experience that a girl needs to "get through" so that she can return to being a "normal" student. Educators do not view pregnancy as a source for learning.[6] Rather, pregnancy is viewed solely as a barrier to learning, achievement, and success. Educators have foreclosed on the question, "What might girls learn about themselves as a result of pregnancy, childbirth, and chil-drearing?" What would schools look like if educators took a stance of *interest* and *curiosity* rather than *discipline* and *punishment* toward girls' fertility?

In the previous chapter I wrote about Adam Phillip's view of psycho-analysis as an exploration of that "part of the person that makes interest despite, or whatever, the early environment" (1998: 12). He writes that the role of the analyst is to "restore the artist" in clients. Among many things, this means serving as an "interested party" to whatever objects of interest the client brings to analysis. He writes:

> In psychoanalysis we treat the objects of interest as clues and cues, as commas that look like full stops. Every object of desire is an ob-scure object of desire, leading us to ask both: why this rather than that, and why anything at all? Free-floating attention itself, as a method, is a tribute to the vagaries of interest. (14)

Phillips thinks that the goal of clinical practice is to restore human interest in the world, and hence promote creativity. In his words, psychoanalysis is "the art of making interest out of interest that is stuck."

Readers will recall that when I first arrived at the PPPT, a report had been issued that characterized the girls as "depressed," including an observ-able lack of interest in school. While Ms. Nelson resented this characteriza-tion of the girls, she cited a long list of social conditions that could account for the girls' lost interest. There was one condition she did not include and that was the program's own stance toward the girls. While each PPPT teacher took her own specific stance, for example, some took a "tough love" approach and others took a "don't give up on yourself" approach, they all viewed the girls' sexuality and pregnancies as cause for correction and dis-cipline, not for curiosity. But we could imagine otherwise, a program in which teachers considered the girls' sexuality, pregnancy, and impending motherhood as laden with meaning and potential insight, as "clues and cues, as commas, that look like full stops." Educational programs could provide free-floating attention, seeking to help the girls make interest out of their changing bodies and lives.

The PPPT girls are not unlike any other group of students, all who bring wide-ranging, provocative, and fraught interests to their classrooms, including interests the culture simultaneously and paradoxically both pro-motes and demonizes, like sex and MTV, and which, for many reasons, teachers avoid. Adolescents bring distinct curiosities (and anxieties) about their bodies, an interest that is not only ignored, but actively suppressed in schools. Despite the fact that children are understood to use their bodies to discover and act upon the world, schooling and most educational practice cease to acknowledge bodies as a primary tool of expression and communication. "Growing up," as Barrie Thorne suggests, can be seen as "a process of reigning in bodily and imaginative possibilities" (1993: 16). This is not to say that the importance of bodies vanishes; indeed, quite the opposite, as the PPPT girls' experiences of being pregnant in school so clearly illustrates. But students' interest in and use of their bodies gets devalued in favor of language, literacy, and other modes of communication. Schools restrain students' bodily movements and expression, setting certain limits and exclusions in which students participate without knowing—sitting in desks, standing in lines, moving through space in routine and regularized ways, and so forth. Equally important, schools "help to code bodies as having gender, race, beauty, grace, ugliness and stink" (Nespor 1997: 122). In short, a school's stance toward how students carry their bodies in school—in terms of dress, manners, and deportment—is key to the formation of their sense of possibility.

There are numerous examples throughout this book where I consider how the PPPT girls' bodies and their bodily interests served as sites of conflict and learning, starting with the graffiti messages calling upon the girls to refuse being "hidden" away from others and to resist the shame associated with teenage pregnancy. There were the traditional desks into which the girls had to squeeze their pregnant bodies and the girls' informal playful performances of pregnancy where, despite school's imposition, they emphasized their "showing." There were the times a girl exaggerated her "showing," carrying herself in defiance of authority as in the argument between Shanille and Ms. Washington that opens this book. There were the persistent and recurring conversations about hairstyles, fashion and glamour—conversations which when allowed to develop and probed further, led to discussions about bodies, social distinctions, stereotypes and evolving gender, race, and class identities (see chapters 3 and 4). There were the "color line" conversations about how much bodies matter, especially skin color, conversations which, had I ventured to cross the color line more than I did, might have opened up important dialogue about the myriad effects of living in a racialized world.

All of this is to say that, rather than being afraid of students' bodily interests, their search for meaning and pleasure, educators could provide the grounds and guidance for it. Admittedly this would mean rethinking the educational enterprise, as aiming for more than academic achievement. It would mean providing students with an authentic audience for their interests, creativity, and work, an audience that is not there solely to evaluate or judge. Developmentally speaking, it would mean tending to three fundamental human needs: "If we are to go on making and taking our pleasure, . . . there are three things we have to be able to do: involve other people, make good our losses, and enjoy (or at least tolerate) conflict" (Phillips 1998: 6). This is the restorative vision of educational practice I have in mind: one that nourishes relationships; helps students recuperate their losses; recognizes social and personal conflicts, including how different bodies matter; and seeks to integrate rather than split students' multiple interests and identities.

It is in this spirit that I propose the educational use of the student self-representation activities, as opportunities for students and teachers to explore the ties between social and personal conflicts, and as a means to develop young people's body-smarts.

The Transformative Power of Play

My work with the PPPT girls has made me more aware of the value of play in learning, teaching, and self-making. I don't mean "play" in the *consumerist* sense, where young people are "markets" for new toys and leisure items and activities, but in the imaginative, *symbol-formation* sense. Regrettably, school environments, but especially high school settings, split off "work" from "play," privileging the former over the latter. The phrase that haunted the halls of the PPPT, and is heard throughout most high schools is: "Now that you are about to become adults you have to give up fun and games and get down to the serious business of adulthood." This strikes me as wrong-headed, particularly for adolescents who are forging new identities.

My view of play and the role of art-making in teaching and learning is rooted in psychoanalytic theories. From this perspective, art-making (in all its varied forms—dance, music, painting, theater, writing) and art-appreciation (when we resonate with a work of art) are basic human capacities. In classical psychoanalytical literature, art-making and -appreciation tend to get lost under the heading of sublimation (i.e., the artist rechannels threatening unconscious emotions into a more acceptable form, say a painting). Sublimation is possible because as individuals we project unacceptable feelings and wishes on to bounded symbols that disguise (and therefore allow us to tolerate) these unwanted feelings and wishes. Freud divided the world into psyche and reality and was most interested in what was *hidden* in art or dreams (both forms of symbolization). He viewed the subject matter of art and dreams as clues about how the psyche (inner wishes and feelings) comes to terms with the "external world" (reality and its demands). But more contemporary psychoanalytic theories, especially those inspired by D. W. Winnicott, challenge this clear-cut division, focusing more on how individuals creatively bridge the space between inner and outer worlds.

Winnicott suggests that it is through play—what he calls the "transitional process"—that individuals come to terms with reality and its demands. For Winnicott, human beings feel most alive when they are able to weave their inner subjective feelings with external objective realities. At the same time, this weaving causes tension, for which we seek relief. According to Winnicott:

> The task of reality acceptance is never completed, no human being is free from the strain of relating inner and outer reality, and that relief from this strain is provided by an intermediate area of experience which is not challenged (arts, religion). This intermediate area is in direct continuity with the play area of the small child who is "lost" in play. (1971: 13)

As part of this continuum of experience, Winnicott describes the transitional object, which is the child's first "not-me" possession. It is an object that comes into use near the end of the first year of life and that allows the child to have the illusion of mother's presence when she is absent. Winnicott stresses that the transitional object is neither the teddy bear nor the blanket that is seen (objective reality), nor is it the child's internal feeling that this teddy bear (or whatever the transitional object) is her or his mother (inner reality). Rather, the teddy bear holds both realities at once, as it provides a bridge between the familiar (of child and mother) and the disturbingly unfamiliar (of the larger world).[7] The art we create or with which we resonate, the interests we make and hold, are like transitional objects that carry us into realizations and feelings about ourselves and/or others more comfortably. This was certainly the case for me in my role-play experience of the "girl" at the clinic, where I was transported to another place and time, "lost" in play, and, consequently, brought to a new awareness about the force of social distinctions in managing feelings of vulnerability, including my own (see chapter 5).

The domain of play is also an invaluable element of culture. Anthropologists Holland et al. (1998) write about play as a source of human agency, as people are addressed by, and must answer to, their cultural worlds. They write:

Play is also the medium of mastery, indeed of creation, of ourselves as human actors. Without the capacity to formulate other social scenes in imagination, there can be little force to a sense of self, little agency. In play we experiment with the force of our acting otherwise. . . . (236)

Imagination and acting otherwise are the great promises of play, but the space for this sort of reflective activity is increasingly in danger. The realm of play is threatened by many converging forces, including war and violence and the demands of a global economy. Play is also becoming commercialized and corporate interests intrude into children's lives today in a way that their parents never experienced. In schools, over the internet, and in their communities, children are increasingly exposed to marketing interests and pressures that shape their imagination and leisure activities.

Sharon Stephens (1995), in her excellent introduction about the contemporary crisis of childhood, notes that there is more at stake in contemporary laments about the lost quality of play in children's lives than one might expect (34). She sees efforts to protect the domain of play—understood as a safe space for open-endedness, surprise, and cultural invention—as efforts to protect a vision of society that entertains new possibilities and change. Her view draws upon a conviction that play is not just a moral, but a political entitlement for both children and adults.

Adam Phillips (1998) also uses play as his metaphor for the blind spot in psychoanalysis, which is surely shared by education. In his words, psychoanalysts' blind spot is their "unwillingness to sponsor people's potential for ease. . . . Amusement is there if you want it. It is one of the most striking things about children that, in their play, good things can come easily" (7).

It was the *ease* with which the PPPT girls played, used their bodies to perform, and made their self-representations—the vitality they brought to the creative process, despite the difficulties of their environment—that is paramount in my argument. The girls' art and interests (bodily and otherwise) speak not only to their creativity, but also to the possibility for a broad social curriculum that is open to educators, possibilities that schools have shut down.

In addition to basic social provisions, there are specific conditions under which play and creativity are made possible. Conditions of trust are key. Trust in educational settings is slowly built (and cannot be taken for granted), and when established, must be unwaveringly maintained. One of the most potent elements of trust is mutual respect—among students, and between students and teachers, teachers and administrators, parents and school personnel. If there was one condition that most interfered with educational practice at the PPPT it was the lack of respect afforded the teachers in a system that neither recognized nor rewarded their efforts on behalf of the girls. Conditions of disrespect like those faced by the PPPT teachers abound in urban high schools—from deteriorating and unsafe facilities, to rigid rules and punitive policies governing teachers' work. There is no telling how many energetic, imaginative teachers leave or lose part of themselves as a consequence of their working conditions.

Resuscitating the domain of play for both students and teachers strikes me as especially urgent in light of a society that excludes and marginalizes so many of its people. Tillie Olsen (1978) begins her book, *Silences,* by asking, "what *is* the work of creation and the circumstances it demands for full functioning?" (11). She warns that "where the claims of creation cannot be primary, the results are atrophy; unfinished work; minor effort and accomplishment; silences" (13). We see the effects of curtailing students' claims to creativity in high schools across the country, but especially in our undernourished urban public schools. In such settings, adolescents are being silenced, refused their creativity, imagination, and importance. In such settings, teachers are also being silenced because their creativity is not primary, and their own search for respect and respectability is not made a priority.

I hope by now it is clear that I am not simply advocating an expanded offering of "arts" classes in education, or even an integration of the arts across the curriculum, although I support both efforts. When I speak about nourishing students' ease and interest, encouraging teachers' creativity, and creating conditions of trust in schools I am thinking of broad-scale and fundamental changes in educational practice and in curriculum so that self-exploration is carefully tied to an examination of students' social worlds. Ultimately, this view of educational practice would also revise the way we think about development. Rather than positioning the "grown up" adult against the "growing" adolescent, and rather than viewing the goal of adulthood as "growing out of things," adults and adolescents could become partners in the developmental journey of "growing into" their desires "again and again" (Phillips 1998: 108). Politically speaking, this view of education—in which students and teachers take nothing for granted and are encouraged rather than thwarted from redefining themselves, their roles, and their images—sets the stage for redefining the kind of society in which we want to live.

Epilogue

Two years after the closing of the PPPT, I am in the food court of a shopping mall in a neighboring town, and I hear my name being called out—
"Ms. Wendy, Ms. Wendy, It's me Alisha, over here." I glance over to the
Sbarro pizza line and recognize one of the former PPPT "girls." I move
quickly, rudely cutting in front of waiting customers to grab Alisha's hands,
that are reaching across the cheese pizzas. Alisha turns to her three, black
women co-workers, "Ms. Wendy was my teacher."

Under many watchful eyes, Alisha and I exchange information about
our lives. Beaming with pride, she shows me a picture of her five-year-old
daughter, a "graduation" picture from pre-school that Alisha has laminated
and carries in her white, starched uniform pocket. She tells me she is getting ready to take the GED exam for her high school diploma. She says she
was sorry when she heard from one of the PPPT teachers that my mother
died; she asks about my youngest daughter, Emma, "she must be grown by
now; does she still have that blond, curly hair?" I am touched by Alisha's
questions. I ask her about her classmates and what they are up to. She tells
me about Tracey who lives in her neighborhood. "Tracey had another
baby—a girl. She works at Walmart. Her boy, Anthony, graduated with
mine from Three Stars Day Care." She says she sees Violet now and again,
but reports that she is "up to no good."

People always want to know what happened to the PPPT girls, perhaps
because they wonder whether the project made any difference in their lives.
These are questions I wish I could answer, but can't. I can say that for the
few girls with whom I have been able to keep touch, there is no single or
predictable "next chapter" in their lives. I know of one college graduate
whose secretarial job does not begin to match her educational qualifica-
tions, another who graduated high school and is a licensed hairstylist, and
another high school graduate who keeps losing her job because she can't

find affordable child care. I know that they struggle to make ends meet, despite their educational attainment and success finding employment.

My exchange with Alisha remains alive in my mind. She has the same enthusiastic voice that I remember, but her face is much thinner and her hair is cut close to her head. I realize that Alisha is no longer a "pregnant teenager"; she's a "minimum-wage, fast-food service worker," a "black, single mother," a member of the "working-poor." I doubt these new designations capture her own sense of self and identity any more than the previous one did. I am also struck that, of all the things that defined our relationship—as researcher and researched; woman and girl; white and black; middle-class and working poor—Alisha chose the bond of teacher and student to characterize who we were to each other. I believe this speaks to the power that *images*—as "teacher" or as "pregnant teenager"—hold in the public imagination and in personal lives. Understanding how these images define us and what we must do to work with and against them is the purpose of this book.

Acknowledgments

It was Halloween, 1997, and I was packing up my files—field notes, transcripts, and hundreds of note-cards with scribbled thoughts I had been collecting since I started this research project. In less than two months I would be a Visiting Scholar at Cambridge University, England, where I could finally sit, undistracted, with all this data and think more deeply and systematically about it. Late that night I received a phone call from my sister-in-law that my mother had suffered a stroke.

The next few days were harrowing. My mother clung to her life for two days as her children and grandchildren gathered at the hospital in disbelief. The morning after my mother died I was sorting through her mail and many treasures. My husband's sister called with news that his mother had died. I was in shock, my husband was numb, and my children were deadly quiet as we traveled across the country from one funeral to the other. This book is dedicated to the memories of these two powerful family figures. Their combined maternal force and its sudden loss has compelled me to think about grief, sorrow, remembrance, and respect in new ways, and as processes that cannot be rushed. I wrote this book over the course of unraveling emotions.

England was the perfect place for mourning—the rain, the darkness and hot tea, the stonewalls and ancient churches, my anonymity—all served to soothe my heartache. I thank several collegial "strangers" who became friends—Madeleine Arnot, Miriam David, Jo-Anne Dillabough, Mary Hamilton, Chris Mann, and Caroline New.

I returned from England without a manuscript, but with a determination to write up the project so it spoke to multiple audiences, especially those in education. I have many people to thank for supporting me in this direction. I am deeply indebted to Naomi Quinn who has served as a model and mentor throughout my career. While I have been fortunate to have many colleagues nourishing my intellectual growth, her interest in and support of my work has been unconditional. She read a draft of this manuscript when she had limited time and managed to provide me the most comprehensive and cogent commentary; my revisions are no match for her editorial brilliance. I am equally grateful for my husband, Robert Shreefter, whose humor, sense of adventure, and passionate endurance facing life challenges is remarkable. Every aspect of this project is informed by his sensitivity and artful ways—from introducing me to book-making as a vehicle of self-expression, to reading endless drafts, to his unwavering support over the years it took to complete this book. His intellectual and emotional companionship shapes this book in ways that words cannot convey.

Many people have read and provided comments on versions of the chapters in this book. I especially wish to thank Annie Rogers, Kathleen Weiler, Catherine Riessman, and Julie Reuben for their patience reading endless drafts, their friendship, and their resolve that I finish. I am also indebted to John Wilson for his keen insights and intellectual rigor in reading drafts; I have always held his perspective in the highest regard. Thanks to Katherine Frank for her thorough remarks, wonderful sources, and repeated offers to read my work. I also appreciate the close reading and constructive comments of writing group members Lynn Johnson and Deborah Levenson.

Mary Casey gave me the courage to speak openly about my research and writing dilemmas as part of my teaching. Her encouragement has lead to key revisions throughout the text, thanks to the insightful suggestions of my students and teaching fellows. I cherish the way that Mary and Jim Holland modeled the meaning of an "interpretive community" as they read and commented on my work. To my independent study student group—Rhoda Bernard, Cleti Cervoni, Charlene Desire, and Corinne McKamey—I owe special thanks for taking up my invitation to read the entire manuscript and for joining my interests with their own passions and curiosities. Jessica Davis was especially generous with her time and offered painstaking commentary from her perspective as a researcher and advocate of the arts in education.

Over the years, I unsuccessfully sought research funds to support this project. Kristin Luker was a steady source of encouragement throughout this process. In the end, the Spencer Foundation awarded me a Small Grant in 2000–2001 for which I am grateful. This financial support lightened my usual academic workload and was just the boost I needed. Nonetheless, without the Harvard Graduate School of Education faculty seminar, lead by Sara Lawrence-Lightfoot, where we talked openly and honestly about the pleasures and the risks associated with authorship, I am sure the manuscript would still be in progress.

I thank Christine Capodilupo for her generous and thorough research assistance; Erin Meyers for her organizational genius and ongoing assistance; and Jenya Murnikov for the crucial role she played in the final push to get the manuscript out. I am indebted to Ilene Kalish for understanding this project at its outset, and for convincing others of its potential contribution.

Two people's support blurs the line between intellectual and personal that I wish to acknowledge. They are Cynthia Enloe and Joni Seager. Their bounteousness is unparalleled and extends to all members of my family. Three other generous-hearted people—my children—deserve special recognition. I thank Mikaela for her wisdom at such an early age and for making her journey from adolescence into young womanhood such a pleasure to witness and be part of. She read early drafts of my writing and actively listened to many paper presentations. Her keen sense of voice and her ability to say when she couldn't hear mine has been essential to my development. I thank Liam for his quiet and steadfast support all along the way. I learned more about reflexivity from his visual ethnography installed at the North Carolina School of the Arts—the taped conversations with elderly people in an old age home, the portraits he drew of them, and his self-reflections as an artist—than from any text I have encountered. His art has been an inspiration to me. Last, but certainly not least, I am indebted to Emma for humoring me and for putting up with all the demands of her mother's "work." I sit at my office computer where a small, white *post-it* has been stuck on the corner of my screen, and on which she has written the following words, "Mom, I love you. Keep up the great work, Emma." She keeps me going.

Finally, I wish I could publicly honor the girls, teachers, and school officials who made this project possible and taught me so much over the years. In order to protect the study participants' privacy I have altered some facts and re-arranged details about lives, and all names are fictitious. Nonetheless, I trust they will recognize their contribution to this book. Any type of endeavor that probes deeply into personal, subjective experiences is bound to be co-constructed—a product of both the researcher and the researched. This is where knowing and understanding meshes and finds form, not as a set of new ideas, but as a willingness to try them out. I thank them all for their willing and energetic participation.

Appendix

Guide for Discussing Individual Self-Representations

(These questions were asked after a girl had explained her self portrait or media collage. Sometimes it was not necessary to ask the question if a girl had already answered it in her presentation of the piece.)

1. What do you see? List the people, objects, and images, and places.
2. What is going on in this piece?
3. Where are you in this piece?
4. What were you thinking or feeling (*what was on your mind?*) as you made this piece? What's going on with others in this piece? (What are they thinking or feeling?)
5. What would you change about this piece if you were to do it again?

Guide for Group Discussion of Self-Representations

1. What do you see in ____'s piece?
2. What do you think is going on? Mention whatever you see happening, no matter how small.
3. What ideas and/or emotions do you think this piece expresses?
4. What do you think you learned about the artist who did this piece?
5. Does anything you have noticed in this self-representation so far remind you of something from your own life?
6. What would you have called this piece if you had made it yourself?
7. Take a look at all the self-representations—What is similar and different about them?

Notes

Notes to Preface

1. All people, places, and school programs are pseudonyms.
2. I first heard this expression from anthropologist Karen McCarthy Brown who attributed it to Renato Rosaldo. Then I read an article by anthropologist Clifford Geertz (1998) entitled, "Deep Hanging Out" in which he reviews two books that claim to do *intensive fieldwork*, which is the sense in which I am using the phrase.
3. Throughout this book I use the label "Black" (lower and upper case) instead of African American when I want to draw attention to the persistent force of racial categorization according to skin color. Indeed, only recently has data been gathered about the incidences of teen pregnancy according to racial and ethnic groups; initially this data was gathered based only on two racial classifications: "black" or "white." I use the label African American, Hispanic, Latino and white when referring to communities of people, and when discussing current research or writings where these labels have been used by the author.

Notes to Chapter 1

1. There is a vast body of literature about teenage pregnancy exploring the sociological and psychological factors involved. Sociological—Furstenberg (1991), Geronimus and Korenman (1992), Ladner (1995), Luker (1996); psychological—Musick (1993), Kaplan (1997); and education and policy oriented—Pillow (1994, 1997a and b), Burdell (1998), Kelly (2000). Debold et al. (1999) argue that we know little about what is positive about poor, urban pregnant teenagers with the notable exceptions of Leadbeater and Way (1996), Way (1998).
2. See Christine Griffin (1993) for her discussion of representations of youth, from which it is hard for researchers to escape. See also Deirdre Kelly (2000) and Wanda Pillow (1997a) for their discussions of writing against dominant representations.
3. Nancy Chodorow (1995, 1999) refers to this as "personal meanings," including "emotions, affective manner and unconscious fantasies" that she argues are under-examined within feminist research.
4. I am paraphrasing Howard Becker (1986: 147–49) whose work has influenced my thinking in more ways than I can count.

5. Hollan puts it this way: "To the extent that both person-centered ethnographers and psychoanalysts engage interviewees as 'respondents' (that is as objects of systematic study and observation in themselves), rather than merely as 'informants' (that is, as knowledgeable people who can talk *about* behavior, motivation, and subjective experience)—the two approaches can be quite similar" (2001: 53). Hollan organizes his review around three questions asked, and data collection strategies used, by person-centered ethnographers: (1) what do people *say* about their subjective experience; how do they report and reflect upon their lives (usually within the context of an interview setting); (2) what do people *do* that enacts or provides clues about their subjective experiences; and (3) how do people *embody* their subjective experiences (for example through somatic experiences). Nancy Chodorow (1999) also provides an excellent review of parallel theoretical developments in the anthropology of self and feelings, the sociology of emotions, and psychoanalysis.

6. Nancy Chodorow's discussion of the parallel developments in ethnography and relational psychoanalysis focuses on the intersubjective exchange between researcher and researched/analyst and analysand. She suggests that in doing person-centered ethnography there is the creation of an "ethnographic third" like the "analytic third" (Ogden 1994), said to occur in psychoanalysis between analyst and patient. What transpires in these exchanges cannot be reduced to either the ethnographer's or her subjects' subjectivities, but is relationally based and created (Chodorow 1999: 213).

7. There is a broader context within which to consider the notion that the PPPT girls were viewed as depressed. Adolescence, for girls, is said to be a particularly vulnerable time in terms of stress and distress. Compared with boys of the same age, adolescent girls are said to be more stressed, more depressed, suffer from greater numbers of eating disorders, and attempt suicide more frequently (Debold et al. 1999: 186). Moreover, girls' "higher rates of depression may actually makes sense, given that persons who are depressed are more realistic than those who are not" (187). These authors also report that "Jennifer Pastor (1993) observed that the Latina and African American girls in her study who appeared depressed and had the lowest sense of possibility for their own lives also had the most acute understanding of racism, sexism and classism" (188). Given the PPPT girls' circumstances, their "depression" might best be viewed as part of a larger gendered developmental phenomenon created by social inequality than as simply a result of their pregnancy.

8. The merger story, but especially the racial and class dynamics that shaped it, deserves a book of its own.

9. This date of 1920 is perhaps based on official policy and not de facto discrimination that occurred as late as the 1950s. My own mother's experience is a case in point. She was trained to be an elementary teacher and told the story of her difficulties in the following way. She was teaching in a Chicago elementary school and was warned by fellow teachers not to let it be known that she had gotten married (this was in 1950). Unwilling to lie, my mother told her principal, who said that he would have to think seriously about whether to renew her contract for the next year, given her new circumstances—which would, in his view, inevitably lead to her getting pregnant. My mother tried to assure

him that this would not be an issue because she intended to wait for many years before having children. According to her, he responded with a smile, saying he had heard this same story from other women. Her contract was not renewed.

10. Wanda Pillow reports discrepancies between program provision and opportunity with urban schools serving African American girls (which she says follow a deficit model of treatment) and suburban schools serving white girls (which follow a reform model) (1994, 1997b).

11. Current data show that girls use teen pregnancy programs differentially, with African American and Latina teens having the highest rate of returning to school when pregnant (Manlove 1998).

12. In other words, teenage pregnancy was framed as a medical rather than an access or equity problem in schools.

13. Burdell (1998) points out that the early evaluation studies of teen pregnancy programs (Pearlman 1984; Zellman 1981; Weatherly et al. 1985) emphasized the same thing.

14. These students are tainted because of pregnancy and, then again, because of "special" education and its associated isolation.

15. Available from WEEA's Web site: www.edc.org/WomensEquity/resource/title9/report/treat.htm

16. Documenting and unpacking PPPT's curricular issues and examining the subjectivities these curricular themes offer students, including the ways in which they fragment girls' subjectivities, would be a study in and of itself, but not the study I chose to do.

17. See Irvine (2002) for an enlightening discussion of the ever-evolving state legislation regarding sex education.

Notes to Chapter 2

1. Here I am drawing upon a Foucauldian analysis of subtle forms of institutional discipline that lead to self-regulation. Foucault writes about prison practices as an example of how normative behaviors can be enforced. Specific practices regulating bodies—inspection, confession, the regularization and normalization of bodily movement and gesture—many of which the prisoner is unaware, create a model of obedience. These practices inculcate into the prisoner a certain subjectivity that keeps him captive in a more fundamental way than the wall of the prison itself; so that ultimately, "he becomes the principle of his own subjection" (Foucault 1979: 203).

2. Also see R. Kenzel (1993) who writes about the development of a "wronged girl" discursive frame for referring to adolescent female sexuality that the evangelical movement adopted, which she compares to a psychoanalytic discourse that social workers used in their professionalization project.

3. Rickie Solinger (1992) points out that this psychological discourse and mental health approach was associated with white girls; that they could be "cured" of their sexual malady. It is only recently that black girls have begun to be treated as in need of such treatment. See R. Kenzel (1993) on different discourses applied to white versus black girls in the 1920s.

4. Elaine Kaplan (1997) argues that these converging forces create a "poverty of relationships" for the black teenage mothers she interviewed.

5. Vinovskis (1988) notes several other reasons why policymakers embraced the epidemic logic of teen pregnancy, including the rising cost of early childbearing and a convergence of political interests focused on the issue of teenage pregnancy as a way to avoid the more controversial topic of abortion.

6. See Frank Furstenberg (1991, 1998) and Martha Ward (1995) for reviews of the research about risk factors associated with teenage pregnancy (for example, low school achievement, drug and alcohol abuse, low self-esteem, and childhood sexual abuse).

7. Leadbeater and Way (2001) focus on "resilient processes" rather than "individual characteristics as resilient" (29) in their six-year New York study of poor, minority group adolescent mothers and their children. They point out that most research on adolescent motherhood focuses on "the predictors of, the risk factors associated with, or the negative outcomes resulting from teenage parenthood. Even research that has examined the pathways toward diverse outcomes for adolescent mothers (Furstenberg et al. 1987; Horwitz et al. 1991; Leadbeater and Way 1996; Way and Leadbeater 1999) has not examined resilient processes in particular" (26–27).

8. I know of no ethnographic data indicating that young black pregnant girls explain their actions as adaptations to poverty. Geronimus' and Korenman's research was about the costs of early child-bearing, and not about individual motivations.

9. Deirdre Kelly (2000) found this same resentment about being prejudged as bad mothers among the girls she studied.

10. This is also a common complaint among urban, poor, adolescent students who, in light of their adult responsibilities, view the school setting and school rules as infantilizing (Burton, Obeidallah, and Allison 1996). I also heard this resentment from the white and black working-class women I interviewed (Luttrell 1997).

11. The in-depth interview data collected for McMahon's study were gathered in 1988–1989, from fifty-nine mothers living in the metropolitan Toronto area. All the women in the sample were white. All had only been educated in Canada (immigrant women were not included in the sample). McMahon makes a point to emphasize that her study was limited to investigating the "identity and the meaning of motherhood under specific social circumstances. The findings do not apply to all women or all stages of motherhood. As social circumstances change, so do identities and meanings" (1995: 31). She also notes that "race relations are often implicit in many cultural representations of motherhood and in public discourses about who should or should not have children. 'Other' women's motherhood provides shadow images that shape the dominant meanings of motherhood and thus the experience of motherhood among the white women in this study" (32). Like McMahon's, my study focuses on the meanings of motherhood for the PPPT girls and should not be applied to all pregnant teenagers.

12. Also see Luker (1996) for her discussion of the demographics of teenage pregnancy.

13. See Ladner (1971/1995) and Stack (1974) for early examples.

14. Jacquelyn Hall (1983) and Angela Davis (1981) give historical accounts of lynching and the social control of black men's sexuality as a way to keep white, patriarchal relations in place. And see Winthrop Jordan (1977) for his discussion of the "southern rape complex."

15. Quote taken from University of California Press Anthropology Catalogue, 1999, pg. i.

16. The family is, above all, viewed as the ideal domain for the nurturance and protection of children. But the UN convention also recognized that many children live outside the domain of families because of war and abandonment, and that many children suffer within families from abuse and neglect (Stephens 1995: 35).

17. Sharon Stephens (1995) writes eloquently about "children at risk—and as risks" (11): "There is a growing consciousness of children at risk. But the point I want to make here is that there is also a growing sense of children themselves as *the risk*—and thus of some children as people out of place and excess populations to be eliminated, while others must be controlled, reshaped, and harnessed to changing social ends. Hence, the centrality of children, both as symbolic figures and as objects of contested forms of socialization, in the contemporary politics of culture" (13).

18. I don't mean to offer a picture of the history of childhood that suggests a linear improvement over time regarding the protected status of children. But I do mean to argue that what is identified in discourses about what children need to flourish has improved over the years. Yet, and still, it is crucial to recognize that black children living in white America have not shared the same kind of protected status as white children. Indeed, one of the most compelling media images that galvanized more wide-ranging support for the civil rights movement was the image of young, black children being hosed by police—an image that shattered any sense that their childhood was being protected. And there was the media image of Ruby Bridges, the young, lone black girl to desegregate Birmingham schools, being escorted by police through angry mobs of white residents, and the four girls who died in the church bombing, which also dashed any illusion of a protected childhood for black children.

Notes to Part II Introduction

1. Self-representation is a term that needs clarification. I am using it in two senses—in both a psychological sense and in the creative sense of how one uses images, symbols, narratives, texts, and performance to tell about one's life.

   Psychoanalytically speaking, self-representations are the stuff of mental life—mental content, associations, and images that are formed out of identifications with significant others—identifications that are both conscious and unconscious. See Kathy Ewing's (1990) article, "The Illusion of Wholeness," in which she lays out and makes an important distinction between three different psychoanalytic definitions of the self. The first, and most general reference to "self" as person, is that which refers to the physical organism, psychological functioning, and social attributes. The second definition refers to self-representations—the relational self, that part of mental life that is formed out of identifications with significant others, which may be explicit and conscious or implicit and outside of conscious awareness; this is "the culturally shaped self that is the object of anthropological study" (245). The third is used by Kohut (1971, 1977) in his self-psychology, which has to do with primary psychic constellations—self as agent or self as actor. Ewing argues that this view of a self is most infused with culturally shaped biases about being bounded and autonomous (Ewing 1990: 245–255). My use of the notion of self-representation combines the second and third, as I am interested in the girls' relational worlds and how the self understands itself as agent or actor.

2. What I have to say about each form of artistic self-representation is based on several layers of information amassed while doing each activity: (1) tape recorded and transcribed classroom "talk" that took place during the activity sessions, including my questions and the girls' responses, the questions the girls asked of each other about their self-representations, and audience responses to the improvisational skits; (2) audio (and at times video taped) and transcribed skits of the girls' "pregnancy stories"; and (3) the statements the girls wrote (and rewrote) to accompany their self-portraits that became part of a collaborative book.

3. I am borrowing this language from cultural anthropologists Dorothy Holland et al. who write about the self- and identity-making process in the following way: "The self is a position from which meaning is made, a position that is 'addressed' by and 'answers' others and the world (the physical and cultural environment). In answering (which is the stuff of existence), the self 'authors' the world—including itself and others" (1998: 173).

4. Lila Abu-Lughod (1985) raises this as do others. Also see Lisa Delpit (2002) about how language form usage (in this case Black English) shapes attitudes toward the speaker, including assumptions about intelligence.

5. This form of popular theater is based on Boal (1979), *Theater of the Oppressed.*

6. Collage is akin to "bricolage," a concept used by the "Dadaists and Surrealists as a method that juxtaposed unrelated, incongruous elements in order to liberate understanding from the mystifications of straight-line thinking" (Paley 1995: 8); cultural anthropologists; and by cultural studies of youth (e.g., Hebdige 1988). The concept of collage also fits nicely with D. W. Winnicott's (1971) notion of the transitional process insofar as people use objects at hand, "found" in their immediate surroundings, to create something of their own that has emotional resonance and meaning. I will discuss this creative process more in part III.

7. I found that the girls were more comfortable with collage than with drawing, which I suspect might be true for many adolescents who equate "drawing" with figurative and representational art forms. The hand-painted paper was first introduced to me by book-artist, Robert Shreefter and is described in the next chapter.

8. I am drawing on an object-relations way of thinking about self-representation and development. From this perspective, "object" is used to mean a person, a part of a person, or a form of a relationship that has been internalized (also called self-other configurations) and is a part of our mental life, which in this case might be projected through an art form.

Notes to Chapter 3

1. Paste paper is a Japanese technique for making paper that my husband, Robert Shreefter, taught the PPPT girls to make. It involves mixing rice paste with tem-

pera paint and covering large sheets of paper with the thick colorful paste mixture. When the mixture is still wet, one can use various tools, such as a comb, to make patterns or give texture to the paper. The girls loved this activity and would proudly label the pieces they made and later would swap their paper goods with one another. One year the head teacher of the program declared that the activity was "too messy" and "unbecoming" for the girls to participate in and thus canceled the field trip to Robert's studio where the paper was to be made. That year, I brought scraps of paste paper from other school programs where Robert held paper- and book-making sessions.

2. In addition to the usual economic barriers that would hinder Tara's pursuit of higher education, I know that Tara, like most of the girls in the PPPT, won't have the necessary course requirements to enroll in the college preparatory track once she leaves the PPPT program and returns to her "regular" high school.

3. I later learned that some of my questions are similar to those designed by Jessica Davis (1996). I also found the work of child psychoanalyst Viktor Lowenfeld (1959) especially helpful. Despite more recent work in cognitive perspectives, his approach to exploring emotional content in children's art forms informed the questions I asked. He examined children's drawings and identified three main variations. First, is that human figures or parts of bodies may be exaggerated in size or some parts neglected or omitted, which conveys a child's subjective feelings about one's self-image being projected onto the drawing. For example, a child's drawing that is missing hands might suggest feelings of powerlessness or lack of agency. A second variation has to do with the form of the body (as stick figures, as witches, as monsters, as disembodied parts, etc.) that conveys subjective judgment of value. For example, a child drawing her babysitter as a monster might be conveying fearful feelings about the babysitter. And the third variation has to do with relationships between figures to suggest whether a situation is good or bad. For example, a child draws a picture of her family members making one sibling oversized compared to the other figures, which may be conveying specific feelings (good or bad) about that sibling. All three variations are found throughout the girls' self-portraits. There are pictures with missing body parts (mostly hands and feet); small figures in relation to bigger figures and objects (like houses, trees); and various bodily forms (e.g., abstract images like large balls; sea creatures meant to represent a girl's feelings; stick figures; paper-doll figures), all of which may or may not convey particular feelings and/or emotional conflicts being projected onto the drawings. I asked the girls about such variations—say, missing hands—to see what reasons they gave. Sometimes, a girl would talk about not wanting to "mess up" her picture by putting hands, a remark I considered related to artistic capabilities or aesthetic choices. Other times, a girl would be surprised by her own omission ("I didn't even notice that") or pay it little attention ("Hm, I see what you mean").

4. I found only two articles on pregnant girls' self and body image: Stenberg and Blinn (1993) and Matsuhashi and Felice (1991). Stenberg and Blinn point out that while "researchers have investigated adolescent perceptions of body and self, little research explores the changes in body image and self image in pregnant adolescents. Adolescent pregnancy is a complex issue. The pregnant teenager must address normal developmental tasks in addition to the challenges

brought on by pregnancy. Because of the dramatic physical changes during pregnancy, it is important to understand the pregnant adolescent's feelings about self and body" (284). They conducted a pilot study to explore changes over time in fourteen pregnant adolescents from school-based programs for pregnant adolescents throughout Idaho. Based on content analysis of daily diary entries from the girls, the researchers found the girls expressed negative feelings toward their bodies, appearing to "have as much difficulty adjusting to their new body image as do adult pregnant women (Slade 1977)" (288). These negative body images were fairly stable over the six-week period of the study, more stable than their negative feelings toward themselves, which tended to fluctuate (many of the girls reported "mood swings," which is common of both adolescence and pregnancy). It would be interesting to have pregnant girls make portraits of themselves over the course of their pregnancies as a way to trace changing body- and self-image. Matsuhashi and Felice (1991) found that third-trimester pregnant girls had a more positive body image than their never-pregnant peers. They also found that the pregnant girls in their study had higher self-identity and physical-self scores than their never-pregnant peers (using the Tennessee Self Concept Scale), suggesting that some girls may "be developing their own sexual identity through pregnancy" (314).

5. There are many ways to interpret the girls' artistic expression about their child-hood—perhaps they were seeking to represent things as they were (i.e., that they remember being cute or small) or to transcend what might have been (i.e., that they felt vulnerable or burdensome). Similarly, they might have written about their pictures as they *wish* they had been, or how they thought I, their peers, or their more general audience might want them to remember themselves.

6. Shannon's blue eyes made me think of Toni Morrison's (1993) book, *The Bluest Eye*, especially in light of the girls' persistent references to skin color and "good" hair. Morrison's main character wishes for blue eyes, and much of the book is about her confrontation with idealized white femininity, which, for the protagonist, generates both self-denigration and self-pride.

7. I will discuss Kendra's concern about offending me in part III, where I talk about negotiating racial and relational issues in fieldwork.

8. See N. Rooks for her discussion of similar sentiments about hair braiding that can be found "within African American culture (literary and recollected)" (1996: 287).

9. Noliwe Rooks (1996) writes about the politics of African American fashion and adornment, including recent cases where white school officials have sent home black schoolgirls for violating the school's ban on "extreme" hairstyling (corn-row braids) that might disrupt classroom learning. She examines recent appropriation of "black" hairstyles by white "trendsetters in fashion magazines," and makes the following astute observation: "beauty is primarily qualified by gender, raced when disqualified as beautiful, yet is always a joy to behold" (294).

It should also be noted that white girls are not exempt from being accused of drawing attention to themselves through dress or deportment at school. The point is that there are distinctive racial (and class) lenses through which girls are viewed and come to view themselves as desirable, worthy, valuable, and so forth.

10. Bonnie Ross Leadbeater and Niobe Way (2001), use this same metaphor, growing up hard and fast, to describe the lives of black, low-income girls in New York City.

11. See Mary Helen Washington (1991) for her analysis of coming-of-age stories among African American girls.

12. See Brumberg (1998); K. Martin (1996); A. Peterson et al. (1991); Rauste-von-Wright (1989) and D. Tolman (1994).

13. Kusserow (1999), argues against the notion that there is an undifferentiated model of self and individualism within American culture. Equally important, she argues that descriptions of the Western self have tended to be "middle class," ignoring the vast religious, ethnic, and class differences that exist among Americans.

14. Just as Kusserow (1999) argues against oversimplifying the East/West dichotomy regarding notions of self, she also seeks to avoid doing the same for differences among groups within the United States. "One of the challenges in defining individualism within an individualistic society is to avoid the temptation to begin stereotyping again, recreating the East/West bipolar homogeneity, only on a smaller scale, within the United States" (212).

15. This association between the "hard" working class and the "soft" middle class is a conventional one in the studies of British working-class culture (Willis 1977; Skeggs 1997). The related focus on "hard" and "soft" individualism proposed by Kusserow (1999) is probably a slightly different version of this same phemonenon. (I thank sociologist John Wilson, a self-declared "hard man" from England, for bringing this to my attention.)

16. See bell hooks's commentary in her book *Black Looks*. According to hooks:

> Indeed, a fundamental task of black critical thinkers has been the struggle to break with the hegemonic modes of seeing, thinking, and being that block our capacity to see ourselves oppositionally, to imagine, describe, and invent ourselves in ways that are liberatory. Without this, how can we challenge and invite non-black allies and friends to dare to look at us differently, to dare to break their colonizing gaze? (1992: 2)

It struck me that Tara was daring to seek a way to break the judgmental gaze she encounters in her everyday experience of teenage pregnancy.

17. This term is borrowed from Carla Massey's (1996) research with teenage girls in an East Harlem, New York City neighborhood. In an essay titled, "Body-Smarts" she explores issues of "language, the performance of identity and the mind-body problem" (75) that were expressed by one of the participants in her study, a girl named Karnett. Massey uses the term "body-smarts" to call attention to both the pain and the intelligence, the "despair and hope," the "pain and humor" with which Karnett spoke about her perceptions of difference (1996: 275).

18. See Carola and Marcelo Suarez-Orozco's (2001) work on immigration for a discussion of the role of emotional ties in the adaptation experience of immigrants. Also see Robert Shreefter's (2001) article in *Harvard Education Review* and the images Mexican American immigrant youth made about their immigration experience.

19. See Behar (1993) for her discussion of motherhood, martyrdom, and images of Madonna.

20. There are four ways that the PPPT girls depicted themselves in relation to their bodies. Each depiction sheds important light on conscious and unconscious identifications, images, and associations that define the girls' sense of self. The most common were "idealized" bodies—bodies depicted in doll-like form, either remembered from an innocent childhood or projected into the future, when life is good and sorted out. There were "imaginary" forms of bodies that were more dream-like or magical and tended to evoke associations with what life in a better world would be like (Clarise's self-portrait is an example). There were "abstract" bodily depictions through which a girl spoke about her inner life and feelings through abstract images, like the "big heavy ball that can't move" (Tara's picture). And finally, there were "real" bodies, those that consciously depicted a pregnant body.

21. This is but one of many examples of the way in which I was positioned as a "teacher," meant to "correct" the girls—a position that I took up in some ways (i.e., "teaching" them about writing haiku poems, for example) and worked against in other ways (i.e., refusing to follow school "rules"). The texts reproduced here represent those that were "corrected" before the collaborative books were photocopied; they are not in their original form with spelling or grammar errors.

22. It is worth noting that the PPPT girls' pictures, like many girls' drawings, were filled with hearts whose meanings are quite complicated and varied (broken hearts, hearts next to rainbows, and so forth). I wonder in what ways girls might use hearts as an expression of their disavowed anger that arises from their social condition and experience of oppression.

23. See Elaine Bell Kaplan (1997) whose book about black teenage motherhood suggests that, among other social injuries with which black girls living in poverty must cope, is what she calls the "poverty of relationships." She writes:

> Institutional oppressions do occur, and they are played out in a relational framework in which girls develop intentional strategies to form and sustain relationships with their significant others. These teenage mothers describe being disconnected from primary family relations, abandoned by their schools and by the men in their lives, and isolated from relations with other teenagers at a time of their adolescence, when it is most important that they experience positive relationships. These teen mothers developed their strategies to make up for the poverty of their relationships. (11)

24. This is what M. Zurmuehien (1992: 1) cites as being at the heart of art-making, moving from "merely doing something with materials" to reflecting on what one has made and thus, "making art" (quoted in Steve Thunder-McGuire 1994: 51).

Notes to Chapter 4

1. *Teen Voices* is a monthly magazine produced by teenagers who apply to be interns. Interns are selected from disadvantaged neighborhoods in Boston and are trained during the summer to do copyediting and learn critical media literacy skills.

2. See Jane Brown et al. (1994) for work on girls' use of media images in creating room culture.

3. These included discussions about Wesley Snipes and his interracial relationships; Vanessa Williams on her divorce and how she was dealing with life as a single mom; and Whitney Houston's stormy relationship with Bobby Brown.

4. Pregnancy was a time when I felt a heightened sensitivity to smells and tastes and I knew with certainty what foods would satisfy me on any given day. And I remembered that with each pregnancy I had had unique desires (hot fudge sundaes; scrambled eggs with crackers; and grits and biscuits).

5. See "consumption as rebellion" literature, Willis (1987), Hebdige (1988), McRobbie (1991).

6. It is interesting to note that in research conducted by Kathleen Bishop (2002) using this same exercise with two groups of girls (eight freshmen and eight seniors) with whom she met weekly over the course of one school year in a Newark, New Jersey, high school, she found that some girls selected media stars to represent themselves, explaining that they did so because these stars had been exposed to public scrutiny just as they felt they were. One girl, Tiffani, explained that she had chosen singer Lauryn Hill because she, Tiffani, is also on a "spiritual journey . . . but I wanna be more spiritual than her. . . . And I see that. I see a lot of respect coming in my future" (164). While none of the PPPT girls explicitly selected a media star to represent themselves, they certainly talked about identifying with this or that star who had faced hardship.

7. See Goldman (1992); Goldman and Papson (1996); McRobbie (1988); O'Barr (1994) for some examples.

8. I felt certain that my adolescent daughter and her friends would not make "Who am I?" collages with pictures of money and credit cards, so as an informal experiment, I asked her and her friends to make a collage (they were unaware of my reasons), and none of these collages contained images of money. It would be a fascinating cross-class and cross-ethnicity study to conduct with youth.

9. Chin cites Regina Austin (1994) and John Fiske (1994) for their work on the black-consumer-as-shoplifter issue.

10. See Eva Illouz (1997) for a similar argument about how class position shapes one's views about the role of commodities and money in romance. She found that the working-class people she interviewed emphasized the importance of money in seeking and sustaining romance, whereas the upper-middle-class, professional people in her study routinely expressed a disinterest in, and at times aversion to, the role that money can play in establishing romantic bonds. Illouz argues that her upper-middle-class respondents could afford to denounce money because they were further removed from economic insecurity.

11. See Luttrell (1997), especially chapter 2, "Stories from the Field."

12. Raymond Williams (1973) uses the term "structures of feelings" to refer to a constellation of emotions that arise from and are associated with specific class-based conditions and values.

13. See Katherine Newman's (1988) book, *Falling from Grace,* for an exploration of different versions of middle-class fears of falling. She compares the experiences of highly skilled engineers who were laid off in large numbers, with working-

class industrial crafts union members and displaced homemakers after divorce to shed insight on the meaning of class.

14. See Nichter (2000) for her discussion of African American girls' more alternative definitions of and standards for beauty. She found that the African American girls she interviewed were "more satisfied with their body weight and were less likely to diet than white or Latino girls" (159) and that they valued "attitude" and "style" and "making what they had work for them" rather than conforming to an ideal standard (166).

15. See my previous work on teachers' pets (1997) and a burgeoning literature on how teachers shape gendered self-understandings and identities in school, including Arnot (2002), and Mac an Ghaill (1994). I am especially interested in how these gendered self-understandings and identities are shaped by different school contexts (for example, how femininity means something different in an all-girls school than in a coed school).

    Skeggs's (1997) idea of performed narratives of gender draws on the groundbreaking work of Judith Butler (1990) and how girls and boys learn and are instructed in gender displays of emotion, deportment, speech, and so forth. Bourdieu (1977) would talk about this in terms of habitus—all the habits of mind and dispositions that boys and girls acquire in order to have a "feel" (as if it were natural) for masculinity and femininity.

16. The idea that black children preferred or envied whiteness was first introduced by Kenneth Clark (1963).

17. She reads from *Ebony,* November 1997, p. 190.

18. The girls' frank statements—like Kaela's, "I love black men" or Tanya's "the importance of men" (spoken as "the importance of black men")—put me in mind of the efforts of Black feminists to divide their critiques of sexism within the African American community from their love of and commitment to black men. See Springer (2002:1074) for her discussion of this tension.

19. Holland and Eisenhart (1990) found that the African American young women (college students) in their study held the same views about not revealing too much information about their romantic interests for fear it might be used against them, which was not the case for the white young women in their study.

20. There are unconscious connections between adult love and maternal love. Anthropologist Chris McCollum (2000) writes persuasively that American cultural models of adult love are premised on the psychodynamics of early maternal-child bonds of love.

21. In North Carolina, legislation mandates that discussions about sex in classrooms emphasize abstinence until marriage. Teachers in the program complained how this legislation makes no sense when working with pregnant teens.

22. See Stack (2001); Stack (forthcoming); and Newman (1999) for discussions about low-wage work among teenagers.

23. I wondered if the silence was related to a "game" the girls had devised and played the week before. The game was inventive and reflective. It went like this. Each girl was to write five positive words about herself. I am . . . Then, Violet gathered the statements and read them aloud. Then she asked if the statements sounded "right." Every statement that sounded "right" to the girls was put in a pile; those that sounded false, were put in another pile. Disagreements were handled case by case, and if no agreement could be found, the phrase was not

put in either pile. The two piles that emerged were as follows. Phrases that sound "right": I am beautiful; I am wise; I am strong; I am smart; I am intelligent; I am funny. The pile for what sounded "false": I am kind, I am sweet, I am nice, I am loving. The phrase upon which they could not agree was, I am responsible. Celia's phrases on her collage echoed those in the false pile. Perhaps, remembering this kept some of the girls quiet (Celia had not been in class for this game). Perhaps not.

24. Later, as I reviewed the tape I realized that the conversation turned to food because one of the girls joked about what was "American" food, whereupon someone answered, "hamburgers."

25. The history of whiteness in America tells us that at one point in time, Irish immigrants and Jewish immigrants were not considered "white." Ruth Frankenberg (1993) suggests that the meaning of whiteness takes place in "an already constituted field of racialized relations, material and conceptual" (142), and these relations need to be acknowledged in any definition.

Notes to Chapter 5

1. I recorded over one hundred improvisations comprising some three hundred pages of transcribed text.

2. See Stanton Wortham's (2001) book on narrative analysis for a good discussion of these two aspects of storytelling. See Riessman (1993, 2002a and b); Bauman (1986); Bamberg (1997); Harré and van Langenhove (1999); Ochs and Capps (1999) for what these narrative theorists call social positioning in stories.

3. See chapter 6, for more discussion about how I selected the particular arts-based activities that I did. Using arts-based activities that are "local" to the specific group of students with whom one is working is key.

4. See Boal (1979) who draws upon the work of Paulo Freire. See also Grumet (1987) in her discussion about autobiographical narratives.

5. See Chodorow (1978). These scenes, which feature pregnancy and motherhood as a means of feminine identification, would seem to confirm Chodorow's argument.

6. Deirdre Kelly (1996) found the same in her work with pregnant teenagers.

7. See Riessman (2000: 113) and her work on rethinking Goffman's concept of stigma.

8. See Emily Martin (1987) for her discussion of the history of medical discourse and how it fragments the self and body, treating the body as machine and doctor as technician. See Ehrenreich and English (1973), Rothman (1994), Shaw (1974), and Rapp (1999) for historical and ethnographic discussions of the medicalization of pregnancy and birth.

9. See Emily Martin (1987) for her description of medical metaphors that separate the self from the body. The following central metaphors organized interviews she conducted with women: "Your self is separate from your body. . . . your body is something your self has to adjust to or cope with. . . . Your body needs to be controlled by your self. . . . Your body sends you signals. . . . Menstruation, menopause, labor, birthing and their component stages are states you go through or things that happen to you (not actions you do). . . . Menstruation, menopause and birth contractions are separate from the self. They are "*the*

contractions," *the* hot flashes (not *mine*); they 'come on'; women 'get them.'"
(77–78)

10. When I was recruited to play the nurse, I always played the "good" nurse, asking a girl if she had any questions or concerns she wanted to talk about. I tended to be asked medical questions, especially about childbirth: "Is it going to hurt? What does it feel like to have your water break? How many hours will it take?" Or I tended to be asked legal questions, "What would happen if I ran away? Could my baby's father take my baby from me?"

11. Here is another example of the "strongblackwoman" image and identity being presented.

12. These scenes were complicated by the fact that it was often the case that a black girl was "turning out" a black nurse, and indeed this was a conversation that occurred when the girls would compare their experiences at a local clinic and at the downtown hospital where, at the clinic, they were more likely to encounter black nurses and, at the downtown hospital, more likely to encounter white nurses.

13. Kelly (1996, 2000) who found these same warnings.

14. See Hinshelwood (1989), Segal (1979), Sayers (1991, 2000) for books that summarize Klein's views.

15. This parallels Bruno Bettleheim's (1987) argument about the role that fairytales with "bad" mother figures play for children, that children are drawn to stories about "bad" mother figures so that they can avoid dealing with their own conflicting feelings toward their mothers.

16. It strikes me that these mother-daughter strategies are also reflective of avoidant cultural strategies, if not policies regarding sexual knowledge, for example, the "don't ask, don't tell" policy regarding homosexuality in the U.S. Armed Forces and the ever-changing battles over sex education in schools.

17. See Kaplan (1997) for her discussion of fraught mother-daughter relationships among black teenage mothers.

18. See Teri Apter (1990) who also emphasizes that the story of female adolescence has overemphasized girls' desires for separation over their search for connection. I agree, and want to extend this argument further to say that by acknowledging girls' simultaneous desires for separation, connection, identification and disidentification, we are also acknowledging another version of selfhood and agency that more closely reflects the logic of decision making that women (as mothers and as daughters) face.

19. See Patricia Hill Collins (1991) for her discussion of alternative meanings of motherhood within Black families, and Suzanne Carothers (1990) on social interactions between Black working mothers and their daughters.

Notes to Re-Representing Youth Worlds, Identities, and Relationships

1. Feminist researcher Deborah Tolman (1996) provides an especially poignant illustration of this familiar way of thinking among girls. She interviewed Inez, a sixteen-year-old Puerto Rican girl who "knows she is feeling desires 'when my body says yes.'" Inez's description of the relationship between her mind and her

body is all-too familiar: "My body does not control my mind. My mind controls my body, and if my body gets into the pleasure mood, my mind is gonna tell him no. And it can happen, because I said so, because I control you, and my mind is lookin' towards my body" (262).

2. The notable exception is feminist research and education. See J. Irvine (2002) for an excellent account of the battles over sex education in the United States and the role feminism has played in shaping the discussion.

3. It is also the case that maternal ambivalence is quite a threatening notion, as is perhaps best exemplified by the sensationalism of news media reports on mothers who abandon or kill their children.

Notes to Chapter 6

1. This is a phrase borrowed from Karen McCarthy Brown (1991) whose ethnographic work has provided me both inspiration and guidance.

2. Martin (1996) also found that girls and boys narrate the experience of adolescence differently, with girls stressing the difficulties and the ups and downs, and boys being more positive. She relates this finding to the fact that childhood produces more difficulties for boys, while adolescence is considered more difficult for girls.

3. American adulthood, in a sense, is marked by the capacity to see one's life with enough distance/perspective so that a life story can be told. Indeed, the American culture of adulthood offers resources and repertoires that adults draw on to construct meaning in their lives. For example, sociolinguist and life narrative theorist Charlotte Linde (1993) argues that the "life story" is one such cultural repertoire that American adults adopt to show that their lives have coherence, and that they are moral members of particular groups. See Mishler (1986), Chase (1995), and Middleton (1993) for examples of people telling career narratives as a means of establishing their adult identities.

    I would argue that American culture provides young people with distinctive resources and repertoires that encourage them to see themselves and their lives in flux (including consumerism, and the fashion, music, and entertainment industries).

4. One criticism of the literature on young people's use of popular culture is that it tends to focus either on popular culture as "toxic" or it tends to celebrate or romanticize young people's use of it (Buckingham 1994). I believe there is a need for more systematic research to provide insight for educators about the role of popular culture in young people's lives and learning.

5. Mostly the girls played the role of "Oprah" with each other, but on a few occasions I was asked to take the "Oprah" part. I wondered whether the girls imagined that my interest in their life stories was akin to Oprah's in that I was looking for "confessions" as the talk show hosts are said to seek.

6. See Linde (1993) for her discussion of the distinction between elicited and spontaneously produced narratives (60–61). One of the characteristics of spontaneously produced narratives is that they are performed, that is, "acted out to give the addressee an opportunity to experience the event" (61). Among other differences, Linde notes that "the form of evaluation in elicited narratives may

differ from that in spontaneous narrative, since spontaneous narrative may include a component of negotiation between the primary speaker and the other interlocutors—a negotiation that an interviewer may be unwilling to engage in, since it involves a direct effort to bias the data the speaker may give" (61). This is definitely the case in the girls' role plays about visiting the clinic or at home telling their mothers, where other interlocutors (including those girls who chose to use the "freeze" option I had introduced) shaped the stories being told.

7. Myerhoff (1978) documented the lives of elderly members of a Jewish cultural center in Venice, California, in a film and an ethnographic text entitled, *Number Our Days*. She was inspired by what she considered to be a crisis of invisibility among elderly and marginalized people, a crisis that she, as an ethnographer, sought to address.

8. Other ethnographers have taken this approach, including Shirley Brice Heath (1983) who used storytelling activities in her comparative study about black and white, working-class children's language use and development in communities and schools.

9. My approach is part of a family of research often called "action-research." However, people seem to be using this term to refer to such a wide range of research, including consulting and evaluation, that it has lost some of its initial resonance for me. Nonetheless, I believe research is most useful when it is participative, when it engages researchers and those who are researched in collaborative and mutually beneficial relationships, and when it is careful not to confuse "what is" with what should or could be. See Peter Reason and Hilary Bradbury (2001) for their inclusive volume about action research.

10. Others have studied the use of teen magazines including Buckingham (1994) and Finders (1997).

11. I could have introduced other arts-based activities, such as photography, and this would have yielded yet another set of insights. In future work I hope to adapt the photo-voice method (Wang 1997; 1999). There are interesting parallels between conversations about representation and misrepresentation generated by the activities I designed and those that are reportedly sparked in response to photographs that subjects take of their own communities.

12. See Lykes et al. (2001) for their discussion of using a version of the photovoice method with rural women in Guatemala.

13. I understand empathy in the case of ethnography as being a way of doing and knowing that is attuned to complex psychological constellations of an "other." Kohut (1971) defined empathy as "a mode of cognition which is specifically attuned to the perception of complex psychological configurations" (300).

14. Psychoanalytically speaking, there are several concepts that help analysts understand the nature of self and other knowledge, including the concept of counter-transference (Brenner 1982), projective identification (Klein 1975; Moore and Fine 1995), and the most recent concept of enactment (Jacobs 1990). See Chodorow (1999) for her excellent discussion of the parallel evolution of the fields of relational psychoanalysis and ethnography regarding transference and counter-transference. I have chosen to avoid using these clinical terms because of the baggage they carry for many readers.

15. See Luttrell (1997) for a discussion of how I experienced myself differently in relation to the two groups of women I interviewed.

16. I am adapting Lisa Delpit's (1995) phrase about "teaching other people's children" because I believe that my experience as an ethnographer parallels the experience of many white, female, middle-class teachers who work with poor children of color in urban schools. Their wide-ranging feelings of maternal guilt, anger, and so forth strike me as being minimized and undertheorized within educational discourse, which does not well serve either the teachers or their student charges.

17. One friendly reader of this chapter remarked that perhaps the difference between the girls and my reaction to the "teasing game" had to do with our respective development—"that the girls were acting like the children they are versus you acting like the grown up mother you are." While this could surely be a partial explanation, it doesn't explain the routine and patterned nature of the game or my heightened sense of discomfort each time it would occur.

18. I was influenced by the work of Jean Briggs (1998), *Inuit Morality Play*, and the varied ways in which parents teach children about the basic values of their worlds.

19. Attention to these dynamics is missing in contemporary discussions about the role of women in girls' development, including feminist accounts such as Brown and Gilligan (1992).

20. Anne Anlin Cheng (2002) writes about the hidden injuries of racism and the process of racial socialization in a way I find useful:

> To reduce the issue of psychical injury to a simplistic and prescriptive pronouncement of black self-hatred is to miss a fundamental insight revealed by Clark's work and the works of those after him: that the psychology being dramatized by those children in the doll tests reveals the results, not the cause of social relations. . . . Kenneth Clark's experiment in those dusty classrooms over fifty years ago does not give us information about the psyche of black children per se: rather it gave us a dramatization of an *education* of black children. (her emphasis, 15, 19)

21. These terms are borrowed from Signathia Fordham (1996: 364–365). See her discussion of the effects of the color line and her insightful commentary that "African Americans are not unique or 'weird' in their preoccupation with 'light skin color'" (365).

22. See Rosaldo (1989), Behar (1996) and Rabinow (1977) in anthropology; Denzin (1989), Ellis (1991a, 1991b), Ellis and Weinstein (1986), Fine (1998), Reinharz (1997), Richardson (1997), Krieger (1991), Riessman (2002a & b), in sociology, all of whom are writing about these issues.

23. Few anthropologists would want their work described this way.

24. The same is said about relational psychoanalysis, see Lewis Aron (1996).

25. See the book, *Crestwood Heights*, by Seely et al. (1956), a classic study of middle-class community life. When I read it I recognized it as an account of upward mobility that resonated with my own experience.

26. Containing is a communicative and interpretive process that takes place initially between infant and mother. The baby puts out a wide range of expressive messages (feelings, thoughts) to which the mother responds. A mother picks up on some (but not all) expressed feelings, needs, desires, and notices which ones might be missing. She may respond differently according to several things,

including her own relational history and the specific circumstances of the day. Containing involves empathy and being receptive to another's mind, including split-off parts of one's own mind, which in the case of mothers, can be unbearable feelings of anger toward or power over the baby, which are not only personally difficult to tolerate, but culturally unacceptable as part of the ideal of motherhood. Bion (1970) suggested that part of human development is learning to make use of symbols, thoughts, and primary relationships to serve the function for which a mother previously used with the infant as we seek to make sense of emotions we have had and can't explain or comprehend. I view the ethnographic relationship, like the analytic relationship, as serving a containing function, for both the researcher and researched. (See Bion 1977, Billow 2000).

27. I write about trying to avoid the strong emotions of one my interviewees in my previous study (1997, chapter 7).

28. "Engaging the unsayable" was formerly called "interpretive poetics" (Rogers et al. 1999).

29. Many others have also written about the co-construction of interviews and storytelling, for example Mishler (1986, 1999), Riessman (2002a and b), Borland (1991). The distinction in the Rogers et al., method is that it is finely tuned to listen for unconscious language play.

30. To find my way through the dilemmas of ethnographic representation I have drawn inspiration from many feminist researchers, including those "women writing culture" whom Behar and Gordon (1995) feature as underappreciated foremothers of anthropology (i.e., Elsie Clews Parson, Ruth Benedict, Ella Cara Deloria, Zora Neal Hurston, Ruth Landes, Margaret Mead, Barbara Myerhoff, Alice Walker, and Jean Briggs).

31. See Wacquant's (2002) critique of recent ethnographic studies of urban poverty and the responses to it by Newman (2002) for a provocative discussion of these issues.

Notes to Chapter 7

1. These critics represent what is often referred to as social reproduction theories or critical pedagogy, and include scholars such as Bowles and Gintis, Bourdieu, Bernstein, Willis, McCarthy, Apple, Giroux. Feminist critics have focused on how schools reproduce gender and class inequalities and critical race theorists have clarified how schools maintain racial inequality. For one of the best reviews of this literature see the introduction to *The Cultural Production of Educated Person*, by Levinson, Foley, and Holland (1996).

2. For example, see Olsen (1997), MacLeod (1995), Fine (1991), Weis (1990), Oakes (1985), Willis (1977) .

3. See also Castenell and Pinar (1993).

4. Sociologist Hinshelwood (1989) calls these organizational responses the "projective life of institutions."

5. See D. Cohen and H. Hill (2001); L. Darling-Hammond et al. (1995); R. F. Elmore, C. Abelmann, and S. Fuhrman, (1996); S. Fuhrman (1999); and Popham (2002) for discussions about varied ways to measure student performance, and to think about accountability as a means of school reform.

6. We might want to ask why pregnancy as a source for learning is so threatening for schools to address. Perhaps this is a way of controlling women's power and their generativity, an argument proposed by Madeleine Grumet (1988) in her book *Bitter Milk*. She describes the educational pitting of mind against body, as well as the cultural devaluation of teaching as connected parts of the process of gender socialization and inequality in schooling.

7. According to Jessica Benjamin (1995), the same is true for the parent who relates to the baby through her or his transitional object: ". . . for the parent is usually excited by the infant's reaction, not by the toy itself. The parent is in fact taking pleasure in *contacting the child's mind*." (her emphasis) (34–35)

References

American Association of University Women Educational Foundation. 1992. *How Schools Shortchange Girls: A Study of Major Findings on Girls and Education.* AAUW Education Foundation and National Education Association.

Abrahamse, Allan F., Peter A. Morrison, and Linda J. Wait. 1988. *Beyond Stereotypes: Who Becomes a Single Teenage Mother?* Santa Monica, CA: Rand.

Abu-Lughod, Lila. 1985. *Writing Women's Worlds: Bedouin Stories.* Berkeley: University of California Press.

Alan Guttmacher Institute. 1976. *11 Million Teenagers: What Can Be Done About the Epidemic of Adolescent Pregnancies in the United States.* New York: Alan Guttmacher Institute.

Altman, Neil. 1995. *The Analyst in the Inner City: Race, Class, and Culture Through a Psychoanalytic Lens.* Hillsdale, NJ: Analytic Press.

Anderson-Levitt, Kathryn. 1996. "Behind Schedule: Batch-Produced Children in French and U.S. Classrooms." In *The Cultural Production of the Educated Person,* edited by Bradley Levinson, Douglas Foley, and Dorothy Holland. Albany, NY: State University Press.

Apter, T. E. 1990. *Altered Loves: Mothers and Daughters During Adolescence.* New York: St. Martin's Press.

Arnot, Madeline. 2002. *Reproducing Gender? Essays on Educational Theory and Feminist Politics.* London and New York: Routledge.

Aron, Lewis. 1996. *A Meeting of Minds: Mutuality in Psychoanalysis.* Hillside, NJ: Analytic Press.

Austin, Regina. 1994. "'A Nation of Thieves': Consumption, Commerce, and the Black Public Sphere." *Public Culture* 7 (1): 225–248.

Balint, Enid. 1993. *Before I Was I: Psychoanalysis and the Imagination.* London: Free Association Books; New York: Guilford Press.

Bamberg, Michael. 1997. "Positioning between Structure and Performance." In "Oral Version of Personal Experience: Three Decades of Narrative Analysis" (special issue), edited by M. G. W. Bamberg, *Journal of Narrative and Life History* 7:335–42.

Bauman, Richard. 1986. *Story, Performance, and Event: Contextual Studies of Oral Narrative.* Cambridge and New York: Cambridge University Press.

Becker, Howard Saul. 1986. *Doing Things Together.* Evanston, Ill.: Northwestern University.

Behar, Ruth. 1993. *Translated Woman: Crossing the Border With Esperanza's Story.* Boston: Beacon Press.

———. 1996. *The Vulnerable Observer: Anthropology that Breaks Your Heart.* Boston: Beacon Press.

Behar, Ruth, and Deborah Gordon (Eds.). 1995. *Women Writing Culture.* Berkeley, CA: University of California Press.

Benjamin, Jessica. 1988. *Bonds of Love: Psychoanalysis, Feminism and the Problem of Domination.* New York: Pantheon Books.

———. 1995. *Like Subjects, Love Objects: Essays on Recognition and Sexual Difference.* New Haven, CT: Yale University Press.

Berger, John. 1972. *Ways of Seeing.* New York: Penguin Books.

Bettleheim, Bruno. 1987. *The Uses of Enchantment: The Meaning and Importance of Fairy Tales.* New York: Vintage.

Bhabha, Homi. 1983. "The Other Question: Homi K. Bhabha Reconsiders the Stereotype and Colonial Discourse." *Screen* 24 (6): 18–36.

Billow, R. M. 2000. "From Countertransference to Passion." *Psychoanalytic Quarterly* 69: 93–119.

Bion, Wilfred R. 1977. "Attention and Interpretation." In *Seven Servants: Four Works by Wilfred R. Bion.* New York: Aronson.

Bishop, Kathleen. 2002. *Moral Development in Context: Urban Girls Tell Tales Out of School.* Dissertation. Drew University. Casperson School of Graduate Studies.

Boal, Augusto. 1979. *Theater of the Oppressed*, translated by Charles A. and Maria-Odilia Leaf. New York: Urizen Books.

Borland, Katherine. 1991. "That's Not What I Said": Interpretive Conflict in Oral Narrative Research." In *Women's Words: The Feminist Practice of Oral History.* edited by Sherna Berger Gluck and Daphne Patai. New York and London: Routledge.

Bourdieu, Pierre. 1977. *Outline of a Theory of Practice.* Cambridge: Cambridge University Press.

———. 1996. "Understanding." *Theory, Culture, & Society* 13 (2): 17–37.

Brenner, Charles. 1982. *The Mind in Conflict.* New York: International Universities Press.

Briggs, Jean L. 1970. *Never in Anger: Portrait of an Eskimo Family.* Cambridge: Harvard University Press.

———. 1998. *Inuit Morality Play: The Emotional Education of a Three-Year-Old.* New Haven, CT: Yale University Press.

Brooks-Gunn, Jeanne, and Anne Petersen. 1983. *Girls at Puberty: Biological and Psychosocial Perspectives.* New York: Plenum Press.

Brown, J. Larry, and Larry W. Beeferman. 2001. "What Comes After Welfare Reform?" in *Boston Review* (December 13, 2001). Retrieved from www.bostonreview.mit.edu/BR26.6/brown.html.

Brown, J., C. Dykers, J. Steele, and A. White (1994). "Teenage Room Culture: Where Media and Identities Intersect." *Communication Research,* 21 (6): 813–827.

Brown, Karen McCarthy. 1991. *Mama Lola: A Vodou Priestess in Brooklyn.* Berkeley: University of California Press.

Brown, Lyn Mikel. 1998. *Raising Their Voices: The Politics of Girls' Anger.* Cambridge, MA: Harvard University Press.

Brown, Lyn Mikel, and Carol Gilligan. 1992. *Meeting at the Crossroads: Women's Psychology and Girls' Development.* Cambridge, MA and London, Eng.: Harvard University Press.

Brumberg, Joan Jacobs. 1998. *The Body Project: An Intimate History of American Girls.* New York: Vintage Books.

Buckingham, David. 1994. *Cultural Studies Goes to School: Reading and Teaching Popular Media.* Washington, DC: Taylor and Francis.

Burdell, Patricia. 1996. "Teen Mothers in High School: Tracking Their Curriculum." In *Review of Research in Education,* 21, edited by M. Apple. Washington, DC: AERA Publishing.

———. 1998. "Young Mothers as High School Students: Moving Toward a New Century." In *Education and Urban Society* 30 (2): 207–223.

Burton, Linda. 1990. "Teenage Childbearing as an Alternative Life-Course Strategy in Multigenerational Black Families." *Human Nature* 1:123–43.

Burton, Linda, and Vern Bengston. 1985. "Black Grandmothers: Issues of Timing and Continuity of Roles." In *Grandparenthood,* edited by Vern Bengston and J. Robertson. Newbury Park, CA.: Sage Publications.

Burton, L. M., D. A. Obeidallah, and K. Allison. 1996. "Ethnographic Insights on Social Context and Adolescent Development Among Inner-City African-American Teens." In *Ethnography and Human Development: Context and Meaning in Social Inquiry,* edited by R. Jessor, A. Colby, and R. A. Shweder (pp. 395–418). Chicago: University of Chicago Press.

Butler, Judith. 1990. *Gender Trouble: Feminism and the Subversion of Identity.* New York: Routledge.

Carothers, Suzanne. 1990. "Catching Sense: Learning from Our Mothers to Be Black and Female." In *Uncertain Terms: Negotiating Gender in American Culture,* edited by Faye Ginsburg and Anna Tsing. Boston: Beacon Press.

Castenell, Louis, and William Pinar (Eds.). 1993. *Understanding Curriculum as Racial Text: Representations of Identity and Difference in Education.* Albany, NY: State University of New York Press.

Chase, Susan. 1995. *Ambiguous Empowerment: The Work Narratives of Women School Superintendents.* Amherst, MA: University of Massachusetts Press.

Cheng, Anne Anlin. 2002. *The Melancholy of Race: Psychoanalysis, Assimilation, and Hidden Grief.* New York: Oxford University Press.

Chin, Elizabeth. 2001. *Purchasing Power: Black Kids and American Consumer Culture.* Minneapolis: University of Minnesota Press.

Chodorow, Nancy. 1978. *The Reproduction of Mothering: Psychoanalysis and the Sociology of Gender.* Berkeley: University of California Press.

———. 1995. "Gender as a Personal and Cultural Construction." *Signs: Journal of Women in Culture and Society* 20 (3): 516–544.

———.1999. *The Power of Feelings: Personal Meaning in Psychoanalysis, Gender and Culture.* New Haven and London: Yale University Press.

Chodorow, Nancy, and Susan Contratto. 1982. "The Fantasy of the Perfect Mother." In *Rethinking the Family: Some Feminist Questions,* edited by Barrie Thorne and Marilyn Yalom (pp. 54–75). New York: Longman.

Clark, Kenneth Bancroft. 1963. *Prejudice and Your Child.* Boston: Beacon Press.

Cohen, David and Heather Hill. 2001. *Learning Policy: When State Education Reform Works.* New Haven and London: Yale University Press.

Collins, Patricia Hill. 1990. *Black Feminist Thought: Knowledge, Consciousness and the Politics of Empowerment*. London: HarperCollins Academic.

———. 1991. "The Meaning of Motherhood in Black Culture and Black Mother-Daughter Relationships." In *Double Stitch: Black Women Write about Mothers and Daughters*, edited by P. Bell-Scott et al. New York: Harper Perennial.

Darling-Hammond, Linda, Jacqueline Ancess, and Beverly Falk. 1995. *Authentic Assessment in Action: Studies of Schools and Students at Work*. New York and London: Teachers College.

Davis, Angela Y. 1981. *Women, Race, & Class*. New York: Vintage Books.

Davis, Fred. 1992. *Fashion, Culture and Identity*. Chicago, IL: University of Chicago Press.

Davis, Jessica. 1996. The MUSE BOOK (Museums Writing with Schools in Education: Building our Knowledge). Cambridge, MA: Presidents and Fellows of Harvard College.

Debold, Elizabeth, Lyn Mikel Brown, Susan Weesen, and Geraldine Kearse Brookins. 1999. "Cultivating Hardiness Zones for Adolescent Girls: A Reconceptualization of Resilience in Relationships with Caring Adults." In *Beyond Appearance: A New Look at Adolescent Girls*, edited by Noreen G. Johnson, Michael C. Roberts, and Judith Worell. Washington, DC: American Psychological Association.

Delpit, Lisa D. 1995. *Other People's Children: Cultural Conflict in the Classroom*. New York: New Press.

Delpit, Lisa and Joanne Kilgour Dowdy. (Eds.). 2002. *The Skin That We Speak: Thoughts on Language and Culture in the Classroom*. New York: The New Press.

Denzin, Norman K. 1989. *Interpretive Interactionism*. Newbury Park, CA: Sage Publications.

Deri, Susan K. 1984. *Symbolization and creativity*. New York, NY: International Universities Press.

Devereux, George. 1967. *From Anxiety to Method in Behavioral Sciences*. The Hague: Mouton.

Dimen, Muriel. 1993. "Anxiety and Alienation: Class, Money, and Psychoanalysis." Presented at the spring meeting of the Division of Psychoanalysis, American Psychological Association, New York.

———. 1994. "Money, Love, and Hate: Contradiction and Paradox in Psychoanalysis." *Psychoanalytic Dialogues* 4: 69–100.

Dimitriadis, Greg. 2001a. "'In the Clique': Popular Culture, Constructions of Place, and the Everyday Lives of Urban Youth." *Anthropology & Education Quarterly* 32 (1): 29–51.

———. 2001b. *Performing Identity/Performing Culture: Hip-Hop as Text Pedagogy*. New York: P. Lang.

Dryfoos. J. G. 1988. "Using Existing Research to Develop a Comprehensive Prevention Program." *Family Planning Perspectives* 22 (3): 211–223.

Ehrenreich, Barbara. 1989. *Fear of Falling: The Inner Life of the Middle Class*. New York: Pantheon Books.

Ehrenreich, Barbara, and Deirdre English. 1973. *Complaints and Disorders: The Sexual Politics of Sickness*. Old Westbury, NY: Feminist Press.

Ellis, Carolyn. 1991a. "Emotional Sociology." *Studies in Symbolic Interaction* 12: 123–145.

————. 1991b. "Sociological Introspection and Emotional Experience." *Symbolic Interaction* 14 (1):23–50.

Ellis, C. and E. Weinstein. 1986. "Jealousy and the Social Psychology of Emotional Experience." *Journal of Social and Personal Relationships* 3 (3): 337–357.

Elmore, Richard. 2002. "The Limits of Change." *Harvard Education Letter,* Jan/Feb.

Elmore, Richard, C. Abelmann, and S.H. Fuhrman. 1996. "The new accountability in state education policy." In *Holding Schools Accountable: Performance-based Reform in Education,* edited by H. Ladd. Washington, DC: The Brookings Institution.

Erchak, Gerald Michael. 1992. *The Anthropology of Self and Behavior.* New Brunswick, NJ: Rutgers University Press.

Erikson, Erik. 1968. *Identity, Youth, and Crisis.* New York: W. W. Norton.

Erkut, Sumru, and Fern Marx. 1995. *Raising Competent Girls: An Exploratory Study of Diversity in Girls' Views of Liking One's Self.* Wellesley, MA: Center for Research on Women, Wellesley College.

Ewing, K. P. 1990. "Can Psychoanalytic Theories Explain the Pakistani Woman? Intra-psychic Autonomy and Interpersonal Engagement in the Extended Family." *Ethos* 19: 131–160.

Finders, Margaret. 1997. *Just Girls: Hidden Literacies and Life in Junior High.* New York: Teachers College Press.

Fine, Michelle. 1988. "Sexuality, Schooling, and Adolescent Females: The Missing Discourse of Desire." *Harvard Educational Review* 58: 29–53.

————. 1991. *Framing Dropouts: Notes on the Politics of an Urban Public High School.* Albany: State University Press.

————. 1998. "Working The Hyphen: Reinventing Self and Other in Qualitative Research." In *The Landscape of Qualitative Research: Theories and Issues,* edited by N. K. Denzin and Y. S. Lincoln. Thousand Oaks, CA: Sage.

Fiske, John. 1994. *Media Matters: Everyday Culture and Political Change.* Minneapolis: University of Minnesota Press.

Fordham, Signathia. 1996. *Blacked Out: Dilemmas of Race, Identity, and Success at Capital High.* Chicago: University of Chicago Press.

Foucault, Michel. 1979. *Discipline and punish: The Birth of the Prison.* New York: Basic Books.

————. 1980. *A History of Sexuality* (Vol. 1). New York: Vintage.

Frankenberg, Ruth. 1993. *White Women, Race Matters: The Social Construction of Whiteness.* Minneapolis: University of Minnesota Press.

Fuhrman, Susan. 1999. "The New Accountability." In *Policy Briefs: Reporting on Issues in Education Reform,* published by the Consortium for Policy Research in Education (CPRE).

Furstenberg, Frank. 1991. "As the Pendulum Swings: Teenage Childbearing and Social Concern." *Family Relations* 40: 127–138.

————. 1998. "When Will Teenage Childbearing Become a Problem? The Implications of Western Experience for Developing Countries." *Studies in Family Planning.* 29 (2): 246–254.

Furstenberg, Frank, Jeanne Brooks-Gunn, and S. Philip Morgan. 1987. *Adolescent Mothers in Later Life.* New York: Cambridge University Press.

Geertz, Clifford, 1973. "Thick Description: Toward an Interpretive Theory of Culture." In *The Interpretation of Cultures*. New York: Basic Books.

———. 1988. *Works and Lives*. Stanford, CA: Stanford University Press.

———. 1997. "From the Native's Point of View: On the Nature of Anthropological Understanding." In *Interpretive Social Science: A Reader*, edited by Paul Rabinow and William M. Sullivan. Berkeley: University of California Press.

———. 1998. "Deep Hanging Out." *The New York Review of Books*. October 22.

Geronimus, Arline T. and Sanders Korenman. 1992. "The Socioeconomic Consequences of Teen Childbearing Reconsidered." *Quarterly Journal of Economics* 107 (4): 1187–1214.

Giddens, Anthony. 1991. *Modernity and Self-Identity: Self and Society in the Late Modern Age*. Stanford, CA: Stanford University Press.

Gilligan, Carol. 1982. *In a Different Voice: Psychological Theory and Women's Development*. Cambridge, MA: Harvard University Press.

Giroux, Henry and Roger Simon and Contributors. 1989. *Popular Culture, Schooling, and Everyday Life*. Granby, MA: Bergin & Garvey, Inc.

Goffman, Erving. 1963. *Stigma: Notes on the Management of Spoiled Identity*. Englewood Cliffs, NJ: Prentice-Hall.

Goldman, Robert. 1992. *Reading Ads Socially*. London and New York: Routledge.

Goldman, Robert and Stephen Papson. 1996. *Sign Wars: The Cluttered Landscape of Advertising*. New York: Guilford Press.

Goodman, Steven E. 1968. "Trends and Goals in Schooling for Pregnant Girls and Teenage Mothers." *Effective Services for Unmarried Parents and Their Children*. New York: National Council on Illegitimacy.

Gordon, Linda. 1990. *Woman, The State and Welfare*. Madison, WI: The University of Wisconsin Press.

Greenburg, Bradley S., Jane D. Brown, and Nancy Buerkel-Rothfuss. 1993. *Media, Sex, and the Adolescent*. Cresskill, NJ: Hampton Press.

Griffin, Christine. 1993. *Representations of Youth: The Study of Youth and Adolescence in Britain and America*. Cambridge, MA: Polity Press.

Grumet, Madeline. 1987. "The Politics of Personal Knowledge." *Curriculum Inquiry* 17:320–329.

———. 1988. *Bitter Milk: Women and Teaching*. Amherst: University of Massachusetts Press.

Hall, Jacquelyn Dowd. 1983. "'The Mind that Burns in Each Body': Women, Rape, and Racial Violence." In *Powers of Desire: The Politics of Sexuality*, edited by Ann Snitow, Christine Stansell, and Sharon Thompson. New York: Monthly Review Press.

Harré, R. and L. van Langenhove (Eds.) 1999. *Positioning Theory*, Malden, MA.: Blackwell Publishers.

Heath, Shirley Brice. 1983. *Ways With Words: Language, Life, and Work in Communities and Classrooms*. Cambridge, Eng. and New York: Cambridge University Press.

Hebdige, Dick. 1988. *Subculture: The Meaning of Style*. London: Routledge.

Hinshelwood, R. D. 1989. *A Dictionary of Kleinian Thought*. London: Free Association Books.

Hirsch, Marianne. 1989. *The Mother/Daughter Plot: Narrative, Psychoanalysis, Feminism*. Bloomington: Indiana University Press.

Hollan, Douglas. 2001. "Activity Theory and Cultural Psychology." In *The Psychology of Cultural Experience,* edited by Carmella C. Moore and Holly F. Mathews. Cambridge, UK and New York: Cambridge University Press.

Holland, Dorothy, and Margaret A. Eisenhart. 1990. *Educated in Romance: Women, Achievement, and College Culture.* Chicago: University of Chicago Press.

Holland, Dorothy, William Lachicotte Jr., Debra Skinner, and Carole Cain. 1998. *Identity and Agency in Cultural Worlds.* Cambridge, MA and London: Harvard University Press.

Holland, Dorothy and Naomi Quinn (Eds.). 1987. *Cultural Models in Language and Thought.* Cambridge and London: Cambridge University Press.

Holland, Janet, Caroline Ramazanoglu, and Sue Scott. 1990. *Sex, Risk, Danger: AIDS Education Policy and Young Women's Sexuality.* London: Tufnell.

Holloway, Karla. 1995. *Codes of Conduct: Race, Ethics and the Color of Our Character.* New Brunswick, NJ: Rutgers University Press.

Holmes, M. E., L. V. Klerman, and I. W. Gabrielson. 1970. "New Approaches to Educational Services for the Pregnant Student." *Journal of School Health* 40: 168–172.

hooks, bell. 1990. *Yearning: Race, Gender and Cultural Politics.* Boston: South End Press.

———. 1992. *Black Looks: Race and Representation.* Boston: South End Press.

Horwitz, S. M., L. V. Klerman, H. S. Kuo, & J. F. Jekel. 1991. "School-age Mothers: Predictors of Long-term Educational and Economic Outcomes." *Pediatrics* 87 (6): 862–868.

Howard, Bill. 1972. *Dropouts: Prevention and Rehabilitation; Schools Rescue Potential Failures.* Washington, DC: National School Public Relations Association.

Howard, Marion. 1968. *The Webster School: District of Columbia Program for Pregnant Girls.* Washington, DC: Department of Health, Education, and Welfare, Children's Bureau.

———. 1972. *Sharing, Consortium on Early Childbearing and Childrearing.* Washington, DC: Children's Bureau.

Hunt, Jennifer C. 1989. *Psychoanalytic Aspects of Fieldwork.* Newbury Park, CA: Sage Publications.

Hunter, Virginia. 1982. "The Impact of Adolescent Parenthood on Black Teenage Mothers and Their Families and the Influence of Two Alternative Types of Child." Dissertation. University of California, Los Angeles.

Hurston, Zora Neal. 1928. "How It Feels to Be Colored Me." *World Tomorrow* (May 1928), reprinted in *I Love Myself When I Am Laughing ... : A Zora Neale Hurston Reader,* edited by Alice Walker (pp. 152–155). Old Westbury, NY: Feminist Press, 1979.

———. 1950. "What White Publishers Won't Print." *Negro Digest* (April) reprinted *I Love Myself When I Am Laughing ... : A Zora Neale Hurston Reader,* edited by Alice Walker (pp. 169–173).

———. 1935. *Mules and Men.* New York: Lippincott, 1935; rpt. Bloomington: Indiana University Press, 1978.

Illouz, Eva. 1997. *Consuming the Romantic Utopia: Love and the Contradictions of Capitalism.* Berkeley: University of California Press.

Irvine, Janice. 2002. *Talk About Sex: The Battles Over Sex Education in the United States.* Berkeley: University of California Press.

Jacobs, Theodore. 1990. *The Use of the Self: countertransference and communication in the analytic situation.* Madison, Conn.: International Universities Press.

James, Daniel. 2000. *Dona Maria's Story: Life History, Memory and Political Identity.* Durham and London: Duke University Press.

Johnson, Barbara. 1987. *A World of Difference.* Baltimore and London: Johns Hopkins University Press.

Jones, Lisa. 1994. *Bulletproof Diva: Tales of Race, Sex, and Hair.* New York: Doubleday.

Jordan, Winthrop. 1977. *White Over Black: American Attitudes toward the Negro 1550–1812.* New York: Norton.

Kaplan, Elaine Bell. 1997. *Not Our Kind of Girl: Unraveling the Myths of Black Teenage Motherhood.* Berkeley, CA: University of California Press.

Kelly, Deirdre. 1996. "Stigma Stories: Four Discourses About Teen Mothers, Welfare, and Poverty." *Youth and Society* 27 (4): 421–449.

———. 2000. *Pregnant with Meaning: Teen Mothers and the Politics of Inclusive Schooling.* New York: P. Lang.

Kenzel, Regina G. 1993. *Fallen Women, Problem Girls: Unmarried Mothers and the Professionalization of Social Work, 1890–1945.* New Haven: Yale University Press.

Klein, Melanie. 1975. *Love, Guilt, and Reparation & Other Works, 1921–1945.* London: Virago.

———. 1989. *The Psycho-Analysis of Children.* London: Virago.

Klienman, Sherryl, and Martha Coop. 1993. *Emotions and Fieldwork.* London and Thousand Oaks, CA: Sage Publications.

Kohut, Heinz. 1971. *The Analysis of the Self; A Systematic Approach to the Psychoanalytic Treatment of Narcissistic Personality Disorders.* New York: International Universities Press.

———. 1977. *The Restoration of the Self.* New York: International Universities Press.

Krieger, Susan. 1991. *Social Science and the Self: Personal Essays on an Art Form.* New Brunswick, NJ: Rutgers University Press.

Kusserow, Adrie. 1996. "Reconsidering American Individualism Culture, Class and the Social Construction of the Self." Dissertation, Harvard University.

———. 1999. "De-Homogenizing American Individualism: Socializing Hard and Soft Individualism in Manhattan and Queens." *Ethos* 27 (2): 210–234.

Ladner, Joyce A. 1995. *Tomorrow's Tomorrow: The Black Woman.* Lincoln: University of Nebraska Press. Reprinted from the original 1971 edition by Doubleday.

Landy, Sarah, J. S. Montgomery, J. Schubert, J. F. Cleland, and C. Clark. 1983. "Mother-Infant Interaction of Teenage Mothers and the Effect of Experience in the Observational Sessions on the Development of Their Infants." *Early Child Development & Care* 10 (2–3): 165–185.

Law, Regina and Margrit Zariani. 1994. "Children Having Children." *Report on the Status of Women* (July 31): 95.

Lawson, A., and D. L. Rhode (Eds.). 1993. *The Politics of Pregnancy: Adolescent Sexuality and Public Policy.* New Haven: Yale University Press.

Leadbeater, Bonnie, J. Ross, and Niobe Way. 1996. *Urban Girls: Resisting Stereotypes, Creating Identities.* New York: New York University Press.

————. 2001. *Growing Up Fast: Transitions to Early Adulthood of Inner-City Adolescent Mothers*. Mahwah, NJ: Lawrence Erlbaum Associates.

Lesko, Nancy. 1990. "Curriculum Differentiation as Social Redemption: The Case of School-Aged Mothers." In *Curriculum Differentiation/Interpretive Studies in U.S. Secondary Schools,* edited by R. Page and L. Valli. Albany: State University of New York Press.

————. 1991. "Implausible Endings: Teenage Mothers and Fictions of School Success." In *Current Perspectives on the Culture of Schools,* edited by N. Wyner. Cambridge, MA: Brookline Books.

————. 1995. "The 'Leaky Needs' of School-aged Mothers. An Examination of U.S. Programs and Policies." *Curriculum Inquiry* 25(2): 177–205.

LeVine, Robert Alan. 1982. *Culture, Behavior, and Personality: An Introduction to the Comparative Study of Psychosocial Adaptation.* New York: Aldine.

————. 1999. "An Agenda for Psychological Anthropology." *Ethos* 27 (1): 15–24.

Levinson, Bradley, Doug Foley, and Dorothy Holland (Eds.). 1996. *The Cultural Production of the Educated Person: Critical Ethnographies of Schooling and Local Practice.* Albany, NY: State University of New York Press.

Linde, Charlotte. 1993. *Life Stories: The Creation of Coherence.* New York: Oxford University Press.

Lowenfeld, Viktor. 1959. *The Nature of Creative Activity.* London: Routledge and K. Paul.

Luker, Kristin. 1996. *Dubious Conceptions: The Politics of Teenage Pregnancy.* Cambridge, MA: Harvard University Press.

Luttrell, Wendy. 1996. "Taking Care of Literacy: One Feminist's Critique," *Educational Policy: An Interdisciplinary Journal of Policy and Practice.* 10 (3): 342–365.

———— 1997. *Schoolsmart and Motherwise: Working-Class Women's Identity and Schooling.* New York and London: Routledge.

————. 2001. "Good Enough Methods for Ethnographic Research." *Harvard Educational Review.* 70 (4): 499–524.

Lutz, Catherine. 1988. *Unnatural Emotions: Everyday Sentiments on a Micronesian Atoll & Their Challenge to Western Theory.* Chicago: University of Chicago Press.

Lykes, M. Brinton, in collaboration with the Association of Maya Ixil Women— New Dawn, Chajul, Guatemala. 2001. "Creative Arts and Photography in Participatory Action Research in Guatemala." In *Handbook of Action Research: Participative Inquiry and Practice,* edited by Peter Reason and Hilary Bradbury. London and Thousand Oaks, CA: Sage Publications.

Mac an Ghaill, Máirtín. 1994. *The Making of Men: Masculinities, Sexualities, and Schooling.* Buckingham, UK: Open University Press.

MacLeod, Jay. 1995. *Ain't No Makin' It: Leveled Aspirations in a Low-Income Neighborhood.* Boulder, CO: Westview Press.

Manlowe, J. 1998. "The Influence of High School Dropout and School Disengagement on the Risk of School-age Pregnancy." *Journal of Research on Adolescence.* 8 (2): 187—200.

Mann, Chris. 1998. "Family Fables." In *Narrative and Genre,* edited by Mary Chamberlain and Paul Thompson. London and New York: Routledge.

Martin, Emily. 1987. *The Woman in the Body.* Boston: Beacon Press.

Martin, Karin. 1996. *Puberty, Sexuality, and the Self: Girls and Boys at Adolescence.* New York and London: Routledge.

Massey, Carla. 1996. "Body-Smarts: An Adolescent Girl Thinking, Talking, and Mattering." *Gender and Psychoanalysis* 1 (1): 75–102.

Matsuhahsi, Yoko and Marianne E. Felice. 1991. "Adolescent body image during pregnancy." *Journal of Adolescent Health.* 124: 313–315.

McCarthy, Cameron. 1990. *Race and Curriculum: Social Inequality and the Theories and Politics of Difference in Contemporary Research on Schooling.* London and New York: Falmer.

McCollum, Christopher Coy. 2000. "The Cultural Patterning of Self-Understanding: A Cognitive-Psychoanalytic Approach to Middle-Class Americans' Life Stories." Dissertation, Duke University.

McDade, Laurie. 1992. "Sex, Pregnancy, and Schooling: Obstacles to a Critical Teaching of the Body." In *What Schools Can Do: Critical Pedagogy and Practice,* edited by K. Weiler and C. Mitchell. Albany, NY: State University of New York Press.

McMahon, Martha. 1995. *Engendering Motherhood: Identity and Self-Transformation in Women's Lives.* New York: Guilford Press.

McRobbie, Angela. Ed. 1988. *Zoot Suits and Second-hand Dresses: An Anthology of Fashion and Music.* Boston: Unwin Hyman.

———. 1991. *Feminism and Youth Culture: From Jackie to Just Seventeen.* Boston: Unwin Hyman.

Middleton, Susan. 1993. *Educating Feminists: Life histories and pedagogy.* New York: Teachers College Press.

Minow, Martha. 1990. *Making All the Difference: Inclusion, Exclusion, and American Law.* Ithaca: Cornell University Press.

Mirza, Heidi. 1998. "Race, Gender and IQ: The Social Consequence of a Pseudo-Scientific Discourse." *Race, Ethnicity and Education* 1 (1): 109–126.

Mishler, Elliot. 1986. *Research Interviewing: Context and Narrative.* Cambridge, MA: Harvard University Press.

———. 1999. *Storylines: Craftartists' Narratives of Identity.* Cambridge, MA: Harvard University Press.

Moore, B. F. and B. D. Fine (Eds). 1995. *Psychoanalysis: The Major Concepts.* New Haven, CT: Yale University Press.

Morgan, Joan. 1999. *When Chickenheads Come Home to Roost: My Life as a Hip-Hop Feminist.* New York: Simon & Schuster.

Morrison, Toni. 1988. *Beloved.* New York: Dutton Signet.

———. 1992. *Playing in the Dark: Whiteness and the Literary Imagination.* Cambridge, MA: Harvard University Press.

———. 1993. *The Bluest Eye.* New York: Knopf.

Musick, J. S. 1993. *Young, Poor, and Pregnant.* New Haven, CT: Yale University Press.

Myerhoff, Barbara G. 1978. *Number Our Days.* New York: Touchstone.

———. 1992. *Remembered Lives: The Work of Ritual, Storytelling, and Growing Older.* Ann Arbor: University of Michigan Press.

Naevestad, Marie. 1979. *The Colors of Rage and Love: The Process of Change in Psychotherapy Elucidated by the Patient's Own Drawings: A Picture Book of Internal Events.* Oslo and New York: Universitetsforlaget; Columbia University Press.

Nash, Margaret A., and Margaret C. Dunkle. 1989. *The Need for a Warming Trend: A Survey of the School Climate for Pregnant and Parenting Teens*. Washington, DC: Equality Center.

Nathanson, Constance A. 1991. *Dangerous Passage: The Social Control of Sexuality in Women's Adolescence*. Philadelphia: Temple University Press.

Nespor, Jane. 1997. *Tangled up in School: Politics, Space, Bodies and Signs in the Educational Process*. Mahwah, NJ: Lawrence Erlbaum Associates.

Newman, Katherine S. 1988. *Falling from Grace: Downward Mobility in the Age of Affluence*. Berkeley: University of California Press.

———. 1999. *No Shame in My Game: The Working Poor in the Inner City*. New York: Russell Sage Foundation and Knopf.

———. 2002. "No Shame: The View from the Left Banks." *American Journal of Sociology* 107 (6): 1577–1597.

Nichter, Mimi. 2000. *Fat Talk: What Girls and Their Parents Say about Dieting*. Cambridge, MA: Harvard University Press.

Nielsen, Harriet Bjerrum, and Monica Rudberg. 1994. *Psychological Gender and Modernity*. Oslo: Scandinavian University Press.

Oakes, Jeannie. 1985. *Keeping Track: How Schools Structure Inequality* New Haven, CT: Yale University Press.

O'Barr, William. 1994. *Culture and the Ad: Exploring Otherness in the World of Advertising*. Boulder, CO: Westview Press.

Ochs, Elinor and Lisa Capps. 1999. *Living Narrative: Creating Lives in Everyday Storytelling*. Cambridge, MA: Harvard University Press.

Ogden, Thomas H. 1994. *Subjects of Analysis*. Northvale, NJ: J. Aronson.

Olsen, Laurie. 1997. *Made in America: Immigrant Students in our Public Schools*. New York: The New Press.

Olsen, Tillie. 1978. *Silences*. New York: Delacorte Press/Seymour Lawrence.

Ortner, Sharon. 1993. "The Ethnography of Newark: The Class of '58 of Weequahic High School." *Michigan Quarterly Review* 32: 411–429.

Osofsky, Howard J. 1968. *The Pregnant Teen-ager; a Medical, Educational, and Social Analysis*. Springfield, IL: C. C. Thomas.

Pakulski, Jan. 1996. *The Death of Class*. London: Sage.

Paley, Nicholas. 1995. *Finding Art's Place: Experiments in Contemporary Education and Culture*. London and New York: Routledge.

Paley, Vivian. 1986. "On Listening to What Children Say." *Harvard Educational Review* 56: 122–131.

Parker, Roszika. 1995. *Mother Love/Mother Hate: The Power of Maternal Ambivalence*. New York: Basic Books.

Pearlman, S. 1984. "Nobody's baby: the politics of adolescent pregnancy." Dissertation, Brandeis University.

Petchesky, Rosalind. 1984. *Abortion and Woman's Choice: The State, Sexuality, and Reproductive Freedom*. New York: Longman.

Peterson, Anne C., Pamela A. Sarigiani, and Robert E. Kennedy. 1991. "Adolescent Depression: why more girls?" *Journal of Youth and Adolescence*. 20 (2): 247–271.

Phillips, Adam. 1998. *The Beast in the Nursery*. London: Faber.

Pillow, Wanda. 1994. "Policy Discourse and Teenage Pregnancy: The Making of Mothers." Dissertation, Educational Policy Studies, The Ohio State University.

————. 1997a. "Exposed Methodology: The Body as a Deconstructive Practice." *International Journal of Qualitative Studies in Education* 10 (3): 349–363.

————. 1997b. "Decentering Silences/Troubling Irony: Teen pregnancy's challenge to policy and analysis." In *Feminist Critical Policy Analysis I: A Primary and Secondary Schooling Perpective,* edited by C. Marshall. London: Falmer Press.

Popham, W. James. 2002. "Preparing for the Coming Avalanche of Accountability Tests." *Harvard Education Letter* 18, 3.

Rabinow, Paul D. 1977. *Reflections on Fieldwork in Morocco.* Berkeley: University of California Press.

Raphael-Leff, Joan. 1995. *Pregnancy, the Inside Story.* Northvale, NJ and London: Jason Aronson.

Rapp, Rayna. 1999. *Testing Women, Testing the Fetus: the Social Impact of Amniocentesis in America.* New York and London: Routledge.

Rauste-von-Wright, Maijaliisa. 1989. "Body Image Satisfaction in Adolescent Girls and Boys: A Longitudinal Study." *Journal of Youth and Adolescence* 18 (1): 71–83.

Reason, Peter and Hilary Bradbury (Eds.). 2001. *Handbook of Action Research: Participative Inquiry and Practice.* London, Thousand Oaks, New Delhi: Sage Publications.

Reinharz, Shulamit. 1979. *On Becoming a Social Scientist.* San Francisco: Jossey-Bass.

————. 1997. "Who Am I?: The Need for a Variety of Selves in the Field," In *Reflexivity and voice,* edited by R. Herz. London and Thousand Oaks, CA: Sage.

Rich, Adrienne. 1981. "Compulsory Heterosexuality and Lesbian Existence." In *Powers of Desire: The Politics of Sexuality,* edited by Ann Snitow, Christine Stansell, and Sharon Thompson. New York: Monthly Review Press.

Richardson, Laurel. 1997. *Fields of Play (Constructing an Academic Life).* New Brunswick, NJ: Rutgers University Press.

Rieder, Jonathan. 1985. *Canarsie: The Jews and Italians of Brooklyn Against Liberalism.* Cambridge, MA: Harvard University Press.

Riessman, Catherine Kohler. 1993. *Narrative Analysis.* London and Thousand Oaks, CA: Sage.

————. 2000. "Stigma and Everyday Practices: Childless Women in South India." *Gender and Society* 14 (1) (February): 111–135.

————. 2002a. "Analysis of Personal Narratives." In *Handbook of Interview Research,* edited by J. Gubrium and J. Holstein. Newbury Park, Calif.: Sage.

————. 2002b. "Doing Justice: Positioning the Interpreter in Narrative Work." In *Strategic Narrative: New Perspectives on the Power of Personal and Cultural Stories,* edited by Wendy Patterson. Lanham, Boulder, New York, Oxford: Lexington Books.

Robinson, T., and J. V. Ward. 1991. "'A Belief in Self Far Greater than Anyone's Disbelief': Cultivating Healthy Resistance Among African American Female Adolescents." In *Women, Girls, & Psychotherapy: Reframing Resistance,* edited by C. Gilligan, A. Rogers, and D. Tolman. Binghampton, NY: Harrington Park Press.

Rogers, Annie G. 1993. "Voice, Play, and a Practice of Ordinary Courage in Girls' and Women's Lives." *Harvard Educational Review* 63 (3): 265–295.

Rogers, Annie, M. Casey, J. Ekert and J. Holland. 1999. "An Interpretive Poetics of Languages of the Unsayable." *The Narrative Study of Lives,* 6, 77–106.

Rogers, Annie with M. Casey, J. Ekert and J. Holland. 2002. *Between the lines: Engaging the unsayable in narrative research.* Unpublished book manuscript.

Rooks, Noliwe M. 1996. *Hair Raising: Beauty, Culture, and African American Women.* New Brunswick, NJ: Rutgers University Press.

Rosaldo, Renato. 1989. *Culture & Truth: The Remaking of Social Analysis.* Boston: Beacon Press.

Rothman, Barbara Katz. 1994. *The Tentative Pregnancy: Amniocentesis and the Sexual Politics of Motherhood.* London: Pandora.

Sayers, Janet. 1991. *Mothering Psychoanalysis: Helene Deutsch, Karen Horney, Anna Freud and Melanie Klein.* London: Hamish Hamilton.

―――. 2000. *Kleinians: Psychoanalysis inside out.* Cambridge, UK and Malden, MA: Polity Press.

Scheper-Hughes, Nancy and Carolyn Sargent. 1998. *Small Wars: The Cultural Politics of Childhood.* Berkeley: University of California Press.

Seely, J. R., R. A. Sim, and E. W. Loosley. 1956. *Crestwood Heights: A Study of the Culture of Suburban Life.* New York: Basic Books.

Segal, Hanna. 1979. *Klein.* Glasgow: Fontana.

Shaw, Jenny. 1995. *Education, Gender and Anxiety.* London: Taylor and Francis.

Shaw, Nancy Stoller. 1974. *Forced Labor: Maternity Care in the United States.* New York: Pergamon Press.

Shreefter, Robert. 2001. "Borders/Fronteras: Immigrant Students' Worlds in Art." *Harvard Educational Review* 71 (3): A1–A16.

Singer, Linda, Judith Butler, and Maureen MacGrogan. 1993. *Erotic Welfare: Sexual Theory and Politics in the Age of Epidemic.* New York: Routledge.

Skeggs, Beverly. 1997. *Formations of Class & Gender.* London and Thousand Oaks, CA: Sage.

Slade P. D. 1977. "Awareness of Body Dimensions during Pregnancy: An Analogue Study." *Psychological Medicine* 7: 245–252.

Solinger, Rickie. 1992. *Wake Up Little Susie: Single Pregnancy and Race Before Roe V. Wade.* New York and London: Routledge Press.

―――. 2001. *Beggars and Choosers: How the Politics of Choice Shapes Adoption, Abortion, and Welfare in the United States.* New York: Hill and Wang.

Springer, Kimberly. 2002. "Third Wave Black Feminism?" *Signs: Journal of Women in Culture and Society.* Vol. 27, no. 4: 1059–1083.

Stack, Carol. 1974. *All Our Kin: Survival Strategies in a Black Community.* New York: Harper and Row.

―――. 2001. "In Exile on Main Street." In *Laboring Below the Line: The New Ethnography of Poverty, Low-Wage Work, and Survival in the Global Economy,* edited by Frank Munger. NY: Russell Sage Foundation Press.

―――. Forthcoming. *Coming Of Age at Minimum Wage,* with Ellen Stein and Joan Zirker. New York: Russell Sage Foundation Press.

―――. Forthcoming. *In Exile on Main Street: Girls, Work, and Schooling.* New York: Russell Sage Foundation.

Stacey, Judith. 2001. "Family Values Forever." *The Nation.* July 9.

―――. 1990. *Brave New Families: Stories of Domestic Upheaval in Late-Twentieth-Century America.* New York: Basic Books.

Steedman, Carolyn. 1986. *Landscape for a Good Woman: A Story of Two Lives.* London: Virago.

————. 1992. *Past Tenses: Essays on Writing, Autobiography and History*. London: Rivers Oram Press.

Stenberg, Laurie, and Lynn Blinn. 1993. "Feelings About Self and Body During Adolescent Pregnancy." *Families in Society: The Journal of Contemporary Human Services*. 745: 282–290.

Stephens, Sharon. 1995. *Children and the Politics of Culture*. Princeton, NJ: Princeton University Press.

Stephenson, Mary. 1991. *My Child Is a Mother*. San Antonio, TX: Corona.

Strauss, Claudia, and Naomi Quinn. 1997. *A Cognitive Theory of Cultural Meaning*. Cambridge and London: Cambridge University Press.

Suarez-Orozco, Carola and Marcelo M. Suarez-Orozco. 2001. *Children of Immigration*. Cambridge, MA: Harvard University Press.

Sullivan, Mercer. 1993. "Culture and Class as Determinants of Out-of-Wedlock Childbearing." *Journal of Research on Adolescence*. 3: 295–316.

Taylor, Jill McLean, Carol Gilligan, and Amy M. Sullivan. 1995. *Between Voice and Silence: Women and Girls, Race and Relationship*. Cambridge, MA and London: Harvard University Press.

Tebbel, John. 1976. "Sex Education: Yesterday, Today, and Tomorrow." *Education Digest* 41: 45–47.

Thorne, Barrie. 1993. *Gender Play: girls and boys in school*. New Brunswick, NJ: Rutgers University Press.

Thunder-McGuire, Steve. 1994. "An Inner Critic in Children's Artists' Bookmaking." *Visual Arts Research* 20 (2): 51–61.

Tolman, D. L. 1994. "Daring to Desire: Culture and the Bodies of Adolescent Girls." In *Sexual Cultures and the Construction of Adolescent Identities*, edited by J. M. Irvine. Philadelphia: Temple University Press.

————. 1996. "Adolescent Girls' Sexuality: Debunking the Myth of the Urban Girl." In *Urban Girls: Resisting Stereotypes, Creating Identities*, edited by Bonnie J. Ross Leadbeater and Niobe Way. New York: New York University Press.

————. 1999. "Femininity as a Barrier to Positive Sexual Health for Adolescent Girls. JAMWA, 54 (3): 133–138.

Victor, Susan. 1995. "Becoming the Good Mother: The Emergent Curriculum of Adolescent Mothers." In *Repositioning Feminism and Education: Perspectives on Educating for Social Change*, edited by J. Jipson, P. Munro, S. Victor, K. Froude Jones, and G. Freed-Rowland. Westport, Connecticut and London: Bergin and Garvey.

Vinovskis, Maris. 1988. *An "Epidemic" of Adolescent Pregnancy?: Some Historical and Policy Considerations*. New York: Oxford University Press.

Visotsky, H. M. 1966. "A project for unwed pregnant adolescents in Chicago." *Clinical Pediatrics* 5: 322–324.

Wacquant, Löic 2002. "Scrutinizing the Street: Poverty, Morality, and the Pitfalls of Urban Ethnography." *American Journal of Sociology*. 107 (6): 1–53.

Walkerdine, Valerie. 1997. *Daddy's Girl: Young Girls and Pop Culture*. Basingstoke, Eng.: Macmillan.

Walkerdine, Valerie, Helen Lucey, and June Melody. 2001. *Growing Up Girl: Psychosocial Explorations of Gender and Class (Qualitative Studies in Psychology)*. New York: New York University Press.

Wang, Caroline. 1997. "Photovoice: Concept, Methodology, and Use for Participatory Needs Assessment." *Health Education & Behavior* 24 (3): 369–387.

———. 1999. "Photovoice: A Participatory Action Research Strategy Applied to Women's Health." *Journal of Women's Health* 8 (Supplement 1): S47–S54.

Wang, Caroline and Mary Ann Burris. 1994. "Empowerment through Photo Novella: Portraits of Participation." *Health Education Quarterly* 21 (2): 171–186.

Wang, Caroline, Yuan Yan Ling, and Feng Ming Ling. 1996. "Photovoice as a Tool for Participatory Evaluation: The Community's View of Process and Impact." *Journal of Contemporary Health* 4: 47–49.

Ward, Janie Victoria. 1996. "Raising Resisters: The Role of Truth Telling in the Psychological Development of African American Girls." In *Urban Girls: Resisting Stereotypes, Creating Identities,* edited by Bonnie J. Ross Leadbeater and Niobe Way. New York: New York University Press.

Ward, Martha. 1995. "Early Childbearing: What Is the Problem and Who Owns It?" In *Conceiving The New World Order: The Global Politics of Reproduction,* edited by Faye Ginsburg and Rayna Rapp. Berkeley: University of California Press.

Washington, Mary Helen (Ed.). 1991. *Memory of Kin: Stories About Family by Black Writers.* New York: Anchor Books.

Waters, Mary C. 1990. *Ethnic Options: Choosing Identities in America.* Berkeley: University of California Press.

Way, Niobe. 1998. *Everyday Courage: The Lives and Stories of Urban Teenagers.* New York: New York University Press.

Way, Niobe, and Bonnie J. Leadbeater. 1999. "Pathways Toward Educational Achievement Among African American and Puerto Rican Adolescent Mothers: Reexamining the Role of Social Support from Families." *Development and Psychopathology* 11 (2): 349–364.

Weatherly, R. A., S. B. Perlman, M. H. Levine, and L. V. Klerman. 1985. *Patchwork Programs: Comprehensive Services for Pregnant and Parenting Adolescents.* Seattle: Center for Social Welfare Research, School of Social Work, University of Washington.

———. 1986. "Comprehensive Programs for Pregnant Teenagers and Teenage parents: How Successful Have They Been?" *Family Planning Perspective.* 18 (3): 73–78.

Weinstein, Matthew. 1998. "The Teenage Pregnancy 'Problem': Welfare Reform and the Personal Responsibility and Work Opportunity Reconciliation Act of 1996." *Berkeley Women's Law Journal* 13: 117–152.

Weis, Lois. 1988. *Class, Race and Gender in U.S. Education.* New Buffalo: State University of New York Press.

———. 1990. *Working Class Without Work: High School Students in a De-industrializing Economy.* New York: Routledge.

Weis, L., E. Farrar, and H. G. Petrie. (Eds.) 1989. *Dropouts from School: Issues, Dilemmas, and Solutions.* Albany: Statue University of New York Press.

White, Paulette Childress. 1989. "Getting the Facts of Life." In *Memory of Kin: Stories About Family by Black Writers,* edited by Mary Helen Washington. New York: Anchor Books, 1991.

Williams, Patricia. 1991. *The Alchemy of Race and Rights: Diary of a Law Professor.* Cambridge, MA and London, Eng.: Harvard University Press.

Williams, Raymond. 1973. *The Country and the City.* New York: Oxford University Press.

Williamson, Judith. 1978. *Decoding Advertisements: Ideology and Meaning in Advertising.* London: Boyars.

Willis, Paul. 1977. *Learning to Labor: How Working Class Kids Get Working Class Jobs.* New York: Columbia University Press.

———. 1978. *The Youth Review: Social Conditions of Young People in Wolverhampton.* Aldershot, Hants, Eng. and Brookfield, VT: Avebury.

Willis, Susan. 1987. *Specifying: Black Women Writing the American Experience.* Madison, WI: University of Wisconsin Press.

Winnicott, D. W. 1971. *Playing and Reality.* New York: Basic Books.

Women's Educational Equity Act (WEAA) Resource Center. 2002. Title IX Report Card-Treatment of Pregnant and Parenting Students. Newton, MA.

Wortham, Stanton Emerson Fisher. 2001. *Narratives in Action: A Strategy for Research and Analysis.* New York: Teachers College Press.

Zellman, Gail. 1981. *A Title IX Perspective on the Schools' Response to Teenage Pregnancy and Parenthood.* Santa Monica, CA: Rand.

Author Index

Subject Index

229